Praise for *The NLP Toolkit*

NLP is a treasure trove of learning ideas. Rich in content, deep, visually engaging, accessible, flexible, comprehensive NLP presents an endless supply of great ways to spark the learner by sparking the teacher. Terry and Churches have furnished us a toolkit that keeps on giving, getting at the learner's mind and feelings in a way that is irresistibly stimulating.

Michael Fullan
Professor Emeritus, OISE / University of Toronto

NLP techniques hold the secret to success for many leaders and teachers. *The NLP Toolkit* turns the theory of NLP into practical activities that all schools can use with individuals or classes. Techniques for helping teachers develop personal effectiveness, communications skills and emotional intelligence in their students are described as a set of simple tasks. This book makes NLP techniques accessible to all and relates them to key issues affecting schools today – behaviour management, motivation, social skills, raising achievement, inclusion and pedagogy for the 21st century. It offers clear guidance on how young people can be coached to better manage their minds and so help them achieve their potential. Use this Toolkit regularly to become a better teacher, a more flexible communicator and an effective life coach for your family, friends and students.

Jackie Beere OBE
Author, Educational Consultant, Trainer, AST, School Improvement Partner and
Master Practitioner of NLP

I was going to start this review by say___ th__ this Toolkit is a gold mine for educators but it is actually better than that. To find gold yc__ h__ve to s__nd time sorting through dross! This Toolkit is a tightly organized and highly accessible r_____ ___ of a powerful strategies which are tried and tested and directly relevant to the daily w___ ___ers and school leaders. The Toolkit practices what it preaches, it models a thought___ ___ ___matic approach to a wide range of learning and social situations in schools. It is encyc___ ___ ___erage and authoritative approach.

The Toolkit will be an invaluable resour__ ___ ___continuing to implement the components of Every Child Matters and in meeting the ___ ___ ___ersonalising learning.

The Toolkit will help school leaders to develop a rich portfolio of strategies to maximise effective learning and create learning-centered schools.

John West-Burnham
Professor of Educational Leadership, St Mary's University College

Highly effective pedagogy secures good results. Teaching, though, is more than pedagogy. It is also the craft of helping the learner realise what is happening and helping them to be predisposed to learning.

This book is packed with well explained strategies that help teachers to support their learners. Through activities that work on the social or emotional aspects of learning the mysteries of why people succeed or survive are exposed.

Using the book will bring learning alive for young people and add inte__st and enjoyment . . . and success.

Professor Mick Waters

The
NLP Toolkit

The
NLP Toolkit

Innovative activities and strategies for teachers, trainers and school leaders

Roger Terry and Richard Churches

Illustrations by Alison Mobbs

Crown House Publishing Limited
www.crownhouse.co.uk
www.crownhousepublishing.com

First published by

Crown House Publishing Ltd
Crown Buildings, Bancyfelin, Carmarthen, Wales, SA33 5ND, UK
www.crownhouse.co.uk

and

Crown House Publishing Company LLC
6 Trowbridge Drive, Suite 5, Bethel, CT 06801-2858, USA
www.crownhousepublishing.com

British Library Cataloguing in Publication Data
A catalogue entry for this book is available from the British Library.

13-digit ISBN 978-184590138-7

LCCN 2008936801

Printed and bound in the UK by
The Cromwell Press Group, Trowbridge, Wiltshire

This book is dedicated to our children
Sam, Lucy and George

Contents

List of resource chapters

Title	What you will learn	In the classroom activities	Emotional and social literacy with children	Stagecraft and presentation skills for teachers and trainers	Personal development and effectiveness for teachers	Leading with NLP	Page
1 A little help from my friends	*How to develop helping and listening skills*	✓	✓		✓	✓	3
2 And now I see it	*How to improve children's spelling, learning and retention*	✓	✓				5
3 Better remember me No. 1	*How to use stories to help children remember*	✓			✓		8
4 Better remember me No. 2	*How to use images to help children remember*	✓			✓		11
5 Better remember me No. 3	*How to use spatial approaches to help with memory*	✓			✓		14
6 Can you find some balance?	*How to improve examination results by supporting learners to think through their exam-life balance issues*	✓	✓		✓	✓	16
7 In character	*How to enhance characterisation in drama lessons (and creative writing)*	✓	✓			✓	20
8 Code word	*How to develop confidence and the right emotional state before exams or tests*	✓	✓	✓			23
9 Logical levels	*How to help children to develop their reasoning skills*	✓	✓		✓	✓	26
10 Model village	*How to enhance learning and listening skills through observation and activity*	✓	✓				29

In the classroom activities

Introduction

Although this book is mostly aimed at teachers and school leaders, there is much in the book that trainers, lecturers and others involved in adult learning and teacher training will find useful. There is also a specific section (*Stagecraft and presentation skills for teachers and trainers*) that has been aimed at people who work with adult learners as well as children. Also many of the activities in sections 1 and 2 (*In the classroom activities* and *Emotional and social literacy with children*) can easily be adapted for use as part of adult learning – indeed, we include a number of these activities in our leadership development work with executives and business leaders. At the end of the day emotional literacy is emotional literacy whether you are 9 years old or 49!

Neuro-linguistic programming (NLP) is an ever growing collection of personal development and personal effectiveness tools. Although these tools frequently overlap with ideas from psychology, coaching and neuroscience, the basis of NLP is not the tools or ideas, but rather a research methodology known as 'modelling'. Modelling differs from other areas of behavioural science research in that it looks at highly effective people and how they do what they do. The processes of modelling were first developed by Richard Bandler and John Grinder at the University of Santa Cruz in the mid-1970s, and although much has changed in NLP over the years the fundamental principle of finding out the 'difference that makes a difference' between people who are just good at what they do and people who excel remains the same. Today, as well as much practitioner-led modelling, there are a number of projects in university departments throughout the world – particularly at the University of Surrey in the UK where NLP is being applied as a formal research methodology by Paul Tosey and Jane Mathison.

A few years ago, if you mentioned NLP in education few people knew what you were talking about. Recently there has been a substantial growth in interest due to the use of NLP within government programmes, as well as emerging recognition of a gap in communication and personal development training for teachers. In terms of our own work, research and the training that we have delivered, the response from teachers has been overwhelmingly positive and suggests that a number of tools from NLP can make a significant contribution to areas of personalisation as well school leadership and classroom effectiveness. If you wish to follow up on this you may be interested in the research that followed the use of NLP as part of the Fast Track Teaching programme in England. This has been written up by Richard Churches and John West-Burnham (*Leading Learning Through Relationships*) and is available from CfBT Education Trust. You can also find a bibliography of research into NLP in education at the end of this book (page 255).

NLP approaches can be said to fit into four categories:

Outcomes – strategies for self-motivation and the motivation of others.

Rapport – approaches for building rapport and influencing others that support notions of *social intelligence* (as discussed by Daniel Goleman).

Flexibility – techniques for enhancing flexibility and awareness of others.

Influential language – language models derived from psychotherapists' communication skills (including, but not exclusively, hypnosis), much of which is now a standard part of sales and presentation skills training in business and industry.

Those of you interested in NLP and the research evidence, may want to read *Neuro-linguistic programming and learning: teacher case studies on the impact of NLP in education* which is available from CfBT Education Trust. This contains the first full literature review of research into NLP and it impact on children and learners (Carey et al. 2009) as well as over 30 teacher-led action research case studies.

Over the years research into effective teaching and learning has increasingly recognised that effectiveness involves more than strategies that create knowledge and understanding. Being a good teacher or trainer is as much about relationships and interpersonal skills as it is about learning approaches, although all of the above are, of course, important – as is subject knowledge. Teachers who are effective are able to draw on a range of skills and approaches and apply these in ways that support the context at the time, recognising that that context and learning situation is constantly changing and shifting. As John West-Burnham and others like Susan Greenfield, Uta Frith and Sarah-Jayne Blakemore note, neuroscience shows us that learning and emotions are fundamentally interconnected. Therefore, the emotional climate that teachers and school leaders create is not just a nice addition – it is essential for effective learning to take place. Alongside this, NLP has always adopted a positive view of the brain, its development and the way in which it can be affected through positive learning environments – ideas which are being reinforced in neuroscience today on a daily basis through research into neuroplasticity and the development of neural networks.

In *NLP for Teachers: How To Be a Highly Effective Teacher* we opened the book with the following thoughts:

> *Teaching is about relationships as well as pedagogy. It is about feelings as well as facts and it is as much about what goes on inside your head as it is about what goes on in the heads of your students. It is about using your senses as well as your subject knowledge.*
>
> *At the end of the day we all know that it is our mood when we enter the classroom that has the greatest effect on the children, our sense of motivation that drives the pace of the lesson and our abilities to relieve the tension in a difficult moment that creates the right classroom climate. Effective teaching begins and ends with our capacity to manage our internal responses and external behaviours.*

Several years on this still seems a good way to start, for if there is a formula for teacher or trainer effectiveness it probably goes something like this:

Passion for your subject (whatever that subject is) – and by subject we mean the range of content that teachers impart – which, of course, can be much wider than the highly important subject areas in your curriculum

+

Passion for learners (and for helping others to learn)

+

Communication skills

As well as subject knowledge, many studies point to the importance of teacher and school leader skills in areas such as engagement, values, questioning, positive atmosphere and teacher expectations. As a 'toolkit' of approaches for developing personal effectiveness, influence and communication we believe that NLP offers many ways to support existing good practice, and in many cases can be the key to moving from being good to being outstanding.

Just after the last book was published someone in a chat room discussing the book called it 'sneaky psychology'. If the application of ideas, without telling the children or learners, is 'sneaky' then we have been doing 'sneaky sociology' (not to mention 'sneaky pedagogy') for years. Social theories have, without doubt, added richness and depth to our understanding of learning processes and how we run schools. Learning is after all a social process. However, as we move into the 21st century, it is also clear that effective social processes involve high-level interpersonal skills and relationship management and that these in turn are affected by our intrapersonal skills (how we manage ourselves and our own minds, and thinking, whilst we are teaching or leading). It is these two elements (the interpersonal and the intrapersonal), we believe, alongside an understanding of social process, that sit at the heart of what writers like Michael Fullan are talking about when they speak about the moral imperatives of school leadership.

What some NLP tools demonstrate (particularly those modelled from hypnosis) is just how simple it can be to create social conformity and compliance through storytelling, metaphor, the effective communication of expectancy and an understanding of influential language (both verbal and non-verbal). This is particularly true if you apply the principles of emotional and social intelligence effectively and get your followers and the children you teach to fall into line without any emotional 'push back' from their amygdalas! Recent fMRI research (by Gregory Berns and others) has shown that social conformity is associated with a shutdown of the amygdala (the brain's gateway to emotions and feelings) and an increase in blood flow in the brain to areas associated with internal imagery compared to the expression of independence (were the amygdala gets involved). Interesting, isn't it? That's why it is also important to understand these tools and the other side of personal development and effectiveness that is included within the range of NLP skills and approaches – such as effective coaching and questioning.

It is also why it is so important for teachers and leaders in schools and the public sector generally to balance such leadership styles with a coaching style and approach. For not only does questioning help to change behaviours – by getting people to think about what they are doing – asking questions helps to ensure that there is a process of genuine interdependence (rather than just dominance and compliance) between you and your learners, or you and your followers. NLP has much to offer in these areas also, and is the reason why it is so widely used in coaching and therapy. We hope that we have practised what we preach and that you can find in this book the right balance between the skills of influencing and the skills of consulting and involving.

We should at this point thank all those people who have made suggestions and given us ideas for this book – in particular the 1,000-plus teachers that Roger and Henrie Lidiard have trained in NLP over the last six years. We should also perhaps mention here Gillian Atkins and Claire MacLean who put so much effort into getting the learning environment right for the training over the years and the *Times Educational Supplement* (*TES*) for enthusiastically profiling *NLP for Teachers: How To Be a Highly Effective Teacher*. Finally, thanks to Emily Terry, Jenni Churches, Geraldine Hutchinson and Nick Austin for their help in the preparation and development of this book, Ali Mobbs for the illustrations – and our children Sam and Lucy for putting up with the loss of family time!

Getting the most out of this book

This book is designed to be accessed in a number of ways:

- You could read it through in a traditional way,
- Plan a professional learning journey for yourself by using the content lists, or
- You can just dip into the resources at any point.

Each chapter aims to give you all the information you need to learn and implement the approaches described without any prior learning, although some of the more advanced tools will suggest some background reading from elsewhere in the book before you begin.

Use the list of resource chapters on pages x to xv to identify the particular areas of learning that you are interested in. Each chapter focuses on one of the following areas, although most chapters have information that is helpful across at least two areas:

- In the classroom activities
- Emotional and social literacy with children
- Stagecraft and presentation skills for teachers and trainers
- Personal development and effectiveness for teachers
- Leading with NLP.

The five core parts of the book also follow this structure.

The chapters are organised in the following way:

- In the top corner of the first page of each chapter, you can find information that tells you about the chapter's focus and its content. These break down into more detail the key areas covered in the book, for example:

Leading with NLP			
Self-awareness	Resilience	Relationship awareness and influencing skills	School improvement
*	* * *	* * *	* * *

- Each chapter starts with an introduction that outlines the areas covered and why these are helpful to teachers and school leaders.

- *Here's how* sections give you step-by-step instructions on how to use or learn the skills in the chapter.

- *Quick starts* give you a way to rapidly make use of NLP in the particular context. Alongside these, you will also find photocopyable resource sheets and templates to support learning and activities.

- The *Learn more about this* parts of the chapters give you some background information. You can also find suggestions for further reading and background information in our book: *NLP for Teachers: How To Be a Highly Effective Teacher*, which you may want to follow up on.

- Finally, each chapter contains a *When else can you use this?* section with additional suggestions for how the tools and ideas can be used. There is also space for you to write your own notes.

Remember, NLP is best learnt experientially and all the tools are practical. Therefore, the most effective way to go about learning a tool is to give it a go in the real world and notice what happens.

- You will notice that there is some repetition of concepts in the book. We have done this so that you can focus on working on a chapter at a time without having to cross-reference too much.

- We suggest that you take it a little bit at a time and play with the concepts and tools in your daily work, noticing how effective they can be in everyday situations. Once you have read a chapter and worked through the activities yourself, you may want to work through the activities again with a friend or a colleague. With some of the tools and techniques it is helpful to have someone read it out loud whilst you work through it. Discussing the activities afterwards can be really helpful too.

- Set yourself the goal of taking one or two ideas, concepts and techniques at a time and have a day when you practise that one thing. Applying some of these strategies will be much more effective than simply reading the book.

- In general, it is best to work through a single chapter in order, as the chapters are frequently structured as if you were learning the tool on a training course.

- Remember, you don't need to absorb it all at once. Allow yourself time to work on one or two tools or approaches at a time.

Learning more about NLP

Any good book about NLP should aspire to be a complement to hands-on practice and training. With this in mind we have included practical exercises throughout the book. If you have not yet had the opportunity to attend NLP training done by a recognised trainer or practitioner we would highly recommend that you do so. NLP is a set of practical skills and there is even more to learn than can be touched on in the context of a written text. Look out for training delivered by registered trainers of, for example, either the International NLP Trainers Association (INLPTA) or the Association of NLP (ANLP) or other organisations which have trainer accreditation and quality assurance processes.

Most of all have some fun!

Part 1

In the classroom activities

In the classroom activities			
Primary	Secondary	Special needs and emotional and behavioural difficulties	Gifted and talented children
* *	*	* * *	* * *

1 A little help from my friends

How to develop helping and listening skills

Have you ever been teaching children and suddenly realised that they were missing a simple piece of knowledge or part of the 'jigsaw', as it were? Sometimes teachers start teaching emotional literacy and social skills without covering and working through some basic practical skills. Again, as with most learning in this area, it is best to find an activity that helps children to understand some core ideas without bombarding them with theory. *Help me* is a simple activity that works well with children of a range of ages to get them to learn without them even knowing it and includes an easy way to introduce some NLP perceptual positioning.

Here's how

1. Get the children to work in threes. In each trio allocate three roles: learner, helper and observer.
   - The learner asks for help with some activity or problem.
   - The helper's role is to act as a support to help the learner to work through the problem or activity.
   - The observer's role is to feed back what they see and what they thought was helpful and what was not.

2. Run the activity several times so that each student has the chance to experience all three of the roles.

3. Debrief the activity by discussing what happened, what the children learnt during the activity and what they learnt from being in each of the different positions. Finally, ask them how they will use and apply this learning and to think of one specific thing that each of them will do differently as a result of this.

Learn more about this

Learning is a social process and as much as we would like children to begin to understand and develop their emotional literacy and social intelligence from reading about it – or being told about it – the truth is that this is not the best way to go about it. In many ways, the simpler the approach is the

Read some more about perceptual positions

- Read Chapter 7, 'Knowing me, knowing you . . . aha!', in *NLP for Teachers: How To Be a Highly Effective Teacher* (page 73)

better, and children can gain much from simply talking and listening to each other in a structured way. Many will also benefit from learning how to ask for help and receiving it, as well as from helping and supporting others. The observer space is also helpful to those children who are not yet good listeners, as this is the core focus of the role and requires responsibility and focused attention.

When else can you use this?

You can use this activity in a wide range of contexts and also adapt it to include other ideas from NLP such as perceptual positions (see the Index to find a perceptual positions tool). This type of activity is sometimes used in management development – you can adapt the activity and use it for a staff development day. Others examples of how you can use it can be found below.

- Use the *Help me* trio approach in revision lessons. Each child identifies an area of the subject that they need help with. Then they find someone else who knows the answer to the problem that they need to understand, so that they can learn from them – whilst someone else listens as observer.

- Combine the approach with learning about perceptual positions and other similar tools.

- Integrate the tool into a set of lessons that tackle bullying by getting the children to use their experiences of bullying and dealing with it within the trios. Use the learning from each other to talk about and define strategies for dealing with bullies.

What are you going to do with this?
(Your ideas and thoughts)

In the classroom activities			
Primary	Secondary	Special needs and emotional and behavioural difficulties	Gifted and talented children
* * *	* * *	* * *	* * *

2 And now I see it

How to improve children's spelling, learning and retention

Studies have shown that excellent spellers almost always use similar strategies in order to spell. They tend to look up or straight-ahead as they spell and visualise the word as they spell it. Spelling is mainly a visual process – we need to visualise or see a word we've seen before in order to spell it.

Robert Dilts, developer of the NLP spelling strategy, talks about spelling as an important and fundamental language skill that does not come 'naturally' to everyone. He says that intelligent people who otherwise excel in the classroom, even in language abilities, can experience strong and even debilitating difficulties in spelling. According to Dilts, ability with spelling is not a function of some kind of 'spelling gene' but rather the structure of the internal cognitive strategy one is using as one spells. Thus, if people experience difficulty with spelling, it is not because they are 'stupid', 'lazy' or have 'learning difficulties' but rather it is because they are trying to use an ineffective mental programme. When good spellers are observed, their eyes generally move up to the left (to access their visual memory) then move down to feel if it's right, or alternatively they may write the word down at this point (this may help them to access the kinaesthetic (feeling) part of their mind (University of Utah, 1987). Then they look up again to check it looks right. In English it is all but impossible to spell words phonetically – if you tried to spell phonetically by sounding it out it is very unlikely that you would succeed. In fact:

Wun wunders wy foenetick spelling methods arr stil tort as tha ownly weigh in sum skools.

However, on a serious note, we have found that using this method can dramatically increase the number of correctly spelled and stored words. And, of course, some phonetic strategies clearly have value in getting early years children to begin to access reading and writing. For those who find spelling a challenge this strategy can help enormously. It is very easy to teach and results are obtained immediately.

Here's how

You can use the strategy below with individual children or in classes. It is also fun to get children to lead the process. Some of the teachers that we have taught this to have become so convinced of the effectiveness of the approach that they have taken to always writing vocabulary lists and spelling word lists in the top left hand corner of their whiteboard to encourage the children to look up to the left when reading the words. How this works is an interesting area for debate – have a go yourself and let us know what happens.

The NLP Toolkit

1. First of all you will need some equipment:

    - a sheet of laminated A4 paper
    - dry wipe markers.

2. On the sheet of laminated paper (so you can wipe it clean and use again) write the word you want the students to learn. Ask the students to think of something familiar that gives them a good feeling (we want to anchor the correct spelling to a good feeling so that they will know by that feeling that the word is correct).

Hippopotamus

Get a good feeling mmmmm

3. Hold the laminated card above your head and have your students look up (to their left) and take a mental snapshot of the word. Turn the card with the blank face towards the students. Ask them to spell the word by visualising it on the card. If they're not able to do that then turn the card round, ask them to get that familiar feeling again and take another snapshot. Repeat this until they are able to spell the word correctly.

4. Take the card away and ask students to spell the word. You should see them look up to the left then down to the right as they spell the word.

5. You can also load words into the visual field in a more informal way by making sure that words that you want students to remember are placed high up on the classroom walls or written at the top of whiteboards. Students can make their mental image clearer by changing its 'submodalities' (the qualities in the image), for example, by making it bigger or brighter, even into a flashing neon light, bringing the image closer, changing the size or colour of smaller chunks of the word, such as prefixes or suffixes or giving a texture to the words.

Top tip

Most people say that looking up to the left works best for them but some people find that the right works best for them. Start in the classroom with 'left-up' looking, then for any children who find that this works less well for them encourage a 'right-up' look.

Learn more about this

The concept of installing or readjusting a person's strategies is a central theme in NLP. Strategies are the 'subroutines' that we run in our mind when we are doing things and frequently seem to relate to visual, auditory and kinaesthetic processing. In this sense strategies are a sort of mental programming. Our visual 'system' works simultaneously and is perfect for storing large amounts of data. When you look at something you can see it all at once – in one go (providing it's not too complex). We are able to access this data very quickly, much quicker than an auditory strategy.

Read some more about the NLP spelling strategy

Read:
- *Heart of the Mind* by Steve Andreas and Connirae Andreas
- *Righting the Educational Conveyor Belt* by Michael Grinder
- *NLP Workbook* by Joseph O'Connor
- Or read the research zone in *NLP for Teachers: How To Be a Highly Effective Teacher* (pages 162-3)
- The University of Utah research into the spelling strategy, and other references, can be accessed at www.kaltmodel.se: *Principles of Teaching Cognitive Strategies* by Thomas Malloy

When else can you use this?

Using a visual memory strategy works well for a range of contexts and not just for the learning of spelling. Just for a start have a go using it in the following ways:

- Use the strategy to support the development of mental arithmetic. People who are good at this often say that they store information on a sort of imaginary whiteboard that they keep up on the left side of their mind, and will glance up at it to write things now and then for storage later in the sum.

- Use to help in the remembering of mathematical or chemical formulas.

- Remember important dates from history by storing them in special places on displays up to the left.

What are you going to do with this?
(Your ideas and thoughts)

PENS

In the classroom activities			
Primary	Secondary	Special needs and emotional and behavioural difficulties	Gifted and talented children
* * *	* * *	*	* * *

3 Better remember me No. 1

How to use stories to help children remember

The next three resources, *Remember me 1, 2* and *3*, are all built on fun ways to improve memory. One of the easiest systems to begin with is the 'story method'. This is good for remembering characters, objects and information that need a sequence, and is based on the way our auditory systems function. It also engages our visual system with images, whilst making it outrageous can connect us kinaesthetically – especially if the story is funny, ridiculous or bizarre. The more outrageous, funny and bizarre you make the things you want to remember, or the circumstances around things, the easier they will be to remember.

Here's how

This activity works best when you apply it to some real knowledge or area of learning that you are covering within your teaching. It can be particularly effective and fun when applied in revision lessons or at the end of a scheme of work.

1. First take a list of things or ideas, say 15 to begin with.

2. Write them down. Read them out to the class and then ask who can remember them, this part is fun – as students will struggle to remember more than five.

3. Now give out one thing or idea to each person. Have one person start a story that must include the thing being portrayed in the story and be outrageous, unusual, ridiculous or bizarre.

4. The next person picks up the story and expands the story more, including their item in the most bizarre way and so on.

5. You will end up with a strange story that contains and connects all of the items.

6. Once you have made a story tell it again from start to finish. You can do this by having the group work together or you can have just one or two people retell the story.

7. Do this a couple of times until everybody has the learnt the story. The test is: can everybody repeat back the items from the original list without telling the story aloud?

Below is an example of this method as a way to remember the planets.

Mercury	Mercury, hot dude who was always rushing around looking for a date, went to ask . . .
Venus	Venus, the most beautiful planet for a date. Venus said he was too late and she was already going out with Earth . . .
Earth	This was news to Earth, who was busy trying to get rid of an infestation of humans that were causing him to itch like mad. He decided to call on . . .
Mars	Mars, as he had heard that Mars had managed to do this some while ago. Mars said that he had managed to get rid of the infestation, using some cream that he got from Jupiter . . . mind you, it had made his skin red and left him really dry . . .
Jupiter	As always, Jupiter was always busy concocting something in his laboratory. At that moment he was making a special potion designed to get rid of rings. He was due to deliver it the next day to . . .
Saturn	Saturn. She was pleased to see Jupiter, as she'd been having trouble with her rings for quite a while – they squeaked and squealed as they went round and round. Saturn was hoping that the potion would help her have a quiet night and stop all the complaints that she was having . . .
Uranus	From Uranus, who was a grumpy old chap who always complained of the cold, and how he didn't get enough sun being this far out . . . mind you, he was not in half as much trouble as . . .
Neptune	Neptune, who due to the cold had been stuck in his frozen bath for so long even the bubbles were solid, and all he could hear . . .
Pluto	Was the incessant barking of Pluto, who always felt that he was not part of the family.

Learn more about this

By engaging the visual, auditory and kinaesthetic systems together in memory exercises we can help both the storage and subsequent retrieval of information. Before paper, right back to Greek and Roman times, memory systems were very common; it was how Greek and Roman orators were able to speak in philosophical or political debates for hours.

Read some more about fun memory games

- Read the next two chapters!

Simple memory systems are easy to learn and great fun – for younger children they can be made into a game.

Top tip

This sort of activity works best when you give the children lots of freedom and allow them to let their creative 'juices' flow. Humour can make a real difference to learning and this is a great way to have fun, encourage creativity and remember things at the same time.

The NLP Toolkit

When else can you use this?

You can do this type of activity as a standalone classroom activity or integrate it into other work. For example, you might get the children to create a dramatic presentation around their story or an online presentation. Other ways that you can use this can be found below.

- This makes a great party game or training activity with trays of random objects.

- Useful for anything that has a sequence and in which the sequence is important, such as dates and historical events.

- Use yourself when you have something to remember.

What are you going to do with this?
(Your ideas and thoughts)

PENS

In the classroom activities			
Primary	Secondary	Special needs and emotional and behavioural difficulties	Gifted and talented children
* * *	* * *	*	* * *

4 Better remember me No. 2

How to use images to help children remember

This chapter explains the 'peg memory system'. This relies on working with the visual system; in this method we create specific images that will represent numbers. These images will stay constant and act like pegs on which we can hang what we need to remember. Once you have this system installed in your mind you can recall items in many ways – forwards in sequence or backwards in sequence. By being given the number of the peg you can tell what the item is, or alternatively, if you are given the item you will be able to tell what number it was in a list.

Here's how

The basis of this memory system is the creation of a set of unique and highly memorable images that you then associate with the things that you want to remember.

1. Create your 'pegs' (or unusual visual images) and memorise them. This may take between 15 minutes and half an hour (see below for some peg suggestions). Take a list of ten random things or ideas.

2. Write them down as a numbered list – or better still, as a demonstration have someone write the list so you cannot see it, using random items given by the group. The great thing here is that you will be given the most ridiculous and crazy items which, of course, are in themselves easier to remember.

3. Let someone read each item from the list one at a time in order from one to ten. You tell them when you want the next item so that you have enough time to attach the item to the permanent peg in your mind (e.g. if your number one was a skyscraper and somebody gave you an elephant to remember you would see in your mind's eye a massive skyscraper with a huge elephant balanced on top).

4. Once you have your items attached to pegs then it is possible to recall the items in sequence backwards, forwards or randomly, even if you are given the number of the peg or asked what number and item is on the list.

Making your pegs

Each peg should have a different shape and be like the number – make them very big, bright and colourful in your imagination, preferably containing some motion. Here are some suggestions; it's best however to create your own personal set of pegs.

1	A skyscraper, a pencil, a sword
2	A swan
3	A hill tipped on its side
4	Sailboat
5	Snake, a hook
6	A golf club
7	An axe
8	Snowman
9	Balloon on a stick
10	Bat and ball, Laurel and Hardy

Learn more about this

This system of visual pegs can be expanded to allow for up to 10,000 items to be remembered. This is often the basis of memory feats that are done for shows and in memory competitions. It works because the system is primarily a visual method – where data is held simultaneously and access is fast.

Read some more about fun memory games

- Read the last chapter and the next one!

When else can you use this?

- Teach children to help them with revision.

- You can use this method for remembering lists when you have no pen and paper – it is quicker than creating a story.

- Use it when you go shopping.

What are you going to do with this?
(Your ideas and thoughts)

In the classroom activities			
Primary	Secondary	Special needs and emotional and behavioural difficulties	Gifted and talented children
*	* * *	*	* * *

5 Better remember me No. 3

How to use spatial approaches to help with memory

The last of our three memory systems is called the 'Roman room' (see the previous two chapters for two other approaches). This system is based on the way Roman and Greek orators would remember their facts. These orators were well known for being able to speak for many hours and to follow a line of argument accurately and with evidence. This is a great technique because you can use your classroom as the setting. The concept with this system is similar to the peg system in that it works by having a constant image where you can store your ideas, concepts and items. The Greeks and Romans would memorise a large public building in such detail that they could walk through and around the building in their imagination. This gave great scope and a massive area in which to store their memories.

Here's how

In the Renaissance, scholars developed a system called the 'temple of Solomon'. The temple of Solomon had seven doors inside the temple. From those seven doors were seven rooms where you could keep information. You could then have a temple devoted to a single subject and have as many temples as you liked. The most interesting thing that happens with this sort of approach is that, once you have your primary data stored in your mind, your unconscious mind begins to weave together new and original thoughts, inventions and concepts – as well as remembering what you wanted to remember. Have a go and see what happens. Pick a room that you know really well – this could be your classroom, living room or bedroom, or you could use your entire house or school.

1. Spend some time in the room, or imagining the room, until you can accurately hold it in your mind and you can recall all of the features of the room. Remember all the cupboards, tables and permanent features.

2. You now have a template upon which to store your information.

3. For each piece of information you want to store create a visual image – make it bright, colourful and larger than life – and put this in a particular place in the room.

4. Decide on a direction or route to walk round the room and keep this constant. Place your ideas in sequence on your walk around the room. Put them in interesting and unusual positions where you would never find them in real life – they don't have to obey the laws of gravity, so you can hang them from the ceiling, suspend them in midair and even have them moving. Spend a little time fixing the image in its place in your room before you move on to place the next one.

5. Go back into your room as many times as you need to, to position new information. When you do this you should walk around the room in the same way and recall the other objects that you have already placed there. This will help embed the memory.

Learn more about this

With memory systems, one or another will be appropriate for remembering different things. The Roman room combines the sequential properties of a story (you can add a narrative to this as you walk around the room) together with the visual quirkiness that makes the peg system work so well (see the previous two chapters). Furthermore, like the Renaissance scholars

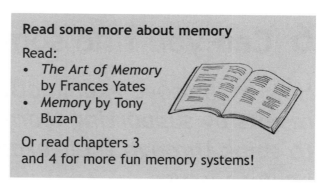

Read some more about memory

Read:
- *The Art of Memory* by Frances Yates
- *Memory* by Tony Buzan

Or read chapters 3 and 4 for more fun memory systems!

you can have many rooms in your memory, each one organised in your own style and designated for different groups of information. These memory systems are a fun way to enhance your ability to store and recall those vital bits of information. By practising these systems you can not only improve your memory but also amaze and intrigue your friends.

When else can you use this?

As with the memory approaches in the last two chapters this tool is great fun and can either be taught as a standalone activity or incorporated into your already planned work. You can also:

- Use it for memorising speeches, talks or what you are going to say in a complicated lesson.

- Use when you are out and about to help you to think through the planning of schemes of work.

- Teach it to children to help them with revision – get them to draw their rooms and fill in the key information around the room.

What are you going to do with this?
(Your ideas and thoughts)

In the classroom activities			
Primary	Secondary	Special needs and emotional and behavioural difficulties	Gifted and talented children
*	* *	* *	* * *

6 Can you find some balance?

How to improve examination results by supporting learners to think through their exam-life balance issues

Life is all about prioritising, we all know that as teachers. In fact we are pretty good at it – well, most of the time. But how often do we stop to share with the children that we teach approaches to ensuring balance and the prioritising of time and effort? The tool below was developed in NLP to help explore values and ensure a balance between core values and purpose, and has been widely adapted and used in executive and life coaching. It is also a great way to explore the things that affect us in a particular context and where we need to adapt and be more flexible in order to achieve our goals.

Here's how

The Balance Hexagon is a useful tool to help identify the areas of life that may need more attention than they are currently being given. It can be particularly helpful in situations like planning for examinations, thinking through what stops children revising and helping to ensure motivation.

1. Photocopy the blank resource sheet on page 18. You will need one copy for each student.

2. Every part of the hexagon is intended to represent an area of life or a personal priority that impacts on success. Get the students to list the key areas of importance in their life, including revision, examination preparation, coursework completion, free time, etc. They should then write the top six things in the boxes at the outside edge of each segment.

3. Next ask them to rank on a scale of 1 to 10 how effective they think that they currently are in each of the areas and how much effort they currently put into improving the areas in question.

4. Tell them to imagine a scale from 1 to 10 extending outward from the hub of the hexagon and get them to mark this point and then shade the area in. Then get them to prioritise areas for action by numbering the arrows on the outside.

5. Finally, ask them to take the two areas that are most in need of action. Shade in the arrows for these two areas. Consider all the current things that stop them moving forward at present then consider all the things that they need to do to overcome these problems. Some people find it helpful at this point to draw a new hexagon just focusing

on this area so that they can drill down into more details and find more solutions (see the example below).

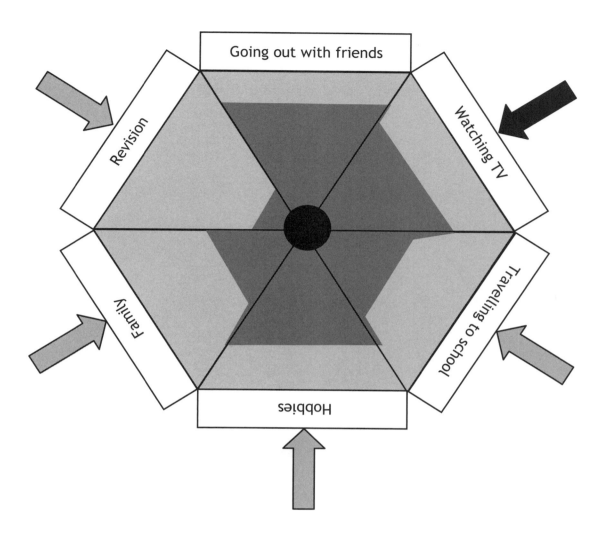

Balance Hexagon resource sheet

1. Write in the white boxes the key areas of your life and what takes up your time

2. Shade the triangles in from the centre to the outside edge, imagining a scale from 1 to 10, to show which areas are currently most important to you.

3. Shade the two arrows to indicate where you need to change.

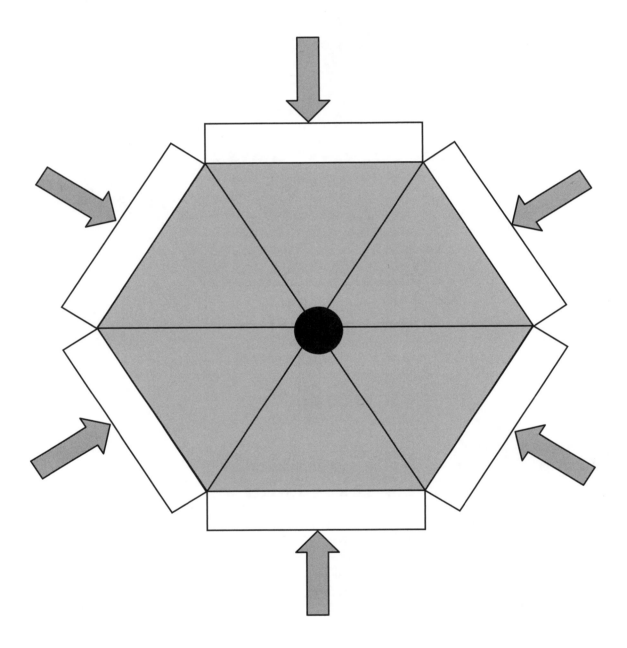

Learn more about this

As is frequently pointed out in NLP, our working memory and therefore our conscious processes are limited to about seven plus or minus two pieces of information. In many cases this limited level of thinking determines many of our future actions, until we notice or think of something else.

> **Read some more about values and NLP**
>
> • Read Chapter 11, 'The teacher within' in *NLP for Teachers: How To Be a Highly Effective Teacher* (page 131)
>
>

Tools like the Balance Hexagon force us to take into account other things that we may have put to the back of our minds but would benefit from engaging with.

When else can you use this?

This is a really good tool for use in a wide range of personal development contexts – with children, colleagues or people that you line manage as a leader. You can also apply the hexagon approach as a tool for supporting classroom activities and discussions.

- Use yourself to prioritise your thinking in an area of personal or professional development.

- Use when coaching colleagues to help them explore work–life balance issues.

- Use with values to coach. Get the person you are coaching to list the top six things that are important to them in life and then work through the process to help them to identify where they are out of balance and what they are going to do about it.

- This is a very flexible tool so enjoy experimenting with how many different ways you can use it!

What are you going to do with this?
(Your ideas and thoughts)

In the classroom activities			
Primary	Secondary	Special needs and emotional and behavioural difficulties	Gifted and talented children
* *	* * *	*	* * *

7 In character

How to enhance characterisation in drama lessons (and creative writing)

Helping children to grasp the ideas inherent in playing a part or becoming a character when they are acting is not always easy. Because it can be difficult to imagine what other ways of thinking or behaving there are, learning about 'metaprograms' is a great way to help learners to recognise the differences between people and how this leads to different ways of thinking and behaving. This is also a really great tool when preparing to do an improvisation.

Here's how

- Get the children to imagine the character they are planning to play. Then explain to them that people are different and are all made up of different combinations of psychological preferences and ways of thinking. That said, there are common areas of preference that we all have. Each of these is a continuum with two very different ways of thinking and being at each end of the continuum. A good example is the metaprogram *options or procedures*: some people prefer to have things kept open and have choices; others like to follow a process step-by-step.

- With older children you could run a little activity to illustrate this. Put two cards on the wall at either side of the room. On one write 'I can play any time' and on the other write 'I need to get my work done before I play' and get them to line up on a continuum between the two places. If you were to do this with a large group of people you would find that you get something like a 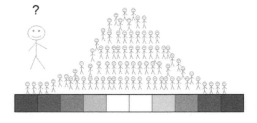 normal distribution curve, like the diagram on the right – with some people extremely *options-orientated*, most people somewhere in the middle and some people extremely *procedures-orientated*.

- You could even draw a diagram, like the one above, and get them to decide where on the continuum their character might be for this type of thinking and what their behaviours might then be.

- Now ask the children to work through the metaprograms worksheet on page 22 and decide what the character they are going to play, improvise or write about is going to be like for each of the areas.

Learn more about this

It has long been known in psychology that people have different personality types, traits and preferences and that these affect people's behaviours. Recently, a personality questionnaire called CDAQ, which is based on NLP metaprograms, has been given British Psychological Society accreditation.

Read some more about metaprograms

- See Chapter 7, 'Knowing me, knowing you . . . aha!', in *NLP for Teachers: How To Be a Highly Effective Teacher* (page 73)

Interestingly, metaprograms do not appear to be fixed in the same way as traits (although we all change over time) but rather are probably contextual. This makes them ideal for modelling excellence in others or for just making an assessment of a person's make up and then applying this to yourself (for personal development or even as a means of developing your acting skills).

When else can you use this?

Having an understanding of metaprograms is helpful in a wide range of situations. For example, you can:

- Notice metaprograms yourself when working with children in the classroom. *Global–specific* is particularly important in relation to how we take in and understand information.

- Use a similar worksheet to help children understand teamworking and working in groups after an activity.

- Use to support creative writing.

- Think about your own metaprograms and what this means for you in your daily life or explore metaprograms from a leadership perspective and reflect on the implications for your leadership style.

What are you going to do with this?
(Your ideas and thoughts)

PENS

In the classroom activities

Metaprograms – characterisation sheet

Preference of my character			How strong is their preference?	How therefore will my character behave in this scene or play?
Internal He/she knows when they have achieved something because they feel it inside		**External** He/she needs to be told by others that they have done well		
People orientation My character notices the people things first		**Activity orientation** My character notices tasks more than people		
Possibility My character has his/her head in the clouds and likes to have new ideas		**Reality** My character is a feet on the ground person		
Towards My character is motivated by future ideas and goals		**Away from** My character is motivated by avoiding fear and mistakes		
Options He/she like choices	**Or**	**Procedures** He/she likes to do things in an agreed step-by-step way		
Accept My character trusts what people say easily		**Evaluate** My character is more wary of people and needs convincing		
Active He/she is a do first person		**Reflective** He/she is a think first person		
Global He/she thinks big picture		**Detail** He/she thinks details		
Perfecting He/she likes to get things absolutely right		**Optimising** He/she can live with some errors		

In the classroom activities			
Primary	Secondary	Special needs and emotional and behavioural difficulties	Gifted and talented children
* *	* * *	* *	* * *

8 Code word

How to develop confidence and the right emotional state before exams or tests

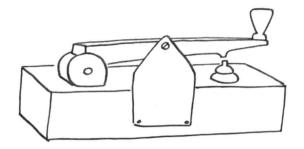

Have you ever been really well prepared for something and then when you came to do it your nerves, internal or emotional state of mind or just your sense of focus, has let you down? The same thing can apply to your students in an examination room – or in any context where they are going to have to perform. Anchoring is an NLP technique based on classical conditioning and is a sort of Pavlovian conditioning for people. We can all learn to associate any feelings with a specific stimulus, visual, kinaesthetic or auditory. In the tool below you can learn how to help your students to have a positive auditory anchor to help them focus and maintain the right emotional state when in an examination situation.

Here's how

As with all guided visualisations an element of trance creation is involved. The effectiveness of this will very much depend on the expectancy that you create in your students and how you present it. Make sure that you use language that presupposes success and be confident about the results.

1. Tell your students to close their eyes and notice their breathing.

   As you sit there listening to my voice you could begin to notice your breathing, so that with each breath you take you become more relaxed.

   Use a calm and gentle voice. There will be a few students who don't close their eyes – that's fine, you will not always get them all to relax the first time they do it but be encouraging.

2. When their eyes are closed and they are looking relaxed use the following visualisation.

   Now you can imagine someone you trust, someone whose views you respect and someone that you look up to . . . Notice yourself meeting that person in a safe and special place. Notice what you see, the colours and shapes – what's there? Now notice what you hear and what you feel whilst you are near to that person. Notice the conversation and begin to notice your feelings of confidence and security. Think about the resources that you have and the sense of confidence, focus and calmness that is in that space. As you do that you could begin to think of a single code word that sums up these positive feelings and internal resources. Knowing that that word will be able to take you back to those feelings whenever you need to in the future.

3. You may want to elaborate on some of the details and leave some pauses to allow the children to create their own internal imagery.

4. Now you are going to 'future pace' the resources.

    Now imagine a line stretching out in front of you towards the future and allow yourself to float up high and into the future. Float up until you see yourself looking down on yourself doing the examination. Notice what you look like down below and when you are ready to . . . float down into your body as you say your secret code word. Experience what it is like to have all those positive resources inside you as you look down at that examination paper. Now when you are ready float back out of yourself and back down your timeline until you find yourself back in your body, still here, still with your eyes closed.

    Again use plenty of pauses.

5. Now you will need to bring the students back into the present. So use words like:

    And as I count down from five to one you could begin to notice your breathing again . . . four . . . the sounds around you . . . three . . . remembering your code word . . . two . . . noticing your eyelids . . . one . . . being wide awake and ready to learn more.

6. Now explain to your students about taking time to practise their code word so that they can use it in the future.

Learn more about this

This is a similar process to the one used by Pavlov when he conditioned his dogs to salivate when they heard the sound of a bell. In the case above the code word is used to trigger positive feelings in a situation that would otherwise prevent us from accessing them. Being consciously aware of such possibilities gives us 'mindfulness' and the ability to modify our feelings and emotions. Using positive feelings helps to prevent the sort of negative and stressful feeling that can cause an 'amygdala' reaction in our brains and prevent learning and effectiveness.

Read some more about anchoring

- Read Chapter 9, 'Anchors away!' in *NLP for Teachers: How To Be a Highly Effective Teacher* (page 105)
- For an early account of anchoring as a process read *Frogs into Princes* by Richard Bandler and John Grinder

Top tip

Anchors work best if they are 'clean' of other stimuli. Encourage the children to choose an unusual code word that they would not use for anything else – otherwise the word could be associated too easily with other feelings and memories.

You will, of course, need to modify the language that you use to best fit the age group that you are dealing with.

When else can you use this?

The process of anchoring can be used in any context where the management of emotions and feeling is important. Below are some ideas to get you going:

- Teach a disruptive child to use anchoring when they need to maintain calmness.

- Get the children to choose the resources that they want to anchor (confidence, calmness, a clear memory) and include a section in the script where they remember having these feelings.

- Use it yourself when you are going to do a presentation or need to be able to access internal resources.

- You can also use auditory anchors covertly in the classroom in order to support classroom management. If you use a slightly unusual word for particular points in the lesson (e.g. clearing up, setting homework, before pointing to certain behaviours) and are consistent in only using this word for this you will gradually condition children to expect that action and over time this will begin to build easier compliance.

What are you going to do with this?
(Your ideas and thoughts)

PENS

In the classroom activities			
Primary	Secondary	Special needs and emotional and behavioural difficulties	Gifted and talented children
*	* * *		* * *

9 Logical levels

How to help children to develop their reasoning skills

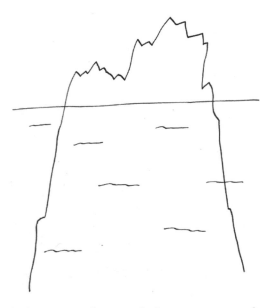

Many things that we need to learn have first to be categorised. This activity is designed to help children and adults categorise in a logical way. This is an essential skill when mind mapping, debating and writing reports. Logical levels can help us understand how things fit together and how we can mis-categorise information. This also has a role in negotiating and helping us reach agreements. Sometimes called 'chunking' in NLP, this model also helps us understand that some people are really comfortable with just the big picture and others need details in order to feel they understand. Everyone has a preference and will access information at different levels of detail. When giving information this preference comes into play as well.

Here's how

We have probably all met the person who when you asked a simple question such as 'How are you?' will spend a long time giving you minute details about their world and their experience whilst there are others for whom just one word will suffice. Being able to identify the chunk size of the person you are communicating with and develop flexibility in your own style will improve your communication and rapport skills. This activity is broken into two parts. The first is a facilitation on the whiteboard or flipchart, where you can guide the group's thinking so that they understand the principle behind logical levels (chunking).

1. On the flipchart or whiteboard in the centre choose a common object and write the word or phrase in the centre. We often find the word 'car' or 'house' to be the easiest to work with.

2. We are now going to work down from that word by asking the question 'What is an example of X?' If we have used 'car' we should get answers like Ford, BMW, Ferrari, etc. – write this below the word car. Next ask 'What is an example of a *Ford* (or whatever category comes up)?' This will give you in this example a model such as a *Fiesta*. Repeat the question until you get to the smallest details, see below.

3. Now we're going to move in the other direction. We're going to be chunking up. Start again at your initial category in this example 'car'. Ask 'What is a *car* an example of? The answer should be a *vehicle* or something similar.

4. We can then move up the logical levels by asking the same question again. This time we ask 'What is a *vehicle* an example of?' The answer should be *transport* or something similar. Continue to ask the question until you can go no further and reach words like existence, life, etc. This gives you the vertical axis and categorisation and is called a logical type.

5. Go back to the *car* in our example and ask 'What are other examples?' This will give you the lateral or logical level information and usually the answer in our example will be bicycle, van, train, etc. You now have a map which helps enormously with understanding categorisation. There are other questions that you can ask which assist in moving up, down or across (see below).

Quick start - Logical levels chunking examples

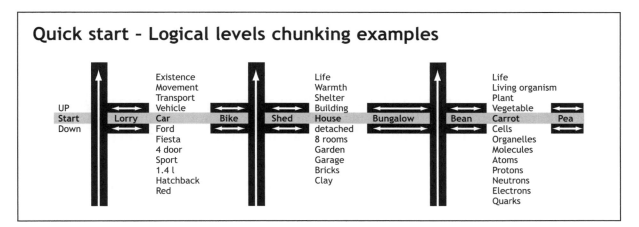

Other questions that can be helpful to ask

Chunking up

- What is that an example of?
- What is the wider context?
- What is important about that?
- What is that part of?
- How could you categorise that?
- What will that do for you?
- What would be the bigger picture?
- What is the purpose?
- What is the intention?
- What are the principles?

Chunking across

- What does this remind you of?
- What else would be in the same category?
- Can you think of other examples of this?

Chunking down

- What specifically or what exactly?
- Where, when, how, who specifically?
- Tell me about a specific instance?
- What are the details?
- What parts is it made of?
- What are the components?
- Tell me exactly how you would do it?
- Give me the precise steps?

The NLP Toolkit

Learn more about this

This idea of logical levels, called 'chunking' in NLP, originally came from Bertrand Russell and Alfred North Whitehead who were trying to find a way to separate classes and types in mathematics. However, in understanding how human beings sort information these are also incredibly useful concepts. They help us get a clear idea of how we can separate, sort and categorise information.

> **Read some more about logical levels, or chunking, and how they can be applied in other areas of life**
>
>
>
> • *Steps To An Ecology of Mind* by Gregory Bateson
>
> Find out more ways to use chunking in the classroom in:
> • Chapter 12 (Questions, questions, questions)

When else can you use this?

Teaching children about logical levels has benefits in all areas of learning and can help learners to think more clearly and organise ideas more effectively. In leadership this activity can also be used to help a team get unstuck when they find themselves focusing on the wrong level of detail. Have a go at using it in the following ways and contexts:

- Use as a negotiating tool. Chunk up until you reach agreement and then chunk down into the detail only as fast as you can maintain agreement.

- Logical levels (chunking) can help categorising information in mind maps.

- Helps sort information and tasks out for projects.

- Steer conversations to the subject you want to talk about.

- If a child is stuck understanding something, notice where they are in terms of chunk size and chunk up, down or across by asking a good question – in order to 'unstick' their mind.

What are you going to do with this?
(Your ideas and thoughts)

In the classroom activities			
Primary	Secondary	Special needs and emotional and behavioural difficulties	Gifted and talented children
* *	* * *	* *	* * *

10 Model village

How to enhance learning and listening skills through observation and activity

Looking for more ways to structure active learning in the classroom? With a little thought you can incorporate ideas from NLP into teaching and learning activities with ease. This can not only make learning more fun but can provide practical ways to create learning to learn opportunities for the children. The activity below works well for debates and learning situations where there will be different views and opinions about a topic and includes elements of the NLP modelling process.

Here's how

Below you can find a way of structuring discussion activities that supports modelling (learning from the expertise of others through observation) and the observer perceptual position (stepping outside the situation to learn and notice things from a more objective space). Both of these ways of thinking and viewing the world can enhance the learning to learn skills of children of all ages and work well with older learners as well.

1. The village group at the centre of the activity needs to be made up of children who have expertise in or interests or experience to do with the area of learning. This small village group sits in a small circle and the other members of the group sit outside in a larger circle.

2. Whilst the village group sits and discusses the area of learning the other learners outside the village adopt an observer/modeller perspective.

3. Those outside the village group should:

   - Listen to the discussion
   - Notice skills and abilities
   - Make a note of things which they hadn't thought of and other perspectives
   - Make a note of things which come into their mind from a listener/observer perspective
   - Be prepared to share their observations and ideas when they join the village.

4. Put empty chairs in the village space so that the group can be joined by observers from time to time.

The NLP Toolkit

The observers

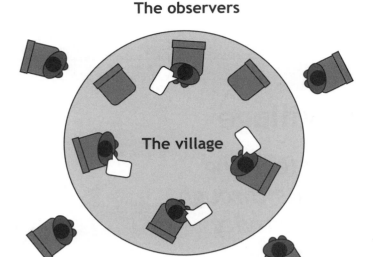

The village

Learn more about this

Gregory Bateson pioneered thinking about learning to learn (although he never used the phrase) in his ideas about Learning Zero, I, II and III. Adopting a 'meta' position (a bird's eye position on the learning that we are engaged in) gives us, as learners, the potential to modify our thinking and our understanding. To do this effectively learners need to develop an awareness of other possible ways of seeing the world, as in the Model village process – a bit like looking in a mirror, where you see a different point of view.

Read some more

- Read the research zone about Bateson's work in *NLP for Teachers: How To Be a Highly Effective Teacher* (page 47)
- For some deeper understanding read Bateson's *Steps To An Ecology of Mind*
- Learn more about modelling by reading *Modelling with NLP* by Robert Dilts

When else can you use this?

You can apply the observer approach from this tool to a wide range of teaching and learning activities. Sometimes this approach is also known as 'the fish bowl' or 'theatre' approach. Below are a few suggestions to get you started:

- Use in performance arts projects as a way of getting children to critically appraise performances.

- Get older children to appraise the process they have been through and the benefits. Get the children to reflect on what else they could do with this process.

- Incorporate mind mapping into the process by getting the children in the centre circle to be designing a large mind map of the learning that they engaged in. The observers can do their own mapping and then the groups can come together to compare thoughts and thinking.

- Modify the content of the activity and use as part of a training or inset day for teachers.

What are you going to do with this?
(Your ideas and thoughts)

In the classroom activities			
Primary	Secondary	Special needs and emotional and behavioural difficulties	Gifted and talented children
* *	* * *	* *	* * *

11 On the job

How to develop interview skills and at the same time learn the power of modelling others

The idea of learning from the excellence of others is at the heart of NLP. Although modelling can be complex and detailed, it can also be straightforward and simply involve noticing the things that people who are good at something do. Getting children to notice this process and recognise it is important because, in many ways, modelling is a life skill that we all have but sometimes are not aware of.

Here's how

This activity has three stages. Firstly, the use of a role play to develop and practise some skills; secondly, a debrief to unpick the key skills that were effective; and thirdly, a practice session to embed and improve skills.

1. Ask the children to think about what sort of questions are important to ask in a job interview, if they were the person employing someone – the sort of questions that would be asked whatever job was being applied for. They could write these on cards or have an interview questions sheet.

2. Get them to form groups of three or four. One person should be the person applying for the job, one person the interviewer and the other person/people observers. The student who is role playing the applicant should decide what job they are applying for and then tell the rest of the people in the group.

3. Allow some preparation time for the interviewers and the interviewees. During this time the observers should come together and discuss what sort of things they think will make a good interviewee. You may want to give them some prompts: voice tone, body language, things to say and not to say, etc.

4. Run the interviews through. After each round of interviews each group should discuss what they saw and what they thought was good, also any things that they thought could be improved. Repeat the activity so that everyone has had the opportunity to work through the process.

5. Run a class discussion about all the things that were observed around the question: what makes an excellent interviewee? Finally, pair the students up with someone they have not yet worked with so they can 'model' and practise the top skills that were identified from the activity.

Learn more about this

Learning is a social process and as well as learning knowledge and facts there is much to be learnt from observing the way that effective people do things. Often this effectiveness is related to things other than the

Read some more about modelling

- Read *Modelling with NLP* by Robert Dilts

words that are being used: such as body language, beliefs and even internal mental pictures and imagery. Learning to recognise, model and adopt approaches to being effective is a life skill and one that is easily learnt as a child.

Top tip

Some groups will pick this up quickly, others will need some prompting and some will need you to scaffold their learning with a little more input. Use skilful questioning to ensure that the children notice and unpick a range of details.

- Voice tone
- Body language
- Internal beliefs and ideas
- Mental imagery (positive or negative that may be having an effect)
- The way that answers to questions are organised, etc.

When else can you use this?

This approach to modelling can be used and applied in a wide range of contexts – you could also use the same approach when supporting other teachers. Here are a couple of suggestions:

- Adapt the activity to support in the teaching of areas such as careers or to help students prepare for university interviews.

- Apply the ideas of modelling in subject areas where there is a strong emphasis on observation and skills development (e.g. Physical Education, Drama).

What are you going to do with this?
(Your ideas and thoughts)

In the classroom activities			
Primary	Secondary	Special needs and emotional and behavioural difficulties	Gifted and talented children
* * *	* * *	* * *	* * *

12 Questions, questions, questions

How to be more precise when using questions in the classroom

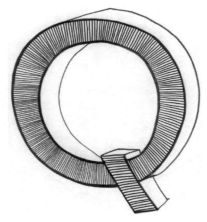

Have you ever asked a question and found your children's or students' thinking taken to a place where you didn't intend it to go? Did you think about what type of question to ask or did you just launch off and ask questions? Questions affect our thinking in lots of different ways and affect the internal processing of the people who are being asked. One key way in which this works is to do with whether a question forces us to think big picture or detail, or whether it forces us to move across to other categories of the same thing. In this chapter you can find some practical applications of the idea of logical levels that was discussed earlier in the book.

Here's how

In NLP we talk about 'chunking up' or 'chunking down' – a process that Bandler and Grinder identified excellent therapists using and being aware of. Chunking up is the process by which we move from detail to big picture, from specifics to generalisation.

For example, a car is a type of transport.

Transport

Car

This concept comes from Bertrand Russell's ideas about logical type and the application of thinking about sets from maths to words and word logic. Thus, a car is a member of the set of things that are transport.

Transport

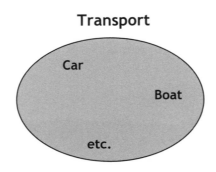

Car

Boat

etc.

A question that would lead someone to think up one 'logical level of type' would be

> *What type of thing is a car?*

Alternatively, we can 'chunk down' to look at what types of car there are, or 'what are the parts of a car?'

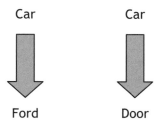

We can also 'chunk across' at any point to talk about other things that are also types of transport, or on another level other types of car, in which case we move within a category within a logical level.

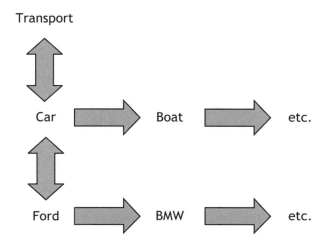

The same principles apply to simple knowledge as well as highly academic concepts. Below you can find a good way to start applying the ideas in practice.

- Reread the explanation above.

- Write the name of an object or idea in the centre of a piece of paper or in the 'What are you going to do with this?' section below.

- Think of a question you could ask.

- Now decide whether that question chunks down, chunks up or chunks across. Is that where you would want to go with learners?

- Now think about where you might want learners to go in their mind and construct some precision questions that will frame their thinking. Have a go with different questions and notice the differences.

Learn more about this

Gregory Bateson noticed that not only does the concept of set and category apply to mathematical logic but also to word logic and the way our minds work.

Thinking and learning about logical levels of type and chunking up and down is another way of helping children to 'go meta', to the details and concepts that they are learning and to 'learn how to learn'.

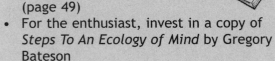

Read some more about chunking

- Read Chapter 5, 'Don't think about chocolate cake', in *NLP for Teachers: How To Be a Highly Effective Teacher* (page 49)
- For the enthusiast, invest in a copy of *Steps To An Ecology of Mind* by Gregory Bateson

Remember the core principle in NLP: what we put in other people's minds, or the frames we set, are what people will think about. Or:

The person who sets the frame controls the communication.

This is because people's conscious processes are limited to seven pieces of information, plus or minus two (the limits of working memory).

When you ask a question you are setting a frame. This frame will either lead people to chunk up in their minds, chunk down or chunk across. As a teacher you want to be the person setting the frames so you remain in control of the processes of thinking in your learners' minds, whilst freeing their minds to explore content and reinforce learning and connections between the content at different levels.

When else can you use this?

Any time that you use questions as a teacher in the classroom or as a school leader you will engage people's minds at one logical level or another. Here are some other examples of how to start using the technique:

- When explaining things or introducing topics, start big picture and chunk down one logical level at a time. Keep your chunks to three pieces of information at each level, so you don't overload their working memory and send them off into different directions in their thinking.

- If you notice that you are working with someone one-to-one whose 'metaprogram' preferences (see Chapter 7, 'In character', for information on this) are for specifics rather than global information, start them off in the details and then chunk up one level at a time.

- When writing reports or proposal documents, start big picture and chunk through logical levels so that the writing is clear.

- Teach children about chunking so that they have a structure in mind when writing essays: big picture chunk, chunk down a level, then chunk across the other details at that level, etc.

- When you are negotiating, chunking up – to find common agreement about the purpose of something – is a really great

36

way to resolve conflict and begin the agreement process; this is because people will often get stuck arguing about a detail when they in fact want the same thing. Once they realise this, people are often more willing to compromise on the small details.

- In meetings notice what logical level people are operating at and challenge their thinking by asking a question that takes people's minds to another logic level. After all, Einstein is reputed to have suggested that the solutions to problems are always to be found at a different level! This was the same principle applied by Bateson to code breaking in the Second World War.

What are you going to do with this?
(Your ideas and thoughts)

In the classroom activities			
Primary	Secondary	Special needs and emotional and behavioural difficulties	Gifted and talented children
* * *	* * *	* * *	* * *

13 Storymaker

How to use a story to support learning

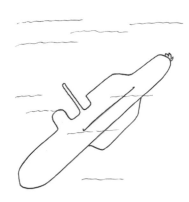

Think about the last story that you were told. What was it about? With stories, as with language, there is often a surface structure and a deep structure. The surface structure consists of the superficial content and the words that are actually used in the story. However, there is often a deeper meaning, moral or message to the story – below the waterline. Just like a submarine these deeper meanings are not easily seen from the surface, but are there nonetheless. In NLP research into highly effective hypnotherapists, like Milton Erickson, it was noted that they frequently used stories to create change in their clients. The same thing is true with learning.

Here's how

Stories with meaning and message help people to grasp concepts and understanding at a level that is simpler to access and frequently easier to remember. A story which mirrors real life, and which has an underlying message, is called an isomorphic metaphor.

1. Take a few moments to think about something that you are planning to teach where there is an underlying concept or idea that you want to get across.

2. Now allow yourself to think of the first sort of story concept that comes to mind. The details are not important at the moment. The more unrelated it is the better in many ways!

3. It may help to have a particular image in mind that sums up the concept you are planning to use.

4. Now use the planning template below to map out the ways in which you might create your story or metaphor.

Here's an example. Some time ago Richard was about to do some training with teachers and Local Authority advisors about Robert Dilts's neurological levels of thinking. A key concept that the learners needed to grasp was the idea that we frequently forget to think about purpose when we begin something and then are surprised when it doesn't work out quite right in the end. The story/metaphor he used went something like this:

Put your hand up if you have ever owned a mug. Put your hand up if you have ever owned a favourite mug. We recently went somewhere where a new coffee machine had been installed. It was one of those automatic machines where you can select a packet from the rack, insert it and then press a button. Hey presto, out comes your drink. It looked sleek, contemporary and was carefully designed with a seriously impressive digital display – but you couldn't fit your mug into it and you had to remove the grill in order to do so. How is it that such things can happen – that extraordinary amounts of effort can be put into something that in the end doesn't work? Often in life we can fail to think about the purpose of things and what they are there for . . .

Although this is a simple metaphor example, you can also do something similar in a *'once upon a time . . .'* format or in a *'have you heard the story about the person who . . .'* type way. The planning sheet below will help you to think through your story and the underlying moral or message that you want to get across. For example, if your story was about a group of people working as a team in a business (to support understanding on a business course about teamwork), first decide on the number of characters and their role (leader, administrator, project manager) then the context (in an office planning something new). Then think of a story context (e.g. a ship). Have the same number of characters on the ship with parallel roles, etc. For example:

Once upon a time there was a ship that was beginning a long and complicated journey. On the ship were a captain, a cook and the first mate as they were yet to hire a crew . . .

Isomorphic metaphor planning sheet

Topic and underlying message that I want to get across

Metaphor or story context I am going to use

Areas to cover	Deep structure The real meaning and content	Surface structure The story I will tell and what will happen
People		
Place		
Problem		
Issues and challenges		
The process or journey		
What the answer or solution was		

Learn more about this

Storytelling is universal and neuroscience and psychology research suggests that the brain may be hardwired to enjoy stories and that narrative has both emotional and cognitive effects. Furthermore, ideas may be more easily accepted when people are in a story-accepting frame of mind compared to a more analytical frame of mind. This may also apply to learning and is, perhaps, the reason why storytelling is widely used as part of hypnotherapy and appears frequently in leadership contexts. Effective leaders tell stories too, and as the leader in your classroom you may want to draw on some of the potential of this way of leading, influencing and supporting learning and change.

Read some more about influential language

- See chapter 5, 'Don't think about chocolate cake', in *NLP for Teachers: How To Be a Highly Effective Teacher* (page 49)
- If you want some great change stories read *My Voice Will Go With You: The Teaching Tales of Milton Erickson* by Sidney Rosen
- Invest in a copy of the *Magic of Metaphor* by Nick Owen which is also full of some great ideas

When else can you use this?

Any time that you are teaching, explaining something or seeking to influence, telling a story or using a metaphor is a powerful way to have a greater impact. Develop your storytelling skills further by:

- Incorporating storytelling and metaphor into your leadership toolkit.

- Use the template to plan a story for a school assembly.

- Collect some funny everyday stories about your experiences that illustrate points and learning.

- Use metaphors with children to help them think about relationships and positive behaviour management.

- Get your learners to close their eyes and tell them a learning metaphor story in which people travel on a path to collect an object that symbolises their journey – bring the object back with them (a journey through a forest to a special place works really well).

What are you going to do with this?
(Your ideas and thoughts)

In the classroom activities			
Primary	Secondary	Special needs and emotional and behavioural difficulties	Gifted and talented children
* * *	* * *	* * *	* * *

14 Why did they do that?

How to get learners to have a deeper understanding of historical contexts

Have you ever been teaching something that involved understanding the past and found that the children were having difficulty relating to the people of the time and why they thought and acted like they did? Or maybe you just want to find an interesting activity to use for those times when you want your students to think more deeply and engage in discussions about what the people of the past might have felt or actually experienced?

Here's how

As well as being a great tool for personal development, perceptual positions (seeing the world from the three perspectives of self, other and observer) can be really helpful in classroom contexts where you need an activity that requires the children to step into the shoes of people from the past or people from another context. This can also be a great way to revise a topic or embed some of the learning.

Children can do this in pairs or in groups.

1. Get them to write the words: self, other and observer on three sheets of paper or use three chairs in a triangle (facing inwards)

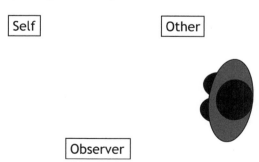

2. Next get the children to coach each other through the process. One child starts by standing on the 'self' space and thinking about the historical context from their own perspective. What do they know about life at the time? What questions would they like to ask someone from the past? What things do they not understand about people's motivations, feelings, values and beliefs?

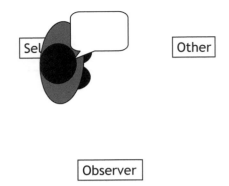

3. When they have finished doing this, the student should move to the 'other' space. In this space they imagine themselves as a real person from that time. They should stand like the person and even have a go at speaking like the person. Now get them to look across at the 'self' space where they were stood before and get them to talk about what it is like from this perspective – from the point of view of the historical person.

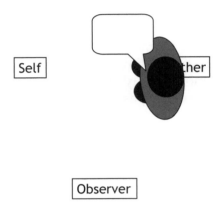

4. Finally, get them to stand or sit on the observer space and imagine themselves as an objective historian. What have they learnt from the experience? What do they now understand from the perspective that they have as an observer? What have they learnt about their own perspective as well as that of the historical character?

5. You can then allow the students to go back to any space that they might find helpful.

With younger children you can get them to cut out and design shoes for the three different positions or draw pictures to represent the historical character(s).

Learn more about this

Empathy is not only useful for developing our existing relationships and behaviours – being able to appreciate the world from different perspectives is a key skill for learners. We all have a preference for whether we see the world from a 'self' perspective or whether we tend to see the world from the point of view of other

Read some more about perceptual positions

- Read Chapter 7, 'Knowing me, knowing you . . . aha!', in *NLP for Teachers: How To Be a Highly Effective Teacher* (page 73)

people. Some people also prefer to adopt a more observer perspective. The truth is no one perspective is better than another. The key is to have flexibility and to have the ability to see things from different points of view.

When else can you use this?

You can use this type of activity wherever there is any learning that involves an understanding of others and where other people are coming from. You may also like to have a go at some of the following suggestions:

- Get the children to work in groups and write about, or do group mind maps, for each of the three perspectives.

- Adapt the tool by making the questions more challenging for older students.

- For older students get them to step out into a fourth perceptual position and think about the historical situation from a system or change perspective. Then go back into the other positions to learn and explore more.

- Use with drama students to help them develop characterisation and method acting approaches.

What are you going to do with this?
(Your ideas and thoughts)

PENS

In the classroom activities			
Primary	Secondary	Special needs and emotional and behavioural difficulties	Gifted and talented children
* * *	* * *	* * *	* * *

15 Yes or no!

How to get children to understand the difference between open and closed questions

Have you ever noticed children getting stuck in discussions? Or particularly finding the leading and questioning part of teamworking difficult? Often this can be because they have not yet acquired some of the understanding and skills that we as teachers take for granted. Helping them to recognise and understand the difference between open and closed questions is a powerful way of enhancing skills and opening doors to higher order thinking.

Here's how

This activity can be done in pairs or in groups.

1. On sticky labels get the children to write down the names of really famous people that everyone in the room is likely to know the names of, e.g. pop stars, footballers, famous historical characters.

2. Stick one of the labels to the back of one of the children in the group. Don't let them see what name is written on their label. The child then turns around and shows everyone in the group that she/he is working in what is on the label.

3. The person with the label on their back now has the task of trying to find out who is written on the label by only using 'yes' or 'no' questions.

4. When all the children have had an opportunity to be the questioner ask the children about what happened. How easy was it to find out with just 'yes' or 'no' questions? Now ask them to think about what other types of questions there are. Explain the difference between open and closed questions.

5. You can then get them to think about the effect of different questions. Get them to pair up and ask each other questions that begin with: *Why? What? When? Where?* or *Who?* Instead of answering the question, the person being asked the question should tell the other person where that question took them in their mind and what the effect of that question was.

6. Again debrief the activity by asking the children what happened. Finally get the children to talk about what they could do with the knowledge and what they will now do differently when working together. You can find below a questions Quick start that you may like to modify to create some teaching materials of your own.

Quick start – Open questions

Where questions take minds

When?

To a place in time (past/present/future)

Where?

To a place or location

How?

To thinking about processes and strategies

What?

To the place in our mind where we keep information
To thinking about outcomes

Who?

To thoughts about people

Why?

To explanation or reasons
or
To justification

Top tip

Why? is one of the most useful and at the same time problematic questions that we have in English. It is essential for prompting thoughts about explanations and reasoning in relation to fact and understanding of knowledge. Be careful, however, in how you use it when exploring behaviours and people's beliefs and values as it tends to imply justification and can put people on the defensive.

Think about it for a moment.

If I were to ask you 'Why are you wearing those clothes today?' where would your mind go?

Learn more about this

Questioning is one of the most powerful tools that we have in life and it is impossible not to respond in some way to a question (even if you do so only in your own mind). Using higher order questioning and more effective questioning with children is a key way to improve their analytical skills and reasoning. Teaching them to be able to question effectively not only enhances their own skills but will make any group working that you have set up as part of your lessons much more effective.

Read some more about questions and NLP

- Read Chapter 10, 'Verbal ju-jitsu' in *NLP for Teachers: How To Be a Highly Effective Teacher* (page 117)

When else can you use this?

It is all too easy to assume that children and even older learners understand how questions work and what their impact is. Find below some more suggestions about what you can do with this.

- With older children get them to think in more detail about all of the ways in which you can use questions.

- Instead of labels get the children to write names on cards and work in pairs.

- Get children to think about a problem or a situation and construct the best possible question that they could ask in this situation. This is great for moral dilemmas or for personal development issues.

- Teach the children questioning and coaching skills and integrate this activity into your lesson planning.

What are you going to do with this?
(Your ideas and thoughts)

Part 2

Emotional and social literacy with children

Emotional and social literacy with children			
Self-awareness	Self-management and motivation	Relationship awareness and empathy	Managing relationships and social skills
* * *	* * *	* *	* *

16 Diamond mine

How to develop self-awareness and explore values with children

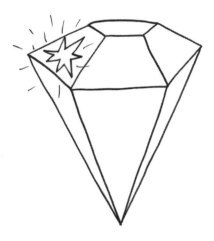

Although children are still developing their values and underlying motivations, in many ways this is the time to start them thinking and exploring such concepts. In fact, many adults would probably function better if they also had some tools to help them understand some of their underlying motivations and values. Teaching children to coach each other is also a great way of developing relationship skills and understanding.

Here's how

You will need nine pieces of card for each learner and some paper.

1. First run a simple 'values elicitation'. Get the children to question/coach each other to define what their values are in relation to a particular context (e.g. learning, relationships). This is easy to do. One child becomes the coach and the other the coachee. The coach simply asks 'What's important to you about . . .?' The answer is written down. Then the question is repeated and another value will emerge. Again the coach should keep asking 'What's important to you about . . .?' until there are nine values.

2. Note: it is really important to keep going as some of the values that we are least aware of may be the ones which we need to pay more attention to or modify.

3. When nine values that are important have emerged the coachee should write them on their nine cards.

4. Then the coachee should sort them into a 'diamond mine' with the most important values at the top and the least important at the bottom.

5. Once this has been done the coach should ask the coachee some good coaching questions, for example:

   • Think of a problem that you have or an issue for you in this area of your life.

   • Are there any of these values which you might benefit from prioritising higher up in your diamond? Re-sort the order.

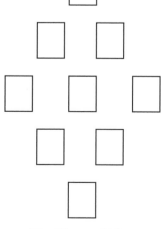

The Diamond Mine

- What behaviours do you need to change in order to achieve this?

- What would the ideal 'diamond mine' look like to solve this problem?

- Are there any values that you currently don't have in your mine which you might want to begin to develop? Write these down and add them in by re-sorting your priorities.

Top tip

Some values will emerge as 'towards a goal values' and others as 'away from values'. With values it is often good to phrase them in our internal dialogue as 'towards' motivations rather than 'away froms'. This is because 'away froms' have no goal in mind, other than getting away, whereas 'towards' values are goal directional and can presuppose behaviours. For example, the value:

I don't want to fail my next test

does not have any positive behaviours presupposed within it. It could include the behaviour to leave school early and never take a test again! It might be better to develop internal dialogue and values awareness with a more specific and 'towards value' such as.

It is important to me that I start early with my revision

This sort of thinking (and reframing) can be particularly powerful in relation to exploring values about relationships and behaviour management.

Learn more about this

Leading figures in education, such as Michael Fullan, have suggested that it is important for leaders in schools to practise and develop the behaviours that go with the values associated with moral purpose and that real breakthroughs in development come not just from doing but also from 'thinking about the doing'. In our experience in applying NLP to other contexts, the same can be said for many other walks of life, including learning how to become an effective learner and in the development of children's self-awareness and self-management.

Read some more about values and NLP

- Read Chapter 11, 'The teacher within', in *NLP for Teachers: How To Be a Highly Effective Teacher* (page 131)

When else can you use this?

Exploring values is a great way to engage any group to begin to develop effective behaviours and understanding. This can be just as effective with adult teams as it can be in the classroom with learners.

- Use the exercise with yourself to support an exploration of your own priorities.

- Use with teams in team leadership contexts. Get the team to agree on its top nine values first (this may take some time) then get them to 'diamond mine' what their current values hierarchy looks like and compare this to the ideal hierarchy for them to achieve their goals as a team. What should they change? Are there any other values that they would benefit from adopting?

- Use in a coaching session with a colleague or someone you line manage.

- The diamond approach is a great training and teaching structure – think of other ways to use it with more content specific activities and learning.

- Use with children who need one-to-one coaching to support their behaviour management and career planning.

What are you going to do with this?
(Your ideas and thoughts)

17 Ear you are

How to change behaviours in a fun way

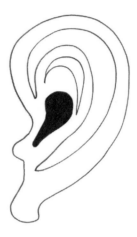

Have you ever blushed? What made you do that? What was it that triggered that automatic response that just seemed to happen before you had a chance to intervene? We are constantly reacting automatically to the environment around us as a result of some form of trigger or other. We can also use this phenomenon to our advantage by deciding to associate a particular behaviour with a trigger in the future so that we can avoid getting caught out again. The process at the heart of this is called 'anchoring'. In the tool below you can learn a way to anchor both a new behaviour and an appropriate trigger for that behaviour.

Here's how

This tool is really useful when a child knows what behaviour they want to replace (e.g. a reaction to a particular situation or person) and needs something to give them the confidence to adopt that behaviour in the future.

1. Identify the target behaviour that the child wants to have in place of what they currently do. Get them to visualise themselves really doing that as if it were through their own eyes.

2. Tell the children that when they can really feel themselves doing the thing they are imagining (with a rich cinema in their minds, including visual, auditory and kinaesthetic information) they should hold their earlobe. Tell them to hold their earlobe until their sense of being in the moment doing this new behaviour is at its strongest. Get them to do this a few times holding their earlobe until this action feels associated with thinking about the new behaviour.

3. Now get them to imagine doing something that they find really pleasing, something that they really enjoy. As they create the image of doing this in their mind tell them to hold their other earlobe. Again do this for a while until they associate this action with feeling the pleasurable feelings and experience the activity in their minds.

4. Now get them to merge the two feelings by holding both earlobes at once. Tell them to allow the two images to switch between each other until they become part of a single internal picture.

5. Test the effect of this by giving them something else to do and then getting them to pinch an earlobe again and notice what happens. Now explain to them that they have a resource that they can draw on when they think that they need to adopt their new behaviour in the future.

Top tip

As with all of these sorts of tools, your confidence and support for the child in working through them is essential. The more confident you are the more 'response expectancy' you will build up and the more effective the tool will be.

Learn more about this

Self-awareness and self-management are the keys to emotional literacy and some would say to effectiveness in general. Having novel or unusual strategies for developing self-management is an effective way of developing self-control and emotional state management. Anchoring combines awareness of internal state and feeling with the recognition that we all have the internal resources and abilities to manage our emotions and to choose our behaviours.

Read some more about anchoring and NLP

- Read Chapter 9, 'Anchors away!', in *NLP for Teachers: How To Be a Highly Effective Teacher* (page 105)

When else can you use this?

Anchoring is useful wherever it is important to manage emotions and internal feelings as part of behaviour management.

- Use the knuckles on the hand with older children or with spaces on the floor marked by pieces of paper.

- Teach anchoring to help children with examination nerves and to create positive states in the exam room.

- Share the technique with children with emotional and behavioural difficulties to help them with in the moment management of their feelings.

What are you going to do with this?
(Your ideas and thoughts)

Emotional and social literacy with children			
Self-awareness	Self-management and motivation	Relationship awareness and empathy	Managing relationships and social skills
* *	* * *	*	* *

18 High flyers

How to help children understand the importance of goals

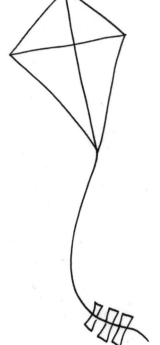

Do you know where you're going to? It is an obvious question but how often do we ask it of ourselves? If you don't know . . . how are you going to get there? This is a fun way to help children to recognise the importance of setting goals and outcomes in a way that includes an activity that you usually don't let them do!

Here's how

To do this you will need some plain paper to use for making paper aeroplanes, some paperclips and clear sticky tape. You will also need a big space to have fun in and a long tape measure or some way of marking out/pacing out distances and measuring.

1. Get all the children to make a paper aeroplane and have a go to see if they fly. To begin with, just get the children to use a single folded sheet of paper.

2. Now get them to collaborate in teams. On another sheet of paper, or in their exercise books, get them to record how far their planes went.

3. Ask them to guess how much further they will be able to make their planes go by developing their design to include clear sticky tape, paperclips and additional pieces of paper.

4. Their team goals should be recorded on the whiteboard so that everyone can see them. They should continue working on and developing their planes until it achieves their goal or until it flies as close to the goal as possible.

5. Any team that achieves this quickly should set itself a new goal.

6. Have a final flight for all of the finished planes and record the results on the whiteboard. Then debrief the activity with a group discussion:

   • What was the benefit of having a goal to aim for?
   • What was the effect of telling other people in the room your goals?
   • How did you work as a team?
   • What could you do to work together better in the future?

7. Introduce them to the idea of a SMART and PURE goal. One that is:

    -   **S**pecific
    -   **M**easurable
    -   **A**chievable
    -   **R**ealistic
    -   **T**ime-related

    -   **P**ositive
    -   **U**nder your control
    -   **R**ight-sized
    -   **E**cological (i.e. if achieved would be beneficial all round and not have negative unintended consequences).

8. With older children you could modify the activity so that the groups critique their goals and identify which of the areas above they had not taken into account. What benefits would there have been in ensuring this area was covered?

9. Finally, ask them to think about their own personal goals. What do they want to achieve in life, in examinations, etc.? Apply the SMART and PURE formula.

10. Introduce the idea of visualising their goal (what will they *see*, *hear* (internal words and externally what others will say) and *feel* (emotions and physically)) when they have achieved this goal. Get them to write their goal out.

Learn more about this

There is much evidence to suggest that positive mental imagery improves performance. Psychology experiments have shown positive benefits from having clear goals and mental images of success in a range of areas. A large part of our behaviours take place quite automatically without our

Read some more about goals, outcomes and NLP

- Read Chapter 2, 'Blockbuster movies', in *NLP for Teachers: How To Be a Highly Effective Teacher* (page 9)

conscious awareness. Alongside this, at a certain level our brain can't really tell the difference between a memory and a future imagined action. Creating a goal in full sensory detail and thinking that goal through may help to ensure that we stay on track with our goals at times when we might otherwise get easily distracted from them.

When else can you use this?

Developing an understanding of goals is an important life skill. Helping children to do this is not only rewarding – it can also significantly improve their motivation to learn and to overcome barriers to success. Use this tool wherever goals and outcomes are important.

- Use this activity to start a piece of work that involves problem solving.

- Modify the activity for use in Design Technology and similar subject areas to help the children understand the key concepts of designing, making and critically evaluating.

- Use as an activity to explore teamworking skills and the importance of agreeing team goals and consensus.

What are you going to do with this?
(Your ideas and thoughts)

---

19 Map and territory

How to get children to understand other points of view

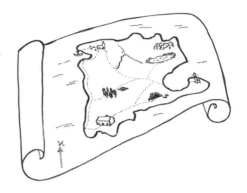

One of the presuppositions of NLP is that 'the map is not the territory'. In other words, the internal map that we create in our minds is not reality. At any one time our maps are influenced by our beliefs, our values and experiences and our unique individual perspective on the world. Teaching children to adopt this mindset is helpful for developing empathy, dealing with bullying and improving relationship skills.

Top tip

This is a challenging tool that is best used in classes and in contexts where you, as a teacher, feel confident about being able to set ground rules and maintain boundaries with the children. This said, it is a very effective tool for use with senior school children in contexts such as sex and relationships education, health education and drama.

Here's how

Start by explaining some of the key concepts that you are going to cover first and set some ground rules about respecting other people's views and where other people are coming from. Ground rules and expectations are particularly important in this sort of activity because the questions being asked are quite challenging.

1. Get the children to work on their own first. They should write four questions like the ones below on separate cards:

    *   A question that you would not want to be asked by someone else and which you would refuse to answer, if you were asked it.

    *   A question that you would like to be asked by someone else.

    *   A question that you think no one in the room will be able to answer.

    *   A question that you desperately want to know the answer to.

    You can photocopy the template on the next page and cut out the squares for the children you are working with, if you think that this will help with your particular students.

For example, in a secondary school lesson about health and relationships with older learners, you may want to get the students to talk about boundaries. In such a lesson the type of questions they may come up with could include:

I would not want to be asked about my personal bodily functions.
I would like to be asked about what makes me feel comfortable.
I think no one could answer the question 'what is normal?'
I want to know what makes others feel insecure.

2. Once your children have completed their cards tell them to walk around the room and find somebody else to show their first card to. Each pair should then explore their different points of view in relation to this area and what lies behind their different ideas, values and beliefs.

3. Once all the children have worked through all their questions with about six other people, get the children together as a group again and debrief the activity. Ask questions like: *What happened? What surprised you? What did you learn? What will you do differently from now on?*

Something that you would not want to be asked by someone else and which you would refuse to answer, if you were asked it.	Something that you would like to be asked by someone else.
Something that you think no one in the room will be able to answer.	Something that you desperately want to know the answer to.

Learn more about this

If developing self-awareness is the key to emotional and social literacy then empathy is the oil in the cogs. Understanding that others have different ways of seeing the world and being sensitive to this is not only a good thing from a moral perspective; it is also the key to effective communication. If we recognise where others are coming from we can adapt our behaviours and language in a flexible way to explain our own points of view through their map of the world. The first step in this understanding is to recognise the differences between ourselves and others, and to develop sensitivity to other people's world views. This activity helps children to begin to do both.

> **Read some more about understanding others with NLP**
>
> • Read Chapter 7, 'Knowing me, knowing you . . . aha!', in *NLP for Teachers: How To Be a Highly Effective Teacher* (page 73)

When else can you use this?

- Apply the same activity structure to specific areas of Personal, Social, Health and Economic education – particularly areas of Personal Well-Being.

- Use with a new form class or tutor group to help them to get to know each other.

- Apply the same structure and similar questions to support an anti-bullying scheme of work.

- Use this activity in conjunction with NLP tools which include an understanding of perceptual positions (see the Index to find tools that use this).

What are you going to do with this?
(Your ideas and thoughts)

PENS

Emotional and social literacy with children			
Self-awareness	Self-management and motivation	Relationship awareness and empathy	Managing relationships and social skills
* *	*	* * *	* *

20 On your head be it

How to help children develop awareness of facial expressions and emotions

How good at reading others are the children that you work with? Do your children sometimes misread emotional signals, or perhaps they are unaware of the signals they are giving out? Social intelligence is partly learnt, and giving the opportunity for children to develop their social skills and abilities to work with others is essential, particularly now that social interaction is reducing and they may find themselves with fewer natural opportunities to develop.

Here's how

This is a great activity for helping children to develop their empathy skills and awareness of others. These things are particularly important in an era when children are engaging in less and less face-to-face contact and therefore may not be learning, as easily as they used to, to read facial expressions and other social displays.

1. Get the children to make paper headbands by cutting strips of paper, bending them in a circle and sticking the two ends together. Write on each headband a particular emotion, expression or attitude.

2. Allocate one of the headbands to each of the children but do it in such a way that the child who is wearing the headband cannot see what is written on it.

3. Put the children in a circle and give them a scenario to act out. They might be all new members of a youth club and need to get to know each other or maybe they have to plan a visit somewhere (choose something that you know will interest them). Tell them that they are to act out the scenario but get them to react to each person they meet according to the emotion, expression or attitude that is written on the headband.

4. Debrief the activity by getting the children to discuss what they thought was written on their headband and what gave this away to them (voice tone, body language, words used). Then discuss what the impact of this was on them. What happened? How did they feel? How could they apply what they have learnt?

Learn more about this

Bandler and Grinder's studies of effective people suggested that highly effective people use 'sensory acuity' to read others and help them to be flexible. Today such ideas are beginning to be understood in more detail as a result of our growing understanding of the importance of mirror neurons. Mirror neurons fire when we perform an action and when that same action is observed by another, and were first noted in primates in the 1990s. In doing so the neuron literally mirrors the behaviour of the other person.

Read some more about NLP, body language and sensory acuity

- Read Chapter 3, 'We like like', in *NLP for Teachers: How To Be a Highly Effective Teacher* (page 23), specifically the research zone on mirror neurons on page 27

When else can you use this?

This is an activity that builds children's skills in recognising and responding to emotional states and the feelings in others. Use with any groups of learners who need to develop their abilities in these areas.

- Use the activity to develop skills in drama.

- Integrate this activity with others that support this area of development in order to help children with social, emotional and behavioural difficulties.

- Run the activity just using body language and without any voicing at all. Teach the children about Satir Categories (see page 91) and run the activity with these.

What are you going to do with this?
(Your ideas and thoughts)

PENS

Emotional and social literacy with children			
Self-awareness	Self-management and motivation	Relationship awareness and empathy	Managing relationships and social skills
* * *	* * *	*	* *

21 Ori-goal-me

How to develop motivation to achieve goals

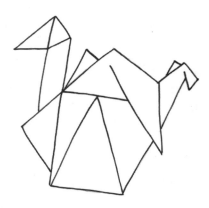

Often as teachers we find ourselves telling children to aim higher or to aspire to something – but how often do we teach them a strategy to help them feel more motivated to achieve a particular goal or desired outcome? The activity below is a fun way to explore the idea of imagining a future goal or desired outcome using all three senses: visual, auditory and kinaesthetic. It can also help children to develop an awareness of their internal thoughts and feelings and how these affect their actions. You can also use it to help children develop coaching skills with each other.

Here's how

To do this activity you will need some blank paper, or if you think that the children you are working with need a bit more scaffolding, photocopy the worksheet at the end of this tool. At some point you will want to introduce the idea of taking control of yourself and the idea that 'you can't control someone else's behaviour, only your own'. Therefore, if something is not working for you, you may need to change what you are doing.

1. Ask the children to put their piece of paper in front of them 'landscape'. Then ask them to fold their paper into three parts.

2. In the middle part they should write down what their goal is and (depending on their age, etc.) draw a picture of what it is that they want.

3. In the right hand column get them to write down:

   - What they will see when they have achieved their goal
   - What they will hear when they have achieved their goal
   - What they will feel when they have achieved their goal.

   Ask them to include lots of details. Who will be there? What will they hear themselves saying in their own self-talk and what will they hear others saying? What will they feel emotionally and physically when they have achieved their goal?

4. In the left hand column get them to write down all the things that they think might stop them from achieving what they want.

5. Now ask them to look at the things that might stop them and get them to sort these into things that are 'inside me' and things that are 'outside of me'. They can do this by simply writing an 'I' or an 'O' next to what they have written.

6. Once they have done Step 5, ask them to reflect on which of these factors are in their control and which are outside of their control.

7. Now get them to fold over the left hand column so that it covers the things that might have stopped them. On this section of paper get them to write down their strategy for achieving their goal – one that will ensure that they have done what they can to overcome the obstacles and have taken control of the things they need to.

8. Now ask the children to fold over the right hand side and decide on what will be their first step. What resources will they need to do this (internally and externally)? Will they need help from someone? If so, who?

9. Get the children to share their goal and outcomes with each other and with the rest of the class. Suggest that they learn their strategy so that they can repeat it to themselves without speaking aloud, like an actor learning lines for a blockbuster movie.

10. Finally, you could get the children to close their eyes and visualise themselves taking all the steps they need to achieve their goal. End the visualisation by getting them to imagine themselves experiencing what they wrote in their final column as if they were actually there.

Learn more about this

Positive mental imagery has been shown to improve performance. Similar results have been demonstrated in relation to the influence of positive self-talk. Of course the opposite is also the case. Therefore, learning to change your internal self-talk and move it from a repetition of problems to an ongoing reinforcement of solutions is a powerful way to improve achievement and motivation.

Read some more about goals and NLP

- Read Chapter 2, 'Blockbuster movies', in *NLP for Teachers: How To Be a Highly Effective Teacher* (page 9)

Top tip

Not everyone is aware of internal dialogue or self-talk when their attention is first drawn to it. Ask the children to close their eyes and sit quietly as they think of something that they are good at or enjoy doing. Tell them to sit there and wait until they notice what words they are saying to themselves about this skill.

When else can you use this?

When we get good pictures, sounds and feelings about our goal then we are able to achieve better results in a wide range of areas, including both academic and personal goals.

- Use before getting children to design revision and examination preparation timetables so that they begin the process with a clear goal in mind.

- Use a similar approach during lessons that involve a problem solving or designing approach (e.g. when the children are planning a musical composition, have a section for resources and instruments and another for the structure of the music).

- Do it yourself to support your own career goals or when coaching a colleague.

- Get the children to work in pairs to help them to develop their coaching skills. One person is the coach and asks questions filling in the sheet for the other person, who is the coachee.

What are you going to do with this?
(Your ideas and thoughts)

Ori-goal-me (goals and desired outcomes sheet)

Things that might stop me from achieving my goal	My goal/ desired outcome is	**What will I see when I have achieved my goal?**
		What will I hear when I have achieved my goal? • Others saying? • My own self-talk?
		What will I feel when I have achieved my goal? • My emotions? • Physically?

65

Emotional and social literacy with children			
Self-awareness	Self-management and motivation	Relationship awareness and empathy	Managing relationships and social skills
* *	* *	* * *	* * *

22 Problem shared

How to develop coaching skills with learners

We are increasingly beginning to recognise the usefulness and power of coaching skills. This is true in school leadership, when supporting others, when self-coaching and in the classroom. Just imagine how useful it would have been if we had been given the opportunity to develop these sorts of skills ourselves when we were at school – instead of having to wait until we were adults and on a training course! Below is a really effective way to get children to recognise and develop the core skills of questioning and listening in coaching and also to help to develop relationship awareness, social skills and empathy.

Here's how

Explain to the children the difference between *mentoring* (telling and sharing of skills by a more experienced person) and *coaching* (as in performance coaching and life coaching, where the coach asks questions and listens, crafting challenging questions to help the other person overcome their problems). You may find the diagram below helpful when explaining the difference between the two definitions. When coaching we believe that the other person has all the internal resources they need to solve their own problems, so avoid jumping in with 'the answer'.

Top tip

Both coaching and mentoring have their place and are useful as support strategies when working with others. Run a discussion with the children first to identify the benefits of both approaches and which contexts they are most suitable for.

---

1. The children should be grouped in pairs and will need to spread out throughout the room to work with each other. Ask them to decide who will be the coach (the person asking the questions) and the coachee (the person being helped).

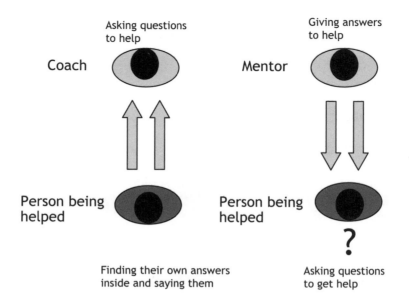

2. Make sure that the children sit appropriately. It is harder to develop rapport and trust when working with someone else if you are sat either side of a table. Get them to sit opposite each other with nothing between them. This will also help them to be more empathic and listen more carefully.

3. The coach should ask the coachee to think about a real-life problem that they have and that they are happy to share with the other person. The coachee then writes down a short paragraph about the problem. While the coachee is writing about the problem the coach should write down between five and ten questions that they think it would be a good idea to ask, whatever the problem is.

4. Now give out the question sheet below and ask the coachees to add their own questions to the sheet. Then get the coach to put the questions to the person they are coaching. Remind them to not interrupt even when the coachee is being silent – this is usually a sign of people being busy in their own minds as they work through the answer to the questions, and is often the time of greatest learning.

5. It is a good idea to suggest that they alternate their own questions with the ones on the sheet, and they may find themselves inventing new questions that just seem right at the time. When the pairs have finished running their coaching session get them to swap roles.

6. Debrief the activity with a discussion in which you ask them questions:

   • What happened? How did they find the activity? How else could they use these skills?

Problem shared – coaching questions sheet

Example questions to use

- What is the problem?

- Tell me more about that . . .

- Which specific things concern you most?

- Thinking about your problem – what are you seeing in your mind?

- What are you hearing?

- What are you feeling?

- How do you know when you have this problem?

- How do you know that this really is a problem?

- Can you think of a time when this situation might not be a problem?

- How do other people deal with these sorts of things?

- If you knew what to do what would that be?

- How do you know who to have this problem with?

- What stops you from changing this?

Your questions

Learn more about this

In his highly influential book *The Inner Game of Tennis,* Timothy Gallwey proposed that tennis players face two opponents: the person on the other side of net and the second, much more challenging opponent – one's self. This second opponent knows all our weaknesses and has all the tools it needs to create self-doubt. Mentoring styles of support can do much to improve our external skills to win through external challenges, but without the right mindset we may be defeated by ourselves. This is the usefulness of questioning and coaching skills when used to help other people to recognise and develop their own internal mindsets and ways of thinking.

> **Read some more about effective questioning and NLP**
>
> - Read Chapter 10, 'Verbal ju-jitsu', in *NLP for Teachers: How To Be A Highly Effective Teacher* (page 117)
> - Read *The Inner Game of Tennis* by Timothy Gallwey

When else can you use this?

Good teaching and learning involves activity. Teaching children coaching skills can dramatically improve the results that you will get when you set up problem solving and group work. You can also use this tool in the following ways:

- The questions in the coaching tool above are just as helpful when coaching adults. Use them when you are coaching and supporting a colleague or as part of a line management meeting.

- Use the tool in a particular teaching context (e.g. motivating yourself to revise more effectively or career coaching).

- Use the questions to self-coach and explore problems with yourself.

- Combine this activity with some of the other coaching related tools in this book.

What are you going to do with this?
(Your ideas and thoughts)

23 Relationship compass

How to help learners develop more effective relationships

Who are the people who are of importance to you? Have you got these relationships right at the moment? What could you do about it? These are tough questions for adults but they are also important for children. It is easy to assume that the children that we work with find it as easy as us to understand the relationships that they have with others and how these relationships inter-relate with one another. The activity below combines the opportunity to explore relationships with a way of stepping outside of a situation to understand it more effectively.

Here's how

1. Ask the children to draw a cross in the centre of a piece of blank paper and label it with a 'north' like the four points of a compass (see below).

2. Now get them to write a list of all the people that are of importance to them in their lives and who affect their lives significantly. Get them to work through the list adding the people to their compass, as described below.

3. The person that means the most to them will be nearest to the centre and the person who is of least importance should be furthest from the centre. All the other people should have line lengths according to their importance.

4. They also should consider whereabouts around the compass it feels right to place the different people. They will start to develop a diagram a bit like the one below.

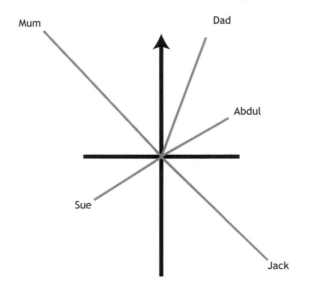

Emotional and social literacy with children

5. When they have finished including all the people on their list ask them to think about all the relationships around them and whether there are any relationships that they have forgotten about which are also important (they should then plot these).

6. Now get them to reflect on their relationship compass by considering the following questions:

   • Which of these relationships are not working as well for them as they could be?

   • What clue does the way in which they have represented the relationship on the diagram give them about what they might need to do to change this?

   • What could they do about this?

   • If they were to make this change how would this be represented on their compass? How would the line length change and the position of the person on the compass?

   • Now get them to close their eyes and imagine making these adjustments in their mind until they feel more comfortable with the changes.

7. Finally get them to plot the changes on their compass and decide on what they are going to do in order to make the changes that they have identified.

Learn more about this

NLP tools and approaches frequently make use of the internal representations that we make of the world. The qualities and characteristics of these internal representations are known as submodalities. Some submodalities relate to the visual, auditory and kinaesthetic characteristics of an internal representation (e.g. colour, weight, volume). The placement of internal representations in our mind within an imaginary 360 degree circle also makes a difference to the way we feel about something and what it means to us.

> **Read some more about submodalities and NLP**
>
> • Read Chapter 8, 'Memories are made of this', in *NLP for Teachers: How To Be a Highly Effective Teacher* (page 91)
> • Read *Insider's Guide to Submodalities* by Richard Bandler and Will MacDonald

When else can you use this?

This is great activity to use when you are stuck trying to think about a way to engage learners in thinking about their own emotions and relationships.

• The compass tool works well for non-NLP activities as well. Get the children to plot aspects of a problem that they are trying to solve and think about the benefits of reprioritising ideas.

• As with all coaching-type tools this tool works well with one-to-one coaching and has frequently been used in management training. Use it also to help people to deal with change. Get people to chart the changes that have happened over a period of time and what their ideal would be. Then get them to reflect on what they could do to fill that development gap.

- Use to support behaviour management development by getting a child to plot all the subject areas and teachers in the school and consider their behaviours in each context.

What are you going to do with this?
(Your ideas and thoughts)

Emotional and social literacy with children			
Self-awareness	Self-management and motivation	Relationship awareness and empathy	Managing relationships and social skills
* * *	*	* * *	* * *

24 Shoe shop

How to guide children to develop empathy and see other people's points of view

Why did you do that? Where were you coming from? Learning to ask these kinds of questions is important for the development of our understanding of others and in our maintenance of effective relationships. This activity makes use of one of the three NLP perceptual positions (self, other and observer) to help children to understand the importance of seeing things from the point of view of others. It combines an exploration of the various perceptual positions with the opportunity to discuss relationships, conflict and empathy. Virginia Satir, the family therapist who was 'modelled' by Bandler and Grinder, used to run sessions with families in which they literally stood in or on each others' shoes to help them to understand the situations they found themselves in and what to do about it.

Here's how

1. Either create the resources yourself or get the children to do it. Imagine a particular challenging scenario, one in which there is a conflict. You should choose something that will be interesting to the particular group of children you are working with (for teenagers you might choose staying out too late or something similar).

2. Have the children create, or create yourself, a cardboard (oversized) picture of a pair of shoes for each of the characters in the conflict (e.g. mum, dad, daughter, sisters, friends, teacher). Working in pairs or in groups get the children to arrange the 'shoes' in a circle.

3. Then one at a time get them to first stand in the middle and talk about what they think about the situation from their perspective as an observer.

   It works just as well if you use pieces of paper with the names of the character on rather than shoes – but it is more fun with younger children if they make a pair of shoes each.

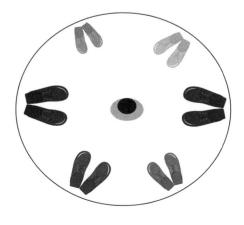

4. Now the person in the middle should move to each of the other places around the circle and in turn stand in the shoes that belong to that character. The other child or children should then ask them questions about what the situation is like from the point of view of the particular characters.

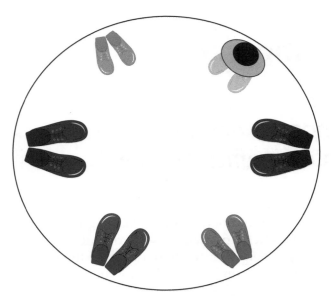

5. Work through the places until all have been covered and all the children have had an opportunity to be in all the character places.

6. Debrief the activity by asking the children about what they learnt: What surprised them? What changed when they moved positions? What will they do differently?

7. Finally get them to work in pairs on a real-life situation that they are in and get them to coach each other to find a solution and develop better understanding.

With older children you can elaborate the game by having more than one person in the circle at a time and getting them to have conversations with each other from the different points of view.

Learn more about this

Empathy is recognised as a key element in social and emotional literacy. It is all very well to have developed self-awareness and the management of our own emotions and feelings, but there are also other people out there with very different maps of the world and different ways of seeing things. Helping children to understand this can support the development of better relationships within their local peer groups and across a school.

> **Read some more about perceptual positions and NLP**
>
> • Read Chapter 7, 'Knowing me knowing you . . . aha!', in *NLP for Teachers: How To Be a Highly Effective Teacher* (page 73)

When else can you use this?

Children love to play games and explore ideas at the same time. This activity allows them to do both of these whilst also exploring some challenging concepts.

- Use this activity to explore other issues in wider curriculum areas: to understand perspectives in a historical context or where there is a particular wider geographic conflict (e.g. global warming) to explore different sides of the disagreement, etc.

- Incorporate into drama lessons to support in character development.

- Use to initiate creative writing projects in English to help children to write more real-life scenarios and characters.

What are you going to do with this?
(Your ideas and thoughts)

---

25 Think, feel, do

How to develop more positive mindsets with difficult children

As with adults, children can sometimes get overwhelmed by a situation to the extent that their attention is focused on only some of the things that they need to pay attention to. A really useful and simple model from NLP that can help children to think through situations, and what they need to do about it, is called the TEA model (which stands for thoughts, emotions and actions).

Here's how

The TEA model is a simple way to sum up and talk about the full range of experiences that we have as human beings. It suggests that all of our experiences can be summed up in three basic areas: our thoughts, our emotions (or feelings) and our actions. When we find ourselves in conflict, difficulty or just not feeling right, one of these areas is almost certainly out of balance. Frequently, this is because we have not considered the importance of, or paid enough attention to, one of the three areas.

1. Use the concept map on the next page to help children explore the idea of 'whole self' and to think through the aspects of a particular problem or issue.

2. Get them to consider it from different perceptual positions also:

   • From their own perspective

   • From the perspective of another person involved in the situation

   • From the perspective of a detached observer.

3. Finally, get them to revisit their first answers in the light of this other useful information and decide what they are going to do about it.

Think, feel, do

1. Complete the questions below from your own point of view.

Thoughts

What do you currently believe about this situation?

What would a more useful belief be?

Emotions

How do you feel about this situation?

What's important to you about this situation (values)?

Is there another value you have that would be more helpful in this situation?

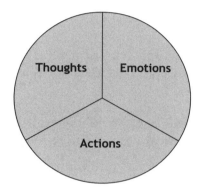

Actions

What are you currently doing?

How does this help?

What other behaviours are there which could be more helpful?

2. Now reflect on each of the areas above from the point of view of the other people in the situation.

3. What would an observer who is not involved say?

4. Look back at your answers, in the light of (2) and (3). What advice do you think that you should give yourself?

5. What will you now do?

Learn more about this

Although there are different views about what emotional intelligence is many writers and researchers suggest that people with some of these characteristics are more likely to be effective and to achieve in their lives. Saying that emotional intelligence is important is one thing but there are fewer examples of how to develop it – and effective tools to support the development of

Read some more about developing flexibility with NLP

- Read chapters 3, 'We like like' (page 23), and 6, 'Streetwise body language' (page 63), in *NLP for Teachers: How To Be a Highly Effective Teacher*

emotional literacy – than there are books extolling the benefits. NLP is somewhat different because it starts from the point of view of seeking to develop self-awareness, self-management, relationship awareness and social skills – for this reason it is sometimes referred to as 'the technology of emotional intelligence and emotional literacy'.

When else can you use this?

Exploring emotions, thinking and actions with difficult students is a good way to challenge them to become more flexible. You can also use this in the following ways:

- Use the TEA model to help children to understand the motivations and actions of key historical figures and to help them to understand other cultures and contexts.

- Apply the same questioning approach when coaching others.

- Use in lessons to support the development of group work and group understanding.

What are you going to do with this?
(Your ideas and thoughts)

Emotional and social literacy with children			
Self-awareness	Self-management and motivation	Relationship awareness and empathy	Managing relationships and social skills
* * *	* * *	*	*

26 Time machine

How to focus children on achieving their goals in the future

Have you ever heard yourself or somebody else say: 'It's about time I did that.' Well, where goals are concerned it's all about time. Getting children to understand that the achievement of goals is a journey – and one that will inevitably have stages and challenges that have to be overcome – is key. The tool below combines the exploration of key questions to help develop thinking about goals and desired outcomes with the idea of travelling forward in time to write an imaginary letter from the future.

Here's how

1. First identify an issue or problem, or a particular goal or outcome, that the children want to achieve. This could be a career aim or related to the passing of examinations.

2. Working in pairs, get the children to co-coach each other by exploring the following questions:

   • Where are you now with this goal or situation and what is happening?
   • What do you want instead? Describe this as a positive outcome.
   • What's important to you about this goal?
   • What will this get you?
   • What are you already doing that can help you with this goal?

3. Now get the children to work individually. Tell them to imagine themselves travelling forward in a time machine to the future. You can just set this up as an activity or run it as a visualisation by getting the children to close their eyes. Suggest details that they might see on their journey.

4. Tell them to imagine themselves in the future at a point in time many years from now and at a time well after they have achieved their goal. Tell them to look around and notice a table with paper and a pen on it. Now get them to write themselves a letter from the future.

Time machine – letter from the future template

Date your letter with the date in the future:

Write about the future that you see *What is going on?* *What do you see, hear and feel?*	Dear me, I thought that I would take a moment to write to you to tell you about . . .
Now tell yourself about the goal that you achieved *What did doing this get you?*	
Looking back at the journey that you travelled, and the challenges you faced, tell yourself about what these challenges were and how you overcame them	
Now give yourself some really good advice about what you need to do first to start the journey that you need to travel	
Tell yourself about the people that helped you and how you went about getting their support for your journey	
Finally, give yourself the best piece of advice that you could possibly imagine	

Learn more about this

Research by Cambridge Assessment has shown that children who have greater emotional control, particularly those who are able to delay their feeling of desire in relation to personal gratification, are more likely to achieve well in academic subject areas. This is probably also true in other curriculum areas. Being able to do this is about understanding the real nature of goals and our personal involvement in achieving them.

Read some more about the use of time in NLP

- Read Chapter 12, 'You can do it . . . and it's about time', in *NLP for Teachers: How To Be a Highly Effective Teacher* (page 143)

Emotional and social literacy with children

When else can you use this?

Although we can be very good in schools at setting short-term goals with learners it is also very useful to be able to support long-term motivation and thinking. As well as using the tool in this context, you may also like to:

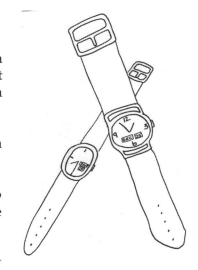

- Do the activity yourself in relation to a career goal or a relationship goal that you have.

- Use as part of departmental planning to create a group vision of what the changes you are implementing will be like in the future.

- Incorporate into creative writing projects to join the activity up with other curriculum work.

- Use the letter from the future to help children understand the thinking of famous historical or dramatic figures.

What are you going to do with this?
(Your ideas and thoughts)

Part 3

Stagecraft and presentation skills for teachers and trainers

Stagecraft and presentation skills			
Self-management	Influencing with words	Body language	Organising learning
*	* * *		*

27 Are you smarter than a dolphin?

How to say 'well done' and change behaviours

Do you care about the learners you teach? Of course you do, but do they know that? Would it be useful to be able to get your learners to follow your rules more frequently with less effort and at the same time feel much better as a teacher or trainer? Teachers, have you noticed that sometimes the school rules and consequences don't always work and you are constantly telling learners off for low-level stuff? Just don't. Stop pointing out what you don't want and start pointing out what you do want by praising those who are doing it – the effect can be contagious.

Stagecraft and presentation skills for teachers and trainers

Here's how

1. Catch the learners you teach doing the right thing and say so, frequently.

2. Be specific about what it is that you like about their behaviour and make sure the whole group hears the praise that you have given, so everyone knows what you want.

3. Never miss an opportunity to praise something that you might normally just ignore – but is what you want to see.

4. Use praise strategically to remind other learners who are not doing the right thing about what you want. For example, in a school if a child turns up late say nothing to the offending child. Instead, turn to the rest of the class and say 'thank you to everyone who is on time – I really appreciate that sort of courtesy and respect', and then carry on. A silent look is very effective in combination with this. Even though you haven't said anything to the child they will often feel compelled to apologise spontaneously. In any case you can always quietly question them later when everyone is working. This sort of strategy avoids the classic 'Where have you been?' argument and backchat.

5. Keep it fresh and constantly adapt so the learners never know where the next piece of praise is coming from.

6. Remember that some learners may actually enjoy or be seeking (at an unconscious level) the negative strokes of attention that low-level punishment brings – don't give them the satisfaction of getting a psychological reward (however low-level) for doing the wrong thing.

85

7. Praise every learner, every lesson or activity, for something specific.

8. If you really have to use a negative to punish, then use five times as much praise afterwards with the whole group and ensure that you find something that the errant learner can be praised about before the end of the session – so that they cannot see your negative feedback as being about them but rather about a specific behaviour you had an issue with. In particular, look out for the first time that they do the right thing that they were previously told off for and make sure you specifically praise them.

14 ways to say 'well done' with children to get you started with the idea

Remember to praise so the rest of the class hears and gets the message.

Thank you to everyone who was on time today.

I like the way that many of you started the task straight away.

Thanks for your answer – you obviously listened really well.

It is nice to see so many of you raise your hand to answer a question.

Thanks for working quietly today, Erica and Mohammed.

Well done to those of you who have already started work.

It's great to see so many of you remembering to bring the right equipment.

Well done for remembering how to underline the title, John, that's what I want to see.

I really like your opening sentence, Sally, it is clear and to the point and lets the reader know what is coming next.

I like the way you have carefully drawn your graph so that the data points are really accurate, Frank.

That's right.

Very good, I like it.

Excellent.

Well done!

Learn more about this

Gregory Bateson, the renowned anthropologist and writer, spent much time researching animal behaviours and found that just using negative and positive reward only worked for a short period of time. If he wanted to get the dolphins that he was working with to really go for it and perform multiple tricks he not only had to consistently reward positive behaviour, rather than give negative punishments, he also had to sometimes give rewards just to preserve the relationship. Relationship rewards are a sort of higher message to say: we have a relationship that is positive

Read some more about positive reward strategies and Bateson's work

- See Chapter 4, 'Dolphin aquarium', in *NLP for Teachers: How To Be a Highly Effective Teacher* (page 39)
- And for the serious amongst you, read *Steps to an Ecology of Mind* by Gregory Bateson
- Find out more about research on praise and reward in the classroom in *Teacher Effectiveness* by Daniel Muijs and David Reynolds

outside of the rewards I give for specific things; and that positive relationship is there whatever happens.

When else can you use this?

Any time that you are working with others it is important to catch people doing the right thing.

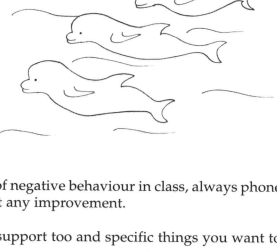

- Apply the same principles as a leader. Catch the people in your team doing the right thing well.

- Apply the negative to positive reward principle with parental contacts. If you have had to phone a parent to inform them of negative behaviour in class, always phone back the next week to praise the child about any improvement.

- If you are a teacher thank parents for their support too and specific things you want to see them carry on doing.

- When you have done something well – reward yourself. Because you're worth it!

> ### What are you going to do with this?
> (Your ideas and thoughts)

28 Be upfront

How to focus learners to have a positive mindset

We often have to 'reframe' students or learners when they have difficulties or objections to what we are teaching. This can be time consuming and have a negative effect on other learners or even become a battle between yourself and your learners. In NLP it is often said that 'five minutes of pre-framing is worth half an hour of reframing' to get back on track. Pre-framing can help you to set expectations in the classroom or training room and give direction at an unconscious level. Consciously designing pre-frames allows a teacher or

trainer to exclude, or include, attitudes and behaviours that could help or hinder learning. Simple frames are composed of the *approach* you want them to take, the *behaviours* required and the *attitude* best suited to the activity. Below are a few simple steps and a worksheet with some examples to help you begin to think in more detail about pre-frames. In essence pre-framing is the covert or upfront suggesting of how you want people to think, feel or behave.

Here's how

Pre-framing starts with the teacher or trainer having a positive mindset and outcome for the lesson – not just in terms of the learning objectives but across the spectrum of what is needed in the classroom or training room to facilitate that learning objective. When our minds know what is expected of us then our natural compliance is activated; this is true for learning activities and for meetings. Any time when we don't know what is expected of us there is the opportunity to generate any sort of behaviour. By framing what we want, rather than what we don't want, we can begin to influence in the direction that will be most beneficial. Pre-frames can be used at the beginning and at the start of each part of a lesson or activity.

> *Today we are going to learn about the way prisms split light. Just as Isaac Newton did when he first investigated prisms we are going use his <u>methodology</u> and work <u>step-by-step</u> and <u>cooperatively</u> in threes <u>drawing</u> diagrams of the light being split. Before the end of the lesson we will all have a clear understanding of how prisms split light and we will <u>discuss</u> where this is useful in science industry.*

In this example, whilst talking about Newton, we have embedded the approach, behaviours, attitudes and expected output and pre-framed the connection back to the real world.

1. Identify the approaches, behaviours and underlying attitudes you want your learners to have. Specifically, the ones that they will need to learn the skills or information you are going teach easily.

2. For each one, think up a statement or experience that illustrates what you want from the learners.

   These statements could be explicit, for example:

   The way I want you to do this is . . .

   Or your statements could presuppose and assume the behaviours, for example:

   As you do this accurately you will find that . . .

3. Decide where in the session you need pre-frames and when you will deliver them. Deliver in sets of three – this makes it easier for the unconscious mind to hold them. More than three will not be taken in. Use the pre-frames think sheet below to help you begin to work out your pre-frames.

Top tip

Marking out the pre-frames with a gesture or vocal emphasis will increase the impact (e.g. drawing a frame in the air with your fingers as you speak).

Learn more about this

Becoming elegant and deliberate with your pre-framing can increase the impact of your work, allowing you to maintain direction and set expectations about approach, behaviour and attitude in your learners that will facilitate the best learning experience. It is also fun to experiment and find

Read some more about framesetting

- Read Chapter 10, 'Verbal ju-jitsu', in *NLP for Teachers: How To Be a Highly Effective Teacher* (page 117)

out which pre-frames were best for which type of student, subject or activity. Pre-framing is used by negotiators, public speakers and trainers and is a way to avoid confrontation or disagreement.

When else can you use this?

There are many times as teachers when we know that there will be objections or challenges. Pre-framing is useful when you know that something like this is coming up. For example:

- Use when leading staff meetings to set expectations.

- If you are a teacher use at parents' evenings to set the frame for a conversation.

- Plan to pre-frame in the early part of a school assembly so that everyone becomes aware of how the assembly is going to be delivered.

Pre-frames think sheet

Area to pre-frame	Example words and phrases you may want to use	What will you say about this area?
Approach	Analytical Creative Imaginative Doing Practical By instruction Coaching Method Step-by-step	
Behaviour	Listen Write Discuss Think Quiet Draw Accurate Fun Sing	
Attitude	Cooperative Interactive Own work Teamwork Challenging Together Collaboratively Curiosity	

What are you going to do with this?
(Your ideas and thoughts)

29 Body talk

How to observe body language when doing lesson observation or when teaching or training

Have you ever had the role of supporting a new teacher or someone less experienced than you and found that although they looked, on the surface, to be doing all the right (and important things) about classroom management and managing learning, there just seemed to be something not quite right and they weren't getting the right responses from the learners? In *NLP for Teachers: How To Be a Highly Effective Teacher* we talked about how Bandler and Grinder, the co-founders of NLP, modelled Virginia Satir (the world famous family therapist) noticing and using a series of simple body postures to influence others. These postures appear to have an almost archetypal significance whether you are doing therapy, teaching, training, presenting or just communicating on a day-to-day basis.

Here's how

Below you can find a brief introduction to five of the body language positions that are important, and an observation sheet to help you to feedback to other teachers or trainers.

1. Familiarise yourself with Satir Categories and experience how they work for you in your own classroom or training room, so that you can share real-life experiences as you feedback and debrief the lesson/session observation. Notice how adopting the postures affects not only the learners you are presenting to and working with one-to-one, but also your own internal state (emotions and feelings).

2. Agree with the person you are observing that you are going to be focusing on presentations skills. However, it is probably best to not mention body language upfront yet as they may become self-conscious.

3. Use the observation sheet to record what you see so that you can feed back later.

4. Begin your feedback by explaining that the area that you were looking at was body language. Talk them through the Satir Categories that they were using. You might also like to ask them to stand and adopt a particular position and then ask them how that changes how they feel inside and what they think that that posture would 'say' to others.

5. Work through your feedback explaining what you saw. You may like to start with a specific piece of praise, then give them some examples of where what they were intending was not necessarily congruent with what they wanted to express, or not the best position, and end with a general positive observation.

Quick start - Body postures

Blaming

Finger pointing and use of stiff gestures. The impact of this is to imply fault, to dictate or imply a superior position. If done to another blaming person it often leads to conflict. Not a useful position generally in the classroom or when training or presenting. Blaming is one body posture that you don't really want to match!

Placating

Palms up. Implies the seeking of sympathy or the giving of a gift. Great for when you want a comment to be seen as a gift not a challenge. It is not assertive, however, but can be effective when reinforcing rules if you then end your sentence with levelling (see below).

Levelling

Centred and balanced stance, with hands palms down. Implies certainty and gravitas. Communicates gentle assertiveness and honesty, and says 'this is how it is – this is correct'.

Computing

Hand on or under chin, other arm across body. In the classroom or training room implies logic and thinking. Good to use when you want others to think (e.g. after or during the asking of a question).

Distracting

Switching between body positions quickly. Can be confusing and says 'don't notice me please'. Not assertive and therefore to be mostly avoided.

Learn more about this

In NLP the term congruence is applied to a person who is communicating consistent messages in relation to the words they say, their voice tone and their body language. Often people who are congruent will be seen as having personal presence and will be perceived as knowing what they are talking about. The term incongruent is used to describe inconsistencies in these messages. Research by Albert Mehrabian at UCLA in the 1970s and 1980s suggests that when there is perceived incongruence people will default to physiology ahead of voice tone and words in the proportions 7:38:55.

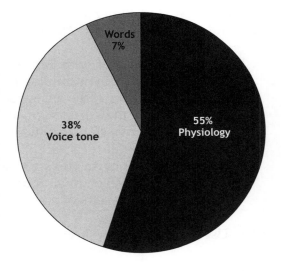

The Satir Categories – lesson observation sheet

Person being observed	
Person observing	
Lesson or session	
Date	

	Number of times used (you could just use a tally for this or make ticks or dots)	Number of times used where the use of the posture was **congruent** with what appeared to be intended/or best use	Number of times used where the use of the posture was **incongruent** with what appeared to be intended/or best use
Blaming			
Placating			
Levelling			
Computing			
Distracting			
Feedback and observations			
Suggested development points			

93

When else can you use this?

Giving structured feedback on body language can improve performance and communication in many contexts.

- As a teacher notice patterns at parents' evenings and use with parents.

- Apply during meetings.

- If delivering a training session or presentation to other teachers, rehearse which patterns you will use when.

- Just have fun noticing this stuff!

Read some more about Satir Categories

- Read Chapter 6, 'Streetwise body language', in *NLP for Teachers: How To Be a Highly Effective Teacher* (page 63)
- For the NLP enthusiast, read the chapter in *The Structure of Magic II* by Richard Bandler and John Grinder (page 27)

Top tip

To give a blaming person what they want (without giving in) - including difficult children and parents - use placating when they are doing blaming but hold your ground verbally. They will default to your body language as the overall message is incongruent and may well end up giving way - particularly if you then skilfully apply levelling to finish.

What are you going to do with this?
(Your ideas and thoughts)

PENS

30 Folders

How to prepare learners' minds to receive information

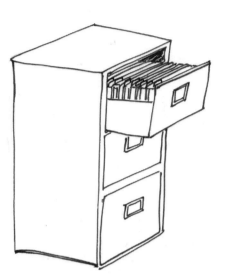

Would it be useful to organise the learner's memory and improve retention of subject matter? Minds, just like a computer or a filing cabinet, need places to put information. Before we had paper or pens memory systems were common – these systems were used to organise information so that retrieval was easy and ordered.

One of the ways we can help our learners remember is to provide a structure to organise information through 'chunking'. This is especially important with children and teenagers whose frontal lobes are still developing; this part of the brain is responsible for organising information and activities. Using this simple approach we can help students have places in their mind to put the information.

Here's how

By creating links to other information we can begin to help the brain organise what we teach in a way that makes remembering easier. Using the metaphor of a computer or filing cabinet as part of the frames for the lesson or session is one method of achieving this. Once you have decided how many main folders or principles you will need for your information this can be broken down into further sections.

1. Break the information down into 'chunks' – three chunks per topic is ideal (a chunk is a big picture element or folder).

2. Using mind maps can be an excellent way of visualising and organising the chunks. With skill and practice you can even learn to speak like a mind map! See below for an example.

3. Examine each chunk and break down that information as if it were files going into a folder. Then have up to three key points for each file.

4. The last stage is to connect or map the connections that this piece of information has to other lessons.

Quick start – Folders

Format the receiver's mind for the information, like creating files on a computer. How many boxes or files will you need to explain this information (e.g. one principle, three keys, three main points per key)?

Here is the example laid out with its levels.

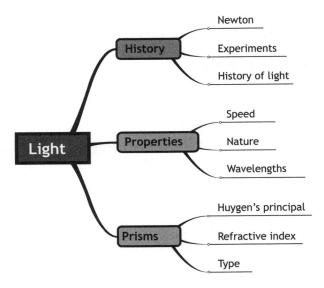

Example (what you might say in the classroom):

> Today we're going to learn about <u>light</u>, firstly a little about the <u>history</u>, <u>Newton's work</u>, his <u>experiments</u> and how <u>light was understood before Newton</u>. We are then going to work with <u>prisms</u> and <u>how the properties of light are affected</u> by prisms, its <u>speed</u>, its <u>nature</u> and the effect on <u>wavelength</u>. We'll learn about <u>Huygens' principle</u>, <u>refractive index</u> and the <u>types of prisms</u> that are available.

Folders worksheet

Use this template to help you to plan what you are going to say.

Principles	Keys	Main points
	1.	
	2.	
	3.	
	1.	
	2.	
	3.	

Stagecraft and presentation skills for teachers and trainers

Learn more about this

The notion of structuring ideas from the general to the specific came into NLP through early ideas from cognitive psychology and the ideas of 'surface' and 'deep' language structure. This is a way of organising information and using your language to great effect by consciously creating ordered maps of information. This can greatly assist your students in retaining more of the lesson content, help with their note taking and will begin to create neural networks of knowledge related to the subject area. This basic system for ordering information is often found in memory systems through the world and throughout history. It provides a logical flow for the information.

> **Read some more about influential language in the classroom**
>
> - Read Chapter 5, 'Don't think about chocolate cake', in *NLP for Teachers: How To Be a Highly Effective Teacher* (page 49)
>
> And find out more about memory systems by reading:
>
> - *The Art of Memory* by Frances Yates
> - *Mind Maps for Kids* by Tony Buzan

When else can you use this?

There are many times when you need to communicate effectively and succinctly. This tool is great for any situation where clarity is essential. Also use it in the following ways:

- Create ordered agendas for meetings and organise ideas for debates and discussions.

- Create quick summaries of dates with connections.

- Plan better report writing and structuring.

- Teach the concept to children to help them to write better essays.

What are you going to do with this?
(Your ideas and thoughts)

31 Hearts and minds

How to create motivation and direction right from the start

Values are about what is important to us and what gives us meaning in a given context. Values are connected to our emotions and drive our behaviours at an unconscious level. As adults we feel motivated to expend our time, energy and resources on those things that are important to us. If we end up having to do things that do not have this connection we will have an emotional response that could range from sadness or a feeling of worthlessness through mild anger to rage. All of these negative emotions increase our level of stress and eventually put us into resistance – life becomes difficult and we become unhappy. The same is true for your learners. On the other hand, if we are engaged in activities or learning that we feel are important and have meaning then our enthusiasm grows – we feel good and actually are able to learn more easily.

Here's how (Part 1)

In the classroom or training room it is critical to align your values and the group's values so that the context has meaning and importance. This takes a bit of thinking through because a lot of this stuff sits in our unconscious mind. Work through the approach below step-by-step using the tools and questions below.

1. Use the first half of the sheet below marked Teacher's values:

   What is your outcome for the lesson or session?

   Think about the subject or an individual lesson and ask yourself:

   What is important to me about this?

   Ask and answer this question at least ten times and notice your answers (usually these are one or two word answers).

2. List your answers as you go – you can even get a colleague to ask the questions as this works particularly well as a coaching activity.

3. Staying with the context ask yourself:

   What is important to my students about this subject?

4. Put yourself in their position.

Outcome for the lesson or scheme of work	
Teacher's values	**Students' values**

Here's how (Part 2)

1. Take the list of values (above) and prioritise them. Ask the following question using the second grid below:

   Which of these is the most important?

2. Then ask yourself:

   Which of these is the next most important?

   and so on. Do this for your values and also your learners' values.

3. The most important values are the top five – these are called IMPACT values. Take the top five in each list and decide how you could meet these values in your lessons or training. Look over your two lists to see where the commonalities are. Are there any? Are there any in the top five? These will be the key ones to focus on.

4. Notice any conflicts. Decide how you might resolve or utilise these values. How can you bring those values alive in your subject? How can you have the group share or work out values that will enhance the learning?

Outcome for the lesson or scheme of work

Teacher's values		Students' values	
1.		1.	
2.		2.	
3.		3.	
4.		4.	
5.		5.	
6.		6.	
7.		7.	
8.		8.	
9.		9.	
10.		10.	

Stagecraft and presentation skills for teachers and trainers

Learn more about this

A value is a like a 'hot button' that drives behaviours. Whatever we do is done in order to satisfy a value – even though you may not be consciously aware of that value and its effect. Some values are 'towards' values and some are 'away from' values. You exercise to fulfil the value of improving your health; you study to fulfil the value of getting on in the world, achieving or not being a failure. Buying designer clothes fulfils the value of looking good, looking right for work or school, being part of a group or not looking scruffy.

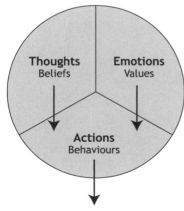

Thoughts / Beliefs • Emotions / Values → Actions / Behaviours

The values we have move us to action. Often we will have thoughts around our values in the form of internal self-talk (like: *I can* or *I can't*, *I'm able* or *I'm not able*). These are the beliefs that form our rule structures. Being aware of these elements can help you to align more effectively your values, beliefs and actions. This is sometimes known as the TEA model.

Top tip

Always work with values in a matter of fact way. Whatever values others have, they are theirs and although they may be radically different from yours they are fundamentally how the other person creates their world. Disrespecting or invalidating another person's values will cause an emotional response and/or war!

An NLP presupposition that is useful here is: 'respect another person's model of the world'.

When else can you use this?

It is important to check in on values in any area in which you want to make progress and create change.

- In a leadership context align the values of your team and share your values with them.

- If you are a school leader use a values elicitation tool, like the one above, to support discussions about school improvement.

- Use the tool to support the development of a more student-centred curriculum and to evaluate your school's whole curriculum.

- Really ask the children what is important to them and do some work on student voice in your school.

Read some more about values

- Read Chapter 11, 'The teacher within', in *NLP for Teachers: How To Be a Highly Effective Teacher* (page 131)
- For another take on this read *Time Line Therapy and the Basis of Personality* by Tad James and Wyatt Woodsmall

---

What are you going to do with this?
(Your ideas and thoughts)

Stagecraft and presentation skills for teachers and trainers

32 In your head and in your body No. 1

How to set yourself up for success when teaching or training

Do you ever get into a situation and know that you are not quite ready, your body feels a bit shaky or you think you might be pushed around (as it were)? If so, or if you want to quickly ground yourself before an important event, then here is a quick mind–body technique you can use to centre yourself. Being centred is really important in the classroom, training room and in any situation where you need to feel in control and be able to be assertive and confident. This comes from the martial arts arena and is a key technique in many spiritual disciplines. Like many things it ended up in NLP training as a result of modelling excellence in a range of fields. Curious? Then read on – below is an experiment that will teach you 'one point'.

Here's how

Use this technique any time you want to align your body and mind. It is a great place to teach from and you feel ready for anything. Find a colleague to help you with this quick experiment.

1. Think about a time when you felt 'unresourceful' or shaky. Have your colleague give you a shove and notice what happens. Do this a few times from different directions – you will most likely find that you go off balance or that you put a lot of effort into resisting the shove.

2. Next think about that time again and this time put a hand (either one) on and over your belly button. Have your colleague shove you again – notice what happens. Practise this a few times with different situations until you are stable in all of them with your hand on your belly button.

3. Now put your attention just below your belly button and test again – you should be stable without the need to put your hand there.

4. Once you have this altogether think of a really positive experience, as if you were there, and say 'one point' to yourself in a way that you can always remember (this is called an auditory anchor). By associating the positive feelings with a phrase you will find that you can pull this feeling back into your mind again whenever you need it. Now test the anchor by thinking of a negative experience and say 'one point'. Then get your colleague to shove you and notice what happens.

Learn more about this

Neuroscience research is constantly pointing to the relationship between mind and body and the need to recognise that they are a single system. This notion of the mind–body system is also a key one in NLP. Keeping 'one point' means that we focus our attention, energy and intention at the very centre of who we are. This puts our attention at the centre of gravity in our body. In martial arts having your attention in one point means your body and mind

Read some more about the mind-body system

- Take up a martial art for more experiences: Aikido is great for balance and being centred!
- Read more about anchoring in Chapter 9, 'Anchors away!', in *NLP for Teachers: How To Be a Highly Effective Teacher* (page 105)

become relaxed and focused and you are ready to move in any direction easily and quickly.

When else can you use this?

Although you may not think this is so your mind and body are always working together, so use this tool whenever you want to consciously be in control. You can also:

- Teach your students to use this before and during exams.
- Teach as part of a train the trainer course.
- Use your anchor during meetings if you don't feel confident.
- Deliver a training session or presentation to other teachers, trainers or parents and teach this to others.

Top tip

Practise using one point whenever you can – the more you do it the more your mind and body will know that this is the right state for you all of the time. Notice how when you can keep the state for a whole day you feel less tired.

What are you going to do with this?
(Your ideas and thoughts)

Stagecraft and presentation skills			
Self-management	Influencing with words	Body language	Organising learning
* * *		*	

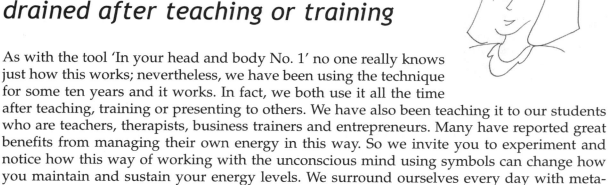

33 In your head and in your body No. 2

How to keep yourself from being drained after teaching or training

As with the tool 'In your head and body No. 1' no one really knows just how this works; nevertheless, we have been using the technique for some ten years and it works. In fact, we both use it all the time after teaching, training or presenting to others. We have also been teaching it to our students who are teachers, therapists, business trainers and entrepreneurs. Many have reported great benefits from managing their own energy in this way. So we invite you to experiment and notice how this way of working with the unconscious mind using symbols can change how you maintain and sustain your energy levels. We surround ourselves every day with metaphors that are intended to create positive feeling and states: the logos on brands, the photos we choose to put in our house, the good luck items and souvenirs we place on our desks, etc. Just take a moment to think of a few of the things that you carry with you in your pocket or in your handbag that have value to you beyond their physical worth and what they mean to you. Have you lost one of these things and spent time and energy locating it again – perhaps more time and energy than you rationally know it is worth?

Here's how

Our unconscious mind takes notice of symbols and makes many connections through them. If you're able to use your imagination then this quick technique can make a big difference to your energy levels over the days and weeks of a busy working life. By using metaphors our unconscious mind is capable of many things and this metaphor helps you to detach from the potentially stressful interactions that occur during the working day. You may already have come across this tool referred to as 'the circles of light'. When you first start to practise this technique find a quiet place, as this will help you to concentrate and focus on the visualisation elements of the technique.

1. When learning the technique, close your eyes. Imagine that you have invisible connections to all your learners and that it is these connections that carry information and energy to them as you teach. You can even imagine energy flowing back and forth along these connections – you may notice that connections to some learners carry more energy than others.

2. Imagine a white disc of light floating above your head – you can imagine it's spinning if you like. Imagine this white disc of light cutting any connections at the top of your head.

3. Now imagine the disc becoming a doughnut shape (the sort with a hole in it) and that it is able to expand and travel all the way down your body. As it does it cuts all the connections you no longer need.

4. Allow the disc to reform briefly under your feet then let it become a doughnut again and notice it travel up your body cutting the last of the connections until it becomes a white disc of light floating above your head once more.

That's it. Once you've practised a few times you will be able to complete this exercise very quickly making it a practice you do before you leave your teaching space. It's a great habit to develop.

Learn more about this

There is growing evidence from research in hypnosis and meditation that the unconscious mind responds powerfully to the use of symbols. Freud and Jung recognised the way the unconscious mind uses symbols. By recognising repeating symbols or patterns they were able to help people restore healthy states. By reversing this process we can use symbols to train our own minds to generate healthy states and manage our energy levels. This metaphor probably says 'it's OK to let go emotionally, now the experience is over you don't need to stay connected'.

> **Read some more about the power of metaphor and symbols**
>
> Read
> - *Metaphors in Mind: Transformation through Symbolic Modelling* by James Lawley and Penny Tompkins
> - *Metaphoria: Metaphor and Guided Imagery for Psychotherapy and Healing* by Rubin Battino

When else can you use this?

There are many stressful things that happen in life. The circles of light tool can help you manage your energy in connection with any situation that involves relationships.

- If you are a teacher use circles of light after any stressful event or after a parents' evening.
- Use it if you have trouble falling asleep.
- Use it when you need to disconnect emotionally from difficult relationships.

What are you going to do with this?
(Your ideas and thoughts)

---

34 It's not really NLP but you should know it

How to understand group behaviours in the classroom or training room

In the spirit of the 'heart of NLP', modelling, there are some times when we feel compelled to include in our training of teachers and trainers something that they really need to know and which we know many teachers have found helpful. Although not strictly from NLP this is a gem and, at the end of the day, NLP is all about the practical application of theoretical ideas from behavioural science and the modelling of successful approaches.

Here's how

Bruce Tuckman and Mary Jensen's group formation model is well worth adding to your repertoire of understanding and skills. As teachers or trainers you will be familiar with the way some groups are full of lots of chatter at the beginning of the learning; in some the chatter turns into more unruly behaviour while in contrast others are ready to go, getting on with the work in hand, ending up producing outstanding results. When we apply an understanding of the model below, we can notice where in the group formation process our groups are, and develop strategies to move the group through to performance. The first step is to begin to think of the group as your team and yourself as the team leader.

1. Familiarise yourself with the stages of group formation (see below in the Quick start). Think about what this might mean for your classroom or training room work. Take an objective look at your groups – they will probably range across the spectrum of stages. Draw a grid or matrix and categorise each class so that you are clear where each group is in the process.

2. Design activities to move towards the performing stage and which take the learners from each stage to the next, paying attention to their linear development as a group. Think about how your teaching style needs to flex for each stage. Here are some examples, although each group will vary according to what it needs, to get it from one stage to another (as is the case with teams):

Forming to storming

- Introduction games
- Debates

- Quizzes in teams, different teams each lesson
- Puzzles to solve in small groups with an element of competition
- Games that engage the groups in physical activities.

Storming to norming

- Develop a group 'value set' that guides the group through conflict and stress (you could use a values elicitation for this, or Robert Dilts's levels of thinking, see *NLP for Teachers: How To Be a Highly Effective Teacher*)
- Find or design problems to solve with an output planned around the learning
- Create projects that involve individuals working together towards a common goal. This is especially good if there is a 'common outside group to benchmark against' or another group to compete with
- Group challenges that increase the status of the whole group preferably visible to those outside the group in some way (e.g. involving praise from another teacher).

Norming to performing

- Design tasks that challenge and push the learners' boundaries
- Have deadlines with a performance element
- Facilitate bigger group goals that mean that individuals must perform for the group to succeed
- Focus on group work and interactions giving more open-ended tasks once the group is 'normed'.

Top tip

As you begin to notice this model at work on a daily basis you may also begin to notice that it works at a micro level as well as a macro level. Frequently, individual team meetings (or even discussions) will go through a forming, storming, norming and performing stage. The same is also often true in the classroom within an individual lesson. Be aware particularly of how you form the group in the early stages and how you then deal with the first storming moment. Often the way in which you deal with this can determine whether the group will recognise you as the leader for the session and norm to your authority. See Chapter 27 ('Are you smarter than a dolphin?') for some positive relationship-based strategies for dealing with low-level storming early and effectively in a lesson or training day. Finally, remember that teams need empowerment at the performing stage and plan for effective devolving of responsibility to the learners once they have effectively 'normed' to you. Throughout the process getting a group normed to you is the key.

Quick start – Tuckman and Jensen's model from the point of view of team leadership

Forming

- Leader provides guidance and direction and a vision of the future direction and what will be achieved in the long term
- Group aims set by leader
- Tasks and responsibilities are clarified
- Be prepared to answer questions about tasks, responsibilities and the process
- Members will test tolerance of system and its leader – leader needs to build rapport and establish position

Leadership style: Directive but creating a vision

Stagecraft and presentation skills for teachers and trainers

Storming

- Group members vie for position as they attempt to establish themselves in relation to other group members and the leader
- Cliques and factions form and there may be power struggles
- Leaders will often receive challenges from group members
- There may be elements of chaos – often groups can get stuck here and no progress is made
- Clarity of purpose must increase to overcome uncertainties
- The group should be focused on goals
- Compromises may be required to enable progress
- It is at this stage in development that leaders may have to deal with people who will not norm

Leadership style: Coaching in a way which clearly shows that you are the leader (e.g. asking challenging questions) and being prepared to step into the leadership space and set boundaries

Norming

- Agreement and consensus grows among group members
- Tasks and responsibilities are clear and accepted
- Some decisions are made by group agreement
- Small teams within the group work on projects together
- Commitment and unity is strong
- The group may engage in fun and social activities
- The group begins to develop its own working style
- There is general respect for the leader

Leadership style: Facilitate and enable

Performing

- The group has a shared vision and is able to stand on its own feet
- There is a focus on over-achieving goals and the group makes most of the decisions against criteria agreed with the leader
- The group has a high degree of autonomy and works towards achieving the goals
- Disagreements are positively resolved within the group
- Group members look after each other and attend to relationship, style and other issues along the way
- Tasks and projects are delegated from the leader
- The team does not need to be instructed or assisted
- Members are guided rather than taught

Leadership style: Delegate and oversee

Forming   Storming   Norming   Performing

Stagecraft and presentation skills for teachers and trainers

Learn more about this

Often we like to see schools and training contexts as separate contexts from the rest of the world. The truth is that there is a wealth of knowledge, research and understanding from the areas of management and organisational behaviour that is just as applicable in an education context (e.g. coaching). In industry, Tuckman and Jensen's model is well known and used to support the creation of high performing teams quickly. In our work using this with schools (where we perhaps need to develop our use of teams more) it is clear that many groups can become stuck in one phase. This is true not only of classes but also of teams that manage specific areas or whole organisations.

> ### Read some more about organisational behaviour
>
> - Read *Forming, Storming, Norming, Performing: Successful Communications in Groups and Teams* by Donald B. Egolf
> - Pick up a book on organisation behaviour and find out more about areas of learning that are also useful in school leadership and management. A great 'cross-over' book is *Management Skills in Schools: A Resource for School Leaders* by Jeff Jones
> - Read *Organizational Behaviour and Management* by John Martin

When else can you use this?

This is a great tool to teach others. Children in particular can find it helpful when understanding how to work together in groups. You can also:

- Design a team-building day for your senior teams with these principles.
- Use in sports or drama for developing high performing teams.
- Use as a discussion topic for raising team dynamics at departmental meetings.
- Use as part of a plenary after a class activity day to understand and analyse how well things worked out for the group.
- Have fun leading!

What are you going to do with this?
(Your ideas and thoughts)

---

35 On the spot

How to manage your emotions

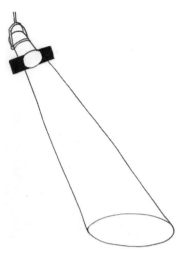

Teaching spaces can become powerful environments – the way we use the space we work in can enhance learning and support behaviour management. Would it be useful if, when you walk to a certain part of your teaching space, your students automatically began to do what you wanted? What we're talking about here is setting up conditioned responses (a sort of Pavlovian conditioning for people – you remember Pavlov, we've mentioned him before – he was the guy with the dogs and the bell). We all have them and they operate in many parts of life. Just think what happens in your class as a teacher when the bell sounds. Is there a burst of activity? Does this happen so quickly that you have to tell the class to quieten down? This is just one example of an automatic response to a stimulus. You can use this process in your teaching space as a teacher or a trainer: you decide what response you want and the location in the learning space. In this case it is your presence and the sound and tone of your voice, together with any gestures, that mark out what it is you want.

Here's how to hit the right spot!

In NLP this is called 'spatial anchoring'. This technique is also used on the stage. When actors want to elicit particular states for their performance they will create the states by rehearsal at a particular point on the stage and mark these places so that walking back into the place will elicit the emotion. You can use the same concept to condition states in yourself and responses from your learners.

1. Think of a response that you would like to have in the group such as being quiet, listening, question-and-answer responses or listening to stories, etc.

2. Choose a place in your learning space from where you can direct that activity. A useful idea is to imagine a circle on the floor in that place – you can give it a colour too.

3. Think of the resources or emotional state(s) that you would like to have – so that you can behave/think/direct in the way that you want to in that situation.

4. You can choose up to three resources or emotional states such as: assertive, confident, congruent, motivational or energised. Be creative and choose just the right states for you.

5. Taking each resource/state in turn:

   - Remember an occasion in which you had that resource. Put yourself into that associated memory (as if you are really there seeing it through your own eyes, feeling it with your body, hearing the sounds) – see, hear, feel and take the emotional state and feelings into the spot or circle.

- Stay there for a few moments fully immersed in the resourceful state then step out.

- 'Break state' by thinking of something completely different and doing a movement of some kind.

- Test the anchor by stepping into the spot or circle – notice what happens. Step out again.

- Future pace by stepping into the circle and noticing how you will be different in future in the way that you behave/think in the situation that you wanted to change.

Top tips

The more consistent you are with the use of your 'spotlights' the better they will work as the learners will begin to recognise (unconsciously) the signals that you are sending them.

Thanking them when they have responded the way you wanted them to will add to the conditioning processes. Be specific (e.g. 'Thank you for stopping straight away').

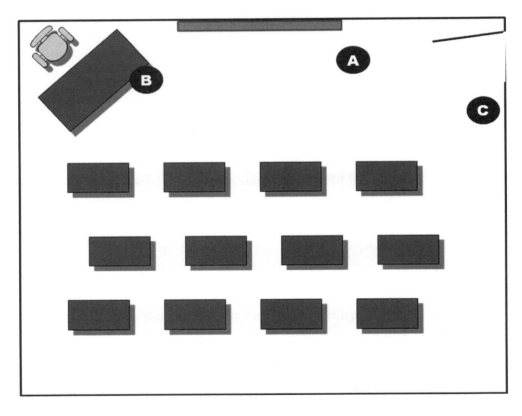

Spots in a teaching space for example

Quick start – Planning your stage spots around the learning space

A few suggestions to get you started in thinking about your teaching space and where you want your spots.

In the diagram above we have suggested three specific spots as a starting point for creating conditioned response anchors for your teaching space. Keep strictly to your purpose for each spot only conducting that particular activity from that place. Let's take a look at each place and consider the states that would be best to utilise.

Spot A

Activity = Teaching

Question: How do I want to be when teaching the information in this session?

Useful states to consider: Eloquent, authoritative, knowledgeable, masterful, open, passionate, playful, brilliant, energised, infallible

Spot B

Activity = Facilitating discussions

Question: How do I want to be when facilitating the group asking and answering questions?

Useful states to consider: Friendly, adventurous, creative, elegant, excellent, good, light-hearted, primed

Spot C

Activity = Calling order and delivering instructions

Question: How do I want to be when bringing a group to order so they can listen to an instruction?

Useful states to consider: Awesome, autonomous, calm, confident, commanding, congruent, gigantic, important, intense, masterful, powerful, together, unstoppable

These are just a few suggestions for states to work with to create your stage anchors. Mix and match three states or think of your own states that would work in these situations. These are not the only spots or collections of states that will work. Begin the fun by designing your own stage – remember you are the star of the show.

Adding some appropriate Satir Category body language will also enhance the effectiveness of spots (see the Index to find chapters that refer to this).

Learn more about this

Anchoring is one of the most useful NLP techniques developed by Richard Bandler and John Grinder. It's a method for using your powerful unconscious resources to get the responses you desire. Anchoring is the process by which a memory, a feeling or some other response is associated with (anchored to) a stimulus such as a sound, a space, a touch or a particular sight. Anchoring is a natural process that usually occurs out of our awareness. For example, when you were young, you undoubtedly participated in family activities that gave you great pleasure. The pleasure was associated with the activity itself, so when you think of the activity, or are reminded of it, you tend to re-experience some pleasurable feeling. In this way anchors are reactivated or triggered.

Read some more about anchors

- Read Chapter 9, 'Anchors away!', in *NLP for Teachers: How To Be a Highly Effective Teacher* (page 105)

Or to explore even more NLP tools read:

- *The Sourcebook of Magic* by Michael Hall

When else can you use this?

Anchoring is not only useful when you are teaching. You can use it in any situation where you need to instantly gain composure or access to a more positive state of mind. You may also like to:

- Use this for teaching students in drama classes – to help them re-access states on stage.

- Use in assemblies. Set up spots and use them regularly. Allied to gestures they can be excellent behaviour control signals that work at the unconscious level.

- Use spots in sport and anchor states to the starting blocks for races, in hockey for shooting or in cricket at the crease or wicket.

What are you going to do with this?
(Your ideas and thoughts)

114

36 The Six Sermons

How to use our natural 'aversion to pain' and 'attraction to pleasure' to motivate

When we want to motivate people to do things, or not to do things, the Six Sermons can be very useful.

I'm wondering whether you want to be the sort of person that has little sway and no influence. Or are you the sort of person that wants to be in command and communicate with clout and so be in charge of all your messages? Perhaps sometimes when you communicate you're not understood, people think you are strange and odd, or even standoffish, and you'd really like to be able to develop a style that is warm and friendly that draws people to you. Maybe you see that if you don't do it in the best way, to the best of your ability, you just won't succeed and you're looking for a way to improve your skills so that you can be successful – whenever you interact with other people.

The Six Sermons brings together two sets of mental pattern: one concerned with what we pay attention to and another set of patterns that indicate our primary motivational drive. We all have a pattern where we move towards pleasure and away from pain, this is known in NLP as the 'towards and away from metaprogram' or 'carrots and sticks'. The second set of three patterns used in the Six Sermons is one identified by the American psychologist David McClelland, who spent many years studying motivation. These three are also sometimes referred to as metaprograms in some NLP writing. McClelland determined from his research that humans have three key motivational patterns that drive our behaviours: power, affiliation and achievement. Put these together with 'towards' and 'away from' and you get the powerful recipe for creating motivational direction in people.

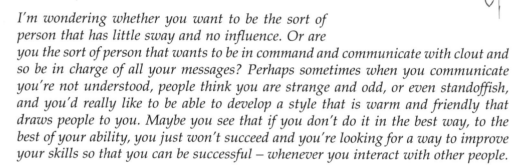

Here's how

People have a natural preference for 'towards' or 'away from' motivation and for either: power, affiliation or achievement. When you describe something from all six possible positions it is called the Six Sermons. Giving such a 'sermon' at the start of a lesson or training session can be very effective.

Think of your context (e.g. something new you are about to teach or train – sport, examinations, a new team direction, etc.). Use the motivational drivers as a focus and imagine the pain and then the pleasure for each one to build what you will say in a way that will have something for everyone:

1. **Power** is about being in control and in charge. If we take a sport example, we may want to move away from the pain of not winning and being under the control of another team, whereas we want to move towards the pleasure of being in charge and in control, in such a way that we can easily overcome the other players.

2. **Affiliation** is about being liked. Again, with a sport example, you might think 'no one likes a loser' and would move away from that, but think that if you are a winner people like you, respect you and sometimes even love you.

3. **Achievement** is all about success and is very often focused on the individual. So we would move away from any circumstance that means we would be a failure and move towards those things that would bring a success. In sport you would be successful beating your own best time even if you didn't win the race.

Quick start - Planning your Six Sermons

Example from above

Driver motive	Metaprogram	Sermon	Example
Power	Away (pains)	1	*I'm wondering whether you want to be the sort of person that has little sway and no control of their communications*
	Towards (pleasures)	2	*Or are you the sort person that wants to be in command and communicate with clout and so be in charge of all your communications*
Affiliation	Away (pains)	3	*Perhaps sometimes when you communicate you're not understood, people think you are strange and odd, or even standoffish*
	Towards (pleasures)	4	*and you'd really like to be able to develop a communication style that was warm and friendly that draws people to you*
Achievement	Away (pains)	5	*Maybe you see that if you don't communicate in the best way to the best of your ability you just won't achieve your target*
	Towards (pleasures)	6	*and you're looking for a way to improve your communications so that you can be successful - whenever you interact with other people*

Quick start – Planning your Six Sermons worksheet

Have a go at completing this worksheet before you start one of your own.

Your context: completing your coursework

Driver motive	Metaprogram	Sermon	Example
Power	Away (pains)	1	Do you want to be the sort of student who will not be able to do what you want, will you end up having to work when others have chosen to go out and enjoy themselves?
	Towards (pleasures)	2	Just think of how it will be to be ahead of the others as you hand your work in completed ahead of time
Affiliation	Away (pains)	3	
	Towards (pleasures)	4	
Achievement	Away (pains)	5	
	Towards (pleasures)	6	

117

Quick start – Planning your Six Sermons

Your context

Driver motive	Metaprogram	Sermon	
Power	Away (pains)	1	
	Towards (pleasures)	2	
Affiliation	Away (pains)	3	
	Towards (pleasures)	4	
Achievement	Away (pains)	5	
	Towards (pleasures)	6	

Learn more about this

Learning to utilise metaprograms and then connect them to value systems can be a powerful way to create motivational direction for individuals and groups. By taking a value (by which we mean something that is important to us, something we will spend our time, energy and resources on) and connecting it to a metaprogram (the way we sort information), we can create a motivation direction. When presented with a potential pain we will naturally tend to move away from it; if we then add a greater

Read some more about metaprograms

- Read Chapter 7, 'Knowing me, knowing you . . . aha!', in *NLP for Teachers: How To Be a Highly Effective Teacher* (page 73)

Or read:

- *Words That Change Minds* by Shelle Rose Charvet
- *People Pattern Power* by Wyatt Woodsmall

potential pleasure just after it we will naturally be drawn to it. Inside we are saying 'Oh no' then 'Yes please'. Repeating this with the key drivers of power, affiliation and achievement not only catches most people's key driver but also sets up three 'yes' responses so it works like a more complex and subtle 'yes set' (see Chapter 45, 'A word in your ear' for more about yes sets).

When else can you use this?

In schools this tool can be useful for talks and presentations to parents when you want them to engage in activities for the benefit of the school. You may also like to use it in the following ways:

- Learn to notice which of the Six Sermons is someone's preference and explain things from their motivational point of view.

- Great for selling ideas to sceptical people – use the 'away from' to handle objections. Use as a leader and a manager to influence individuals and teams.

- As a school leader use in assemblies to create whole school motivation when a new direction is being presented.

- If a particular approach is not working with a child use a different sermon, until you find the right one!

What are you going to do with this?
(Your ideas and thoughts)

37 Tell tale

How to use metaphor in the classroom, or training room

A little while ago a friend of ours who works as an NLP coach in schools was telling us about a teacher. This teacher had an exceptional reputation for handling students that most of the other teachers found disruptive and difficult to work with. Our friend told us that as part of her work as a coach she would often be required to complete teacher observations. Her task was to help come up with strategies that would improve the behaviour management of the students. During her time at the school she observed a number of teachers and in particular observed this exceptional teacher. Her task was to find out just what the difference was and how this teacher was able to get results that others were not. Nothing striking stood out about this teacher at first. Her subject was art, she herself was small in stature and sometimes older students would tower over her. She had a quiet voice and yet somehow she commanded the group and they got on and did everything she suggested. The lesson plans were no different, her objectives were very similar to other teachers, she coached well and knew her subject.

The difference was the way this teacher started her class. She would gather all the students together around the table and in her quiet voice she would begin to tell a story. Often this story would be connected to the subject matter and sometimes it would just be about her own experiences over the weekend. There would always be something exciting, slightly strange or some question that remained unanswered and she would often leave the story at an exciting part and say, 'Well, let's get on with our work now. I'll tell you what happened later.'

Here's how

Metaphor and stories are one of the most powerful ways to elicit internal states (positive feelings and emotions, etc.) in people. As we listen to stories our unconscious mind generates pictures, sounds and feelings and we begin to experience the stories as if we were part of them. In NLP we use stories to pass messages to the unconscious mind, to give instructions and to help create the sort of learning states that are going to be useful for learners.

Below is a simple step-by-step recipe to get the key parts of a *learning story* in the right places.

1. What is the important message that you want to deliver? Keep this simple – one idea or concept is usually enough.

2. Decide on what sort of states (emotions and feelings) you would like to create or elicit in those you're going to tell a story to.

3. Decide on the source and the 'mechanism' for telling a story – a story about yourself, a story that somebody else has told you or a story from a book, the radio, a film or TV.

4. Think of a theme for your story. This may be directly connected to the subject. For instance, if you are teaching biology you may want a story about Darwin. Alternatively, you can use any theme that will work with your outcome and that will enable you to create the sort of states that you want.

5. Create your story but keep it simple and interesting. It is a good idea to collect stories from books, magazines and on the internet, so that you have plenty of base material that you can adapt for your own purposes.

6. Beginnings should have the intention of creating curiosity and include a hook (something useful or desired, interesting or just plain mad) – the idea is to create in the unconscious mind a need for completion. At the beginning you can explore the present situation, define the barriers and obstacles and set out the problem.

7. The middle is the place to put your key message, states and information. This is the place where solutions to difficulties are described and where resolutions occur – where the hero finds a way to defeat the demons, as it were.

8. Think carefully about how you want to finish your story. Leaving a story open will encourage the unconscious mind to be in search mode waiting and listening for the end. In this mode we are more motivated to take in more facts and information. It's as if the 'unconscious mind' and its 'filters' are forced to remain open. Closing the story is a place that you can go later – perhaps at the end of the lesson to round things off.

There are three positions you can tell a story from: your own position (a story about you), a second position (a story that someone has told you) or, alternatively, you can tell the story from the point of view of a source unconnected to you (third position). There are advantages and disadvantages to each of these positions depending on the effect you wish generate.

Position 1 (Your own position – through your own eyes)

Builds rapport and empathy with the teller by sharing something of yourself and your life experience.

Position 2 (Told to you by someone else)

Is useful when you want to give advice or subtle instructions and be less direct.

Position 3 (Told from the point of view of another source outside of you and your circle)

Is great for delivering harder messages because it does not seem consciously to come from you – it is just what your characters are doing.

Use the metaphor making template at the end of this tool to help you plan your story. The opening story in this tool may give you some ideas about how this works.

Learn more about this

We all know that we love listening to stories and all good storytellers know that as well as a beginning, a middle and an end, stories have meanings too. Humans are meaning-making animals. Our brain makes meaning about us in relation to our environment using the information that flows through our senses moment by moment. This automatic and largely unconscious process can be utilised brilliantly when you want to communicate an idea or a meaning to someone else. A well-crafted story is one of the best vehicles for delivery.

> **Read some more about metaphor**
> - Read Chapter 5, 'Don't think about chocolate cake', in *NLP for Teachers: How To Be a Highly Effective Teacher* (page 49) for more information on influential language and metaphor
>
> Or read:
> - *The Magic of Metaphor* by Nick Owen
> - *The Hero's Journey* by Joseph Campbell

When else can you use this?

At the end of the day teaching is all about persuading others. One of the more subtle ways to influence others (such as difficult children, parents, delegates or colleagues!) is to make use of metaphor and story. Use these approaches whenever more direct strategies are less likely to work. You can also:

- Use stories to create a team identity metaphor and reinforce a whole school vision or when training to establish the core of the learning experience.

- Storytelling is great for assemblies. Use to build rapport and create compliant states.

- In class create a storytelling game where different groups come up with a beginning, middle and end, then have fun putting it all together.

What are you going to do with this?
(Your ideas and thoughts)

Quick start – Metaphor making template

What are you going to do with this (your ideas and thoughts)?

1	What is your message?	Be focused and clear about your outcome for the story
2	What states do you want?	e.g. curiosity, listening . . .
3	Source and mechanism	1st position = about you 2nd position = told to you by someone else 3rd position = another source outside you
4	Theme	Adventure, heroes, heroines, personal tale . . .
5	Beginning	Hook, present situation . . .
6	Middle	Your message . . .
7	End	Leave them wanting more . . . .

38 That's me

How to understand your preferences and biases as a presenter/trainer and teacher

Have you ever done something without noticing, and there you were doing it? What was it that led you to do it in that way? What happened in your brain as a result of something you heard, saw or felt that led you to do it? In NLP we talk about attention filters (or metaprograms). These are our big preferences – the sorting principles and the models which people use to organise all the sensory inputs they receive. Metaprograms probably relate to the idea of schema in cognitive psychology and therefore relate to largely automatic behaviours and processes. Of course, as with all behaviour, having awareness of what you do, and why you do it, is the first step on the journey to self-development and change. This tool gives you quite a detailed view of metaprograms – so if you are new to NLP, you might want to first explore some of the simpler applications in Chapter 48 ('Mixing desk') and Chapter 59 ('Comfort zone'). If you have already read these chapters you will notice that we are using some different metaprograms in this resource and some are being applied in a slightly different way. This is because there are lots of types of metaprograms (some suggest perhaps as many as 60), each has different applications (from an NLP perspective) and different combinations are more or less helpful in different types of personal development.

Here's how

Our brains receive a huge amount of information all the time, perhaps as much as two to three million pieces of information a minute. Most of this is processed unconsciously without our awareness. In order for the mind to deal with this vast array of information, it needs to organise the information into categories (what in NLP we call attention filters or metaprograms). Metaprograms have a significant influence on what we do and what we do not do. They determine, to a large extent, our attitude and approach within a context. These sorting principles are often very contextual and therefore you should bear this in mind when using them. Awareness of our preferences can help us change our communication style and increase our impact in many arenas. Attention filters sit on continuums – they are neither negative nor positive, merely different focuses of attention. In this tool we are going to focus on the teaching/presenting context. Attention filters are easy to understand and once understood you need no fancy techniques to shift them and achieve a quick change in your attitude and approach.

1. Decide on the context to be examined. Use the summary sheet to get an understanding of each attention filter.

2. Answer the questions from your own perspective in that context, or even better have a colleague ask you these questions as they can be used to form an excellent coaching tool. For each attention filter ask yourself: 'What can I change or adjust to enhance my presenting/teaching/training?'

Summary sheet of attention filters or metaprograms

Attention filter continuum

Name	Description of the metaprogram	Name
Towards (goals)	Directs the way we move about our values. Towards pulls us to the positive benefits of our values. Away from pushes us away from our undesired values creating a sense of aversion. Everybody moves towards some things and away from others.	Away (from pains)
Global (big picture)	Deals with the 'chunk size' of information people prefer. There are two basic positions, with a lesser third position. Deductive (philosophic) thinkers start globally and move down. Inductive (scientific) thinkers start with details and specifics and move up. Abductive (poetic) thinkers prefer the use of metaphor and analogy.	Specific (details)
Self (focus)	Self and other relate to the starting point for attention in relation to the people aspects of a context, whether the person starts from a self-perspective or from the perspective of others.	Others (focus)
Sameness (match)	There are two basic ways of operating mentally when we work with data. We can look for what matches what we already know (sameness) or for what differs or mis-matches (difference). This metaprogram plays an important role in our overall thinking patterns.	Difference (mis-match)
Internal	This is a key focus when judging, evaluating, deciding responses and behaviour. Refers to where the source of authority and responsibility resides; where a person places the responsibility for their actions. Also refers to the source of motivation and validation for the self.	External
Procedure (must, will, have to, should . . .)	The linguistic markers for detecting this pattern are referred to as 'modal operators'. Modal operators express the contingent relationships we believe to exist between people, outcomes, and ourselves. You can think of modal operators as expressing an 'operative mode' (or mindset) that greatly influences a person's responses and consequently behaviour.	Options (can, maybe, perhaps, might, may . . .)
Past (focus)	The English language allows for time distinctions to be made between past, present and future. How we naturally externalise the passage of time makes it possible for us to think we can organise, structure, manage and control time. We will have a preference for where our focus of attention is placed, either past, present or future.	Future (focus)
Task (focus)	Our preference for focus on task or relationship will determine our communication and organisational style and determine behaviours.	Relationship (focus)

Metaprograms assessment sheet

The sheet below will help you to notice metaprogram preferences that are particularly useful for 'modelling' practice and which you can notice by listening to the language people use when they have been asked a question. You can use the assessment sheet in a variety of ways. In this chapter we will use it to analyse your current metaprograms/attention filters in a particular context and to reflect on whether these are the right ones. To use it for modelling find someone you know who is really excellent at something that they do. Get them to imagine themselves really doing the activity and work through the questions. Notice what the differences are between this and other practice (your own for example). Or you could do some research with a group of colleagues.

Stagecraft and presentation skills for teachers and trainers

Questions to ask	Pattern being looked for	Metaprograms (in bold) and words to listen for in the language people use	Which metaprogram is being used by the person?
What is important in your presenting/teaching/ training? Ask 3 times or more	Values and motivators		
Why is that important? Ask 4 times	Direction of motivation	**Towards:** attain, gain, achieve, include **Away:** avoid, exclude, solve/ recognise problems	
When you plan to teach a new topic do you want to start by gathering all the details together or by getting the general picture first?	Big picture Details	**Big picture:** overall, overview **Specific:** details, sequences, exactly, precise	
Attention direction – Who are you presenting/ teaching/ training for?	Self Others	**Self:** short monotone responses **Other:** animated, expressive, automatic responses	
Describe the connection between presenting/ teaching/ training this year and last year?	Decision factors	**Sameness:** same, no change **Sameness with exception:** more, better comparisons **Difference:** change, new, unique **Sameness with exception and difference:** new and comparisons	
How do you know you've done a good job of presenting/ teaching/training?	Reference	**Internal:** knows within oneself if something is right **External:** needs to be told by others, uses facts and figures to verify	
Why did you choose (your current work or activity)?	Reasoning	**Options:** Choice, possibilities, variety **Procedures:** a story or sequence, how, necessity, didn't choose	
What do you like about presenting/ teaching?	Organisation focus	**Relationships:** people, feelings, reactions **Tasks:** tools, ideas, activities	

Learn more about this

Metaprograms are likely to relate to the cognitive psychology concept of a schema. In cognitive psychology and neuroscience the term 'automaticity' is applied to the recognition that we often perform many activities on 'automatic pilot' (whilst our minds turn to other things). Much of everyday life (including feeling, thinking and doing) is automatic and is driven by current features of the environment (e.g. people, objects, behaviour of others). Fully conscious awareness, or partial awareness, is triggered only when it is needed and in response to a novel situation or those which require conscious analysis.

> **Read some more about metaprograms**
>
> Read:
> - *Words That Change Minds* by Shelle Rose Charvet
> - *Figuring Out People: Reading People using Meta-Programs* by Michael Hall

When else can you use this?

Any time that you need to work with a group of people or an individual your metaprograms will affect the other person. Recognising this is a key step on the journey to flexible behaviour and influence.

- Use the assessment as part of a coaching programme to help people reflect on their behaviours and the impact on others.

- Use it to plan what metaprograms would be best stimulated for learning in different contexts.

- Notice the metaprograms that people use in their language and explain things from their point of view for more impact and influence.

- Use with children to get a much richer picture of learning preferences. Notice the metaprogram preferences of the children that you teach and modify your teaching accordingly (particularly in relation to 'big picture' versus 'detail' preferences).

Stagecraft and presentation skills for teachers and trainers

What are you going to do with this?
(Your ideas and thoughts)

39 Then there were four

How to give your lesson structure 'learning impact'

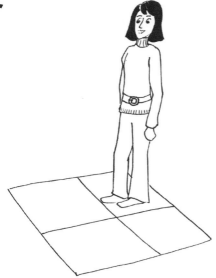

Are you familiar with David Kolb from your training days and those lectures about learning preferences? All very interesting. However, did you ever get a 'HOW to' use the concept? Bernice McCarthy developed the 4MAT Cycle to take Kolb's work into the classroom or training room in a practical and impactful way. Teachers are often looking for that 'silver bullet' that will improve their lessons. Here are four really useful bullets. The 4MAT model breaks down into just four questions that can be used to rapidly format the shape of the lesson and make sure that each learning style and preference is covered. Even if you don't believe in learning styles, it's a great way of structuring thinking. This method can be easily integrated with your lesson planning and so enhance your own unique style as a teacher. With this you can create learning experiences that involve and inform and are practical and meaningful in the wider context of the outside world. Why 4MATs? Well, just imagine yourself standing on each of four mats on the floor as you work through the cycle. You can even use specific spaces in the classroom or training room to introduce each stage. Doing this will help to get your learners 'anchored' to the lesson processes that you use – so that they know what's coming next.

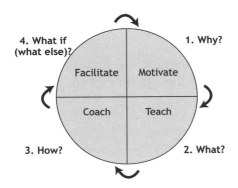

Here's how

There are four stages in the 4MAT model and four accompanying behaviours:

1. **WHY?** is the key question to ask. Why should anyone listen to you? What has it got to do with them and how will it benefit them? What can you do to motivate and create a curious listening state?

    Your role is to *motivate* and develop meaning.

2. **WHAT?** is the information you want them to grasp. What concepts do you want to develop? Use the folders model (see Chapter 30) to help format your data for their minds. Think about the *concepts* that are involved first, then the *principles*, after that a

process overview (a flow chart can help here), then describe the *procedures* (the steps they will take).

Your role is to *teach*.

3. **HOW?** is the active part where they will be doing and following the *procedure*.

Your role is to *coach*.

4. **WHAT IF (WHAT ELSE)?** What connects the information to the real world? Have them investigate what they will be able to do as a result of the learning.

Your role is to *facilitate*.

Use the Quick start planner at the end of this chapter to start reflecting on your own lessons and how you could use this model.

Learn more about this

When NLP developers first looked for a model to underpin the training of NLP they found many excellent trainers using this structure. Preferences and learning styles are linked and describe the ways people perceive and process their experience. Bernice McCarthy's cycle works with the way our mind processes through our preferences; it allows access to the different learning styles very simply with the four key questions. The model helps learners move through the stages of:

> **Learn more about the 4MAT Cycle and how to use it**
>
> Read:
> * *Teaching Around the 4MAT Cycle: Designing Instruction for Diverse Learners with Diverse Learning Styles* by Bernice McCarthy and Dennis McCarthy

- Reflective observation
- Abstract conceptualising
- Active experimentation and problem solving
- Integration of new knowledge and skills.

Learning happens when we integrate the meaning and value of our experiences. The 4MAT procedure and actions allow us to examine those meanings for ourselves, and by moving through this cycle each learner is helped to have an experience that relates to their particular preference.

When else can you use this?

- Brainstorming and meetings. This is a great model for structuring team meetings and discussions, or use as a negotiation structure when negotiating one-to-one as a leader.

- Create talks and speeches that seem coherent and well structured.

- Writing newsletters, papers and reports. You can even teach the model to students to support essay writing.

Quick start planner	
Concepts	**My lesson content notes**
Stage 1. WHY? = MOTIVATING Connect, examine and motivate the students a. What activities will you use to start with: listening, speaking, brainstorming, group interaction, storytelling, games (and any activities that create sameness in the group in order to create rapport) b. Create an experience – **connect** c. Reflect and analyse the experience – **examine** – are interesting questions that build curiosity	
Stage 2. WHAT? = TEACHING Develop concepts a. What are the big ideas to be grasped? – **define these** b. **Principles** – What makes it work? c. **Process** – What is the overview? d. **Procedure** – What are the steps to be taken?	
Stage 3. HOW? = COACHING a. **Practice** – use the procedure with worked examples, get the learners doing something b. **Your ideas** – use questions to support learners to practise the procedure	
Stage 4. WHAT IF (WHAT ELSE)? = FACILITATING a. **Refine** the topic with student experiences through discussion and questioning b. **Integrate** with the real world, ask questions like: How could you use this?	

What are you going to do with this?
(Your ideas and thoughts)

40 Top of the vox No. 1

How to develop your vocal talents

How often have you spent the week teaching and found that your voice was giving out towards the end of the week? All of us who train, present or teach have one thing in common: we all earn our living by using our voice. By taking some simple steps we can look after our voice and also improve our range, intonation and stamina. In the next few resource tools we offer a few well-tried techniques that are quick to do and fun to play with. The first two techniques are designed to warm up and loosen the voice box. The third exercise will help you experiment with the natural range of your voice. You can do them on your own or it can be just as much fun to use with your colleagues or with your class.

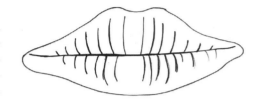

Here's how

When working with the voice your posture is important and this is where we will start.

1. To warm up begin by shaking your hands then arms, moving your head gently, move on to shake your body then legs and feet until all of you is shaking. Stay loose and floppy and say 'AAAAAHHH' – allow your voice to move up and down, loud and soft. Notice how, as you loosen your body, your range begins to increase even if the sound is strange. Do this for two to three minutes.

2. Get your posture right – start with the posture from the tool in Chapter 32 ('In your head and in your body No. 1').

   - Make any movements smooth
   - Have your head up
   - Have your chin level
   - Allow your jaw to relax
   - Let the front of your neck be loose
   - Let your shoulders slope and be relaxed
   - Have your knees soft
   - Allow your back muscles to relax
   - Allow your abdominal muscles to relax
   - Stay with your weight on heels and soles.

3. Practise this until you can do it easily.

4. Now you can experiment with vocal exercises from this warmed up and relaxed posture – see the exercises below.

Exercise 1 – The two parts to this exercise will loosen the muscles around the vocal cords

Start with your tongue on the right hand side of your mouth. Make a figure of eight, so that your tongue goes across your top teeth, to the middle, then crosses to the bottom teeth, along to the left hand side of your mouth, then up and across the top. Keep your mouth closed for this. Repeat this four to six times.

Put the tip of your tongue behind your bottom set of front teeth. Let your jaw drop and gently push out your tongue. Repeat this four to six times.

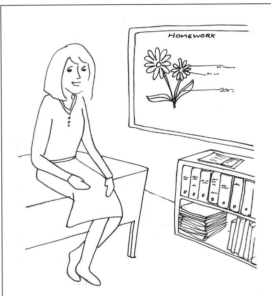

Exercise 2 – These exercises are to help with vowel sounds which help to create richer tones

1. Take a deep breath in, hold and then exhale naturally.

2. Take another deep breath. This time exhale longer on the way out – 20 seconds is excellent.

3. Take another slow deep breath in. Begin to hum, increase the volume slowly and keep the sound even. You can imagine your voice resonating in your nose, forehead, eyes and eventually in your whole head. Repeat this four to six times.

4. Have a relaxed jaw and allow your mouth to open to the maximum without strain or tension. Begin humming 'mmmmmm' then open your mouth and allow your voice to come out with the sound of 'aaaaarrrrrr'. Allow the sound to fade away towards the end of the exhale.

Using one breath, repeat the exercise with all of the vowel sounds. You can experiment with stretching and shortening the vowel sounds.

A	Mmmm maaarr
A	Mmmm mmaaye
E	Mmmm mmee
I	Mmmm mmii
O	Mmmm mmow (the lawn)
U	Mmmm mmoow (like a cow)

Exercise 3 – The next exercises are for exploring and extending the range of your voice. Use different pitches and experiment with rising and falling pitches.

1. Ga-ga! – Make baby noises up and down, then try out using all the vowel sounds, e.g. ga-ga, ge-ge, gi-gi, go-go, goo-goo.

2. Bzzzzzz! – Make buzzing noises like a bee to find resonances in your mouth and sinuses.

3. Innnnnnng-uh! – This helps you to feel the natural resonances in your sinuses. Then use words like 'ding', 'ping', 'zing', 'ting'. Hold the 'i' sound so that it makes your sinuses tickle.

4. Hah! – Imagine you are digging (it works better if you do the actions too!): as you dig into the ground, exhale with a 'HUH!' sound. Lift the soil, and as you chuck it over your shoulder, make a 'HAH!' noise.

   Repeat until it gets silly. You can do this by pretending to do karate moves – kicks and punches. Make sure you do this from your diaphragm (at the base of your chest) not from your throat.

5. Oooooh! – Sliding sounds up and down your natural range. You have to move your arms for this one: high notes – arms up in the air; low notes – try bending your knees and hanging your arms like an ape.

6. Yah! or Yar! – For this one, just let your jaw drop loosely to a loose hanging – don't force it open. Do it for a while – 20 times or so.

7. Wow! – Start low and go up high, then back down again. 'Wwwww-aaaaaaaa-oooooo-wwwww'. Open your mouth wide to let the sound out.

Learn more about this

What's all this got to do with NLP you might ask? Well, in NLP we are not only interested in the words we use and the effect these have on people's minds. NLP is also about the relationship between our minds and our bodies and how by developing this relationship we can learn to also be more effective with others. We are always communicating and the more control and skill we can develop in subtle areas such as voice tone the more effective we are likely to be able to become.

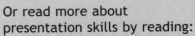

Read some more about voice work

See in this book:
- Chapter 41 ('Top of the vox No. 2')
- Chapter 43 ('Word salad')

Or read more about presentation skills by reading:
- *Presenting Magically: Transforming Your Stage Presence with NLP* by David Shephard and Tad James

Research by Albert Mehrabian suggested that most of what is being communicated comes across mainly through body language and voice tone. Developing your flexibility of vocal tone can make a real difference to how you come across as a teacher, trainer or presenter. Teachers are using their voices for longer during a day than professional singers and opera singers, both of whom understand how important such vocal development is. If you want to run a marathon then you would take up an exercise programme in order to be fit enough. Presenting and teaching is a marathon for the voice. Simple exercises can prevent fatigue and keep the muscles around the voice box loose and stress free.

When else can you use this?

As a teacher or school leader your voice is a key part of your toolkit. Looking after your tools and keeping them well oiled (as it were) is what all good craftspeople do. You can also use this tool in the following ways:

- Use as a warm-up exercise or icebreaker before a training day

- Just for FUN

- Try this at parties!!

What are you going to do with this?
(Your ideas and thoughts)

PENS

---

41 Top of the vox No. 2

How to have more fun with your voice

You should work through 'Top of the vox No. 1' before learning more skills in this tool . . .

Now we have warmed up your voice, we can begin to experiment with ways of using your voice to great effect in the teaching space. Have you ever wanted to give a command to one person when there are many in the room? Would it be useful and fun to be able to target your voice? Here are a couple of ways you can learn to get precision with your voice by projecting it just where you want – the difference between a blunderbuss and a top archer.

Here's how

As with most things in life, what happens inside your head is just as important as what you do physically. The exercises below will help you to create some positive imagery to draw on when presenting – to support the development of better voice projection. The first exercise is best done in a large room where you can move about and experiment with voice targeting.

1. Start with the warm-ups from 'Top of the vox No. 1'.

2. Imagine a bell in front and above you. Using words like 'ping', 'ding', 'zing', 'ting', aim them at your imaginary bell. You will quickly find that you begin to get a sense of your voice arriving at the target. You can also place an imaginary cup in the corner of the room and imagine throwing your voice into it as you vocalise (do this loudly and very quietly and see what happens).

For the next exercise you will need the help of a colleague and a thin-walled wine glass.

3. Have your colleague hold the glass lightly with their fingertips and tilt the glass towards you. Starting close (1–3 metres) aim your voice into the glass – your colleague may feel the vibration as your voice arrives in the glass.

4. Move around holding the glass in different positions and distances until you can target your voice precisely.

5. You can take it in turns to practise voice targeting. Have fun, and when you have learned how to do this you can drop your voice right where it will be most effective.

Stagecraft and presentation skills for teachers and trainers

Quick start – Gym for the voice

Tongue twisters are a great way to improve diction and are fun too

- She sells seashells by the seashore
- Each sixth chick sat on a stick
- Does your shirt shop stock socks with spots?
- Round and round the rugged rock the ragged rascal ran
- Eat fresh fried fish free at the fish fry
- Three gray geese in the green grass grazing; gray were the geese and green was the grazing
- Sixth sheik's sixth sheep's sick
- Sixty-six sick chicks
- Strange strategic statistics
- Lemon liniment
- Rubber baby buggy bumpers
- She stood on the balcony, inexplicably mimicking him hiccupping, and welcoming him in
- A big black bug bit a big black bear and the big black bear bled blood
- Imagine an imaginary menagerie manager imagining managing an imaginary menagerie

Top tip

To look after your voice and to keep your throat clear of phlegm, before speaking to groups, avoid milk and dairy products. A drink made of half a lemon squeezed into a pint of water can be used to clear phlegm. Eating late at night can cause acid reflux, which can come back up the throat and might damage the vocal cords. Oh, and it is best to avoid smoking (for lots of reasons!).

What professional singers do

Although it's tempting, when you first start to develop your vocal skills, to think that projection and voice control is all about what happens in your throat, it couldn't be further from the truth.

At the base of your lungs is a part of your body called the diaphragm. It is this that supports your lungs and affects the air pressure that you can push out from the base of your lungs. Developing the strength and control of your diaphragm is key. Here are a few ways to do it.

- Tie a scarf around your waist just below your ribs and practise pushing out and holding pressure against the scarf, without breathing out. You will soon get to feel where your diaphragm is. Continuous pressure from here is the way to create greater volume and projection in your voice without straining your vocal cords. Always breathe from here (the base of your lungs) when speaking in public, rather than from the top of your lungs.

- Take a deep diaphragm breath and slowly blow the breath out of your mouth with your lips in a tight little 'O'. Hold your hand out in front of you and try to push the air so that you can feel it hitting the palm of your hand.

- Practise the above exercise whilst walking somewhere to build extra strength. You may need to miss the hand bit off if there are people around.

- Vocalise 'Ha' loudly a few times by pushing from your diaphragm, not your throat, to build strength, power and control.

Learn more about this

In NLP we often talk about the relationship between mind and body and see these as a single system. Using your voice effectively is a combination of physical technique and mental application. If done effectively it also has an effect on the people that you are presenting to or teaching. Taking some time each week to develop your vocal skills, particularly if you are new to teaching or training, will reap great rewards and allow you to come over more confidently and assertively.

Read some more about voice work

See:

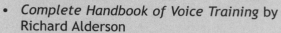

- *Finding Your Voice: A Complete Voice Training Manual for Actors* by Barbara Houseman
- *Complete Handbook of Voice Training* by Richard Alderson
- *Voice of Influence* by Judy Apps

When else can you use this?

- Use tongue twisters as a fun icebreaker on training or as starter activities in classrooms.

- Have a tongue twister competition in class. Get the learners to write them and then perform them.

- Use the techniques in drama lessons or to support singing lessons or as preparations for doing a class assembly.

What are you going to do with this?
(Your ideas and thoughts)

PENS

Stagecraft and presentation skills for teachers and trainers

42 What a state?

How to create a learning state of mind

Have you ever tried to teach or train a group that is not quite ready to learn? They take time to settle and much of the lesson disappears before the real teaching can begin. There is no one way to create a learning state and the types that you create will depend very much on what it is you want to teach. If you go out to teach sports on a cold frosty morning then the state might need to be energetic, enthusiastic and fun. On the other hand, in the classroom or training room, other states will be more useful.

Here's how

There are some core attributes that contribute to a learning state – then there are the extra things that are required depending on the subject matter. Let's take a look at the core attributes. Firstly, in order to learn we must open our senses in order to look, listen and pay attention. If we are focused on what just happened in the break, or what's going to happen later, then our senses will not be ready for us to take in the information. We also learn well when we are comfortable, so another key part of a learning state is to create a relaxed state. With senses open and feeling relaxed we can then move on to the next stage. We may need energy and enthusiasm for sports, or concentration, questioning and focus for the classroom. Of course, these are not the only states that will be useful and are just examples of the way you can begin to think about the process of teaching using states.

1. Decide on the sort of states that are needed in order for the particular piece of teaching that you're going to do to be absorbed in the best possible way.

2. Think about how you are going to relax and open senses (in the Quick start box below are some ideas to get you started).

3. Think about the senses that are going to be involved in your session and the ones that will best carry the learning:

   - Visual – good for taking in large amounts of data
   - Auditory – for sequential learning
   - Kinaesthetic – for learning involving doing or learning that needs an emotional connection.

Think of how you are going to create sequences of senses and what those sequences should be through the lesson. Here we are talking about types of attention rather than brain regions.

Quick start – Learning states
(some ideas about how to create them)

Visual-based states Opening the visual system	• Slide shows with lots of interesting pictures. Include some that contain lots of information about the subject and stimulate the curiosity 'What was that?' • Optical illusions • Spot-the-difference quizzes • Spelling • Mind maps
Auditory-based states Opening the auditory system	• Music • Sequencing games • Spoken puzzles
Kinaesthetic-based states Opening the kinaesthetic system	• Activities that will pre-teach the content • Stories that stimulate appropriate emotional states • Use pre-set anchors in the classroom or training room (see Index for more on anchoring)
Creating relaxation	• Use visualisations that can combine all three senses. See the example below at the end of this tool entitled *Quick relaxation routine*

Stagecraft and presentation skills for teachers and trainers

Learn more about this

Learning to work with students' 'learning states' is an important skill and can take much of the hard work out of a lesson or training session. By thinking at the beginning, in your planning, about what it is that you want and what states are going to be useful, you can dramatically increase the speed and depth of knowledge that students are able to absorb and their engagement with the topic. At the very least, activities generate rapport in the classroom or training room and bring everybody together before you start. Also creating something in the first five minutes of a lesson, or part of lesson, will often set the tone for the rest of the time – particularly if it opens up the right senses for the learning that will follow.

> **Read some more about states and language**
>
> • Read Chapter 5, 'Don't think about chocolate cake' (page 49) or Chapter 9, 'Anchors away!' (page 105), in *NLP for Teachers: How To Be a Highly Effective Teacher*

When else can you use this?

Learning is not just about what you do when you are delivering content, it is also about preparing your learners to receive and understand the information. This is important in a wide range of contexts including when working one-to-one with learners in the classroom training room or in school leadership situations.

- Use these ideas to create states before assemblies.

- Make a recording of yourself introducing sections of a lesson and reflect on what learning state you are creating.

- Think about and plan for learning states when doing training or setting up whole staff discussions.

- Apply the same ideas as a leader and think about what 'follower' states you want to create when leading others or teams.

What are you going to do with this?
(Your ideas and thoughts)

Quick relaxation routine using some NLP language patterns

You easily can adapt this to your context. It starts with the cover all bases (CAB) pattern and then uses yes sets (YS) to pace the listener into a relaxed state. This is followed by soft language suggestions to shift into peripheral vision which creates a great learning state.

Find out more about using language patterns from hypnosis in Chapter 45 ('A word in your ear'). There is also a more extended chapter on influential language in *NLP for Teachers: How To Be a Highly Effective Teacher* (Chapter 5, 'Don't think about chocolate cake').

Your tone should be soft and encouraging. Pause for a few moments after giving an instruction to allow time for students to comply – then you can say 'That's right' or 'Very Good' to emphasise and encourage them.

Good morning/afternoon everyone. We are going to be learning about [topic] today.

Some of you will have heard about this before, some of you might even know a little bit about it, and some of you will not have had any information about it yet. (CAB)

Before we start on [topic] and now we are all sitting here after [last lesson/break/journey here] would you like a few minutes to relax and chill so you are ready to learn? (YS) OK, then here is what to do.

First of all perhaps you might like to empty your mind of all the stuff that's been going on before you got here – you can just leave it to one side for now and pick it up later if you want to; very good. Now all you need to do is to find a spot on the wall that is just above eye level and rest your eyes on it, that's right.

Once your eyes are resting on the spot, keeping them open, you can allow the muscles around your eyes to relax . . . that's right. As they relax you will be able to keep the spot in view and slowly be able to notice that you can begin to see things that are both to the left and to the right – this is your peripheral vision. Very good.

Whilst you enjoy this relaxation you can also loosen your jaw and as you do this you may begin notice any movements at the periphery of your vision. You'll become aware of all the different sounds around you from the loudest sound to the smallest sound – you can now allow your hearing to expand and take it all in.

Stagecraft and presentation skills for teachers and trainers

You may feel your back against the chair and your feet resting on the floor as you can begin to be aware of your breathing and being more relaxed. (YS) Stretch out your hands to either side taking care not to bump into your classmates and wiggle your fingers. Can you see them moving? Move them back slowly and see how far back they will go – with you still being able to see your fingers moving. As you let your hands come back to your sides you can keep your focus like this and any time during the class you can regain this peripheral focus and feel relaxed and ready to learn.

And now it's [time]. You've been sitting down and had a few minutes of relaxation so are you ready to learn about [topic] now? (YS)

Photocopy and use the spiral below as a fun way to focus attention.

Stagecraft and presentation skills			
Self-management	Influencing with words	Body language	Organising learning
*	* * *	* *	* * *

43 Word salad

How to improve your delivery skills in the classroom or training room

Have you ever wanted a quick way to get more out of the way you teach? Would it be useful to have techniques that are fast to practise and will really help in the classroom, training room, in school assemblies or when you give talks? This exercise is based around the idea of separating your words, gestures and voice tone in order to improve each one.

Here's how

'Word salad' is a fun way of improving your delivery in the classroom or training room. Get together with a group of colleagues and have some fun whilst practising key skills at the same time. Use it if you are a teacher trainer – it is great fun in a larger group as part of a seminar or training session.

1. Gather one or two colleagues together, people you are comfortable with and whose feedback you would appreciate.

2. Prepare a five-minute presentation on any topic, preferably something fun, interesting or gripping. This should focus on you delivering the information rather than using PowerPoint images or games involving others. Find a time and space where you will not be interrupted and can be relaxed and focused for the activity. It's best if you all agree to take turns doing this exercise and give each other feedback.

3. Deliver your five-minute presentation to your colleagues – they then will each have one minute to give you feedback (see the sheet below for guidance on the type of feedback required). We are not interested here in feedback on the content of your presentation: the emphasis will be on physiology, tone and gestures. The feedback you receive should be in the form of a sandwich:

   • Two things you did really well
   • One thing to improve on
   • And an overall comment that is not just 'I liked it!'

4. Once you have received the feedback you can go on to the next part. This time you will deliver your presentation using only gestures. You can run the words for your presentation in your mind silently using your gestures to emphasise the communication. Avoid miming or using sign language – use normal gestures and movements. Your colleagues must give you one minute of feedback using gestures only in the feedback sandwich format.

5. You are now going to do your presentation once more, but this time you're going to keep perfectly still and deliver your presentation using 'word salad'. Word salad is a kind of 'nonsense speak' that has no real words in it – but contains all the tonality to convey your message. This forces you to use your tonality to deliver your message. You may end up sounding like Bill and Ben the flowerpot men, the Clangers or someone from an alien land! Again your colleagues will give you feedback using word salad of their own.

6. The last part of this exercise is to do your five-minute presentation once more incorporating what you have learnt from the other part of the exercise. You may find you have surprising results when you put back together the gestures, your voice tone and the content of your presentation.

Quick start feedback sheet – things to look for	
Part 1: Words and gestures	Gestures • size • descriptive quality Movements • pacing • nervous tics Voice • tone • strength • volume • speed Pace of presentation • over-run • under-run • on time Overall impression

Part 2: Gestures only	Gestures • size • descriptive quality Movements • pacing • nervous tics • level of understanding produced
Part 3: Word salad	Voice • tone • strength • volume • speed • level of understanding produced
Part 4: Repeat a complete presentation	Gestures • size • descriptive quality Movements • pacing • nervous tics Voice • tone • strength • volume • speed Pace of presentation • over-run • under-run • on time Overall impression

Top tip

Learn about Satir Category body language patterns and incorporate this into your presentation skills workshops or practice sessions. You can find out more about this in Chapter 29 ('Body talk').

Learn more about this

Those of us that teach and present (just as with everything else in life) can slip into unhelpful patterns of behaviour. Using an exercise like this can really help to break out of patterns that work against what we want to achieve. Over time we may develop ways of dealing with nervous energy that can come out in our gestures and speech patterns – and are thus noticeable to others.

Read some more about voice work

See:
• Chapters 40 and 41 ('Top of the vox' Nos 1 and 2)

Or read more about presentation skills in:
• *Presenting Magically* by David Shephard and Tad James

Stagecraft and presentation skills for teachers and trainers

Because 'Word salad' isolates each part the exercise it allows us to focus our attention on getting clean communication signals for each 'channel' of communication: the physical, the tonal and the verbal. You may find this quite challenging at first but with practice you can rapidly improve your skills.

When else can you use this?

- This makes a fun party game.

- Great for children to improve their presentation skills.

- Useful when coaching a new colleague in presentation skills or with newly qualified teachers or as part of teacher training.

- 'Word salad' is also great for warming up the voice.

- A really good way to improve your 'presence' and impact as a leader. Practising in front of the mirror works well too.

What are you going to do with this?
(Your ideas and thoughts)

44 You know you want it

How to make it easier next time you teach or train

If you have read any of the serious research literature on hypnosis you will know that a large number of writers suggest that the key to hypnosis, as a phenomenon, is expectancy. In fact, hypnotic depth is affected by the expectations of the people who are about to experience it and indeed the very use of the word 'hypnosis' before doing a hypnotic procedure deepens trance. Not only that but the hypnotic-suggestive communication level of advertisements has been shown to have an effect on perceptions of brand effectiveness. The same can be said in the classroom or training room. In other words, the expectations of learning and learning effectiveness that you build up in the learners that you are going to teach in a moment, over the next hour or over the next year, are critical to their acceptance, beliefs and ultimately of their achievements and attainment.

Here's how

We all have expectations. No matter where we go or what we do we are always expecting something. Sometimes we don't know what to expect and are surprised. Sometimes we know exactly what to expect and are disappointed before we arrive. On other occasions we are excited by what we think is going to come – this is usually because we have received messages before we get there that have put us in the mood, tantalised us or presented us with a mystery that will be solved when we get there. This is called 'response potential' and we experience it almost every day. Trailers for films, adverts, previews of new television programmes all tell us that something worth waiting for is on the way. Usually there is just enough information and a cliffhanger that makes us want to know more. This is a well-proven technique in advertising and one you can use in your teaching and presenting. How much better would it be if you could have a state of expectation and excitement in your learners before you even begin? This is where you become your own advertising agent creating temptation, excitement and mystery.

1. First some questions to ask yourself:

   - What are you going to teach next time?
   - What are the most interesting parts of the lesson?
   - What will they be doing that will be fun?
   - How can you create a cliffhanger?
   - What expectations can you set up for next time?

2. Then follow the steps below to formulate your thinking. Use the simple formula below to advertise what will be coming next. The AIDA structure is a formula that is frequently used by advertising and copywriting professionals to create response potential.

A – is for **attention**, a statement or fact that will grab their attention.

I – is for **interest**, something about what is to come that creates interest and curiosity.

D – is for **desire** – what would make them want to be there?

A – is for **action** – what do they need to do, bring with them or think about for next time?

3. Use the Quick start table below to work out the trailers for your next lesson so you can set expectations and build response potential. Once you've got your ideas together for each part of the formula, work towards being able to deliver this quickly. When you have everyone listening use it almost as an aside and a link to what you're doing in the current lesson.

Quick start – Building response potential using AIDA

Area to cover	How will you do this?
Attention Grab their attention with something funny, unusual or bizarre	
Interest Create interest with something that will be useful, fun or exciting	
Desire Make them want to know more – set up expectations for something they won't want to miss	
Action Tell them what you want them to do (e.g. be here on time, bring something, think about something)	

Learn more about this

We all want to make life easier for ourselves and using the AIDA formula is a great place to start. AIDA was developed in the 1930s by advertising executives in order to build response potential to products. Although this form has been around for a long time it still works. This is something you can have fun with as you tantalise and tempt your class. On a serious note, building response potential is a critical part of teaching and training. By leaving a topic open with no answer, much like a metaphor, the unconscious mind seeks an answer. The unconscious mind stays listening ready to pick up the information. This is also a way to set minds up for the information you want to teach. By building response potential, motivation is increased and the desire to find out what will come next keeps the attention focused.

Read some more about building response potential

- Put your analytical head on and then watch film/TV trailers, adverts, soaps
- If you want to read some fascinating research then read the following paper by Oren Kaplan (2007): 'The effect of the hypnotic-suggestive communication level of advertisements on their effectiveness', *Contemporary Hypnosis*, 24(2): 53-63
- There is also a 2009 paper by Richard Churches on the Society for Organisational Learning in the UK website (www.sol-uk.org) that you might find interesting too: 'Look Into My 'i's: A Conversation About Leadership as Hypnosis', Society for Organisational Learning in the UK seminar, University of Surrey School of Management, 19 March 2009

When else can you use this?

Response expectancy is critical at the start of lessons and when beginning new sections of learning, so think carefully about how you are going to create those all-important expectations and response potentials.

- Use for headlines in your school magazines or other school literature.
- Use the formula for writing posters for events or teach the structure to children as part of creative writing.
- Get your classes to build their own AIDAs for upcoming events or learning.
- Be aware of the power of response expectancy as a school leader and think carefully about what this means for your whole school work.

What are you going to do with this?
(Your ideas and thoughts)

Stagecraft and presentation skills for teachers and trainers

Part 4

Personal development and effectiveness for teachers and trainers

45 A word in your ear

How to be influential with language

In NLP we frequently say that 'you cannot not communicate'. In other words, everything that we say or do says something. Understanding what this means for the language that you use in the classroom, or in other parts of your role, can significantly increase your effectiveness.

Here's how

Hypnotic language or soft language patterns are very useful in the classroom. These patterns can enhance your abilities to work with difficult students, help to ensure that your instructions are followed and encourage learning and positive thinking.

1. Understand presuppositions

Surface structure

Deep structure

An important idea to grasp is the concept of presupposition. Presuppositions are the deeper meanings in language that are under the surface. If we said:

> *Now that you have read this, you can think of the last time that you had to influence a child in the classroom or a parent in a meeting.*

you may well have found yourself doing just what we suggested. This is because the sentence presupposes that you were going to do what we suggested. Another useful concept is the double bind. Double binds work by giving you two choices, either one of which would be a desirable outcome. In the classroom you could say:

> *Would you like to begin by doing the graph or by answering the questions?*

The presupposition is that the child will start work whichever way is chosen. Presuppositions exist all the time in everyday sentences as well as in deliberate suggestions. For example, if we were to say to you: *A university professor we know is pregnant*, you would immediately also know that this person is female even though this is not stated in the surface structure of the sentence.

2. Using yes sets and yes tags

Yes sets are frequently used in sales and are a form of pacing and leading (where you acknowledge someone else's current situation first before attempting to influence them). If you hear something that is a fact, your mind has a natural tendency to 'nod' to itself in agreement. You can extend this phenomenon by stating three undeniable facts one after another before making your suggestion (or 'embedded command').

You have read about presuppositions (fact), *learnt about yes sets* (fact) *and have started to read this example* (fact), *so now would be a good time to learn another pattern* (suggestion), *wouldn't it?*

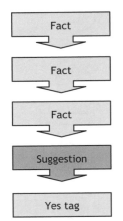

In a classroom context you might say:

We have learnt about the Romans, know the names of famous emperors, know what the Romans thought about war, so now would be a good time to reflect on what lessons we can draw from history for our own time, wouldn't it?

In both the examples above, notice the language pattern that sits at the end of the yes set (*wouldn't it?*). This is called a yes tag and is hard to say no to when used in this sort of context. You can also enhance its effectiveness by nodding at the same time. Other yes tags include: *isn't it?* and *can't you?*

Top tip - Watch your words

There are some words that have presuppositions, or suggestions of response, built into them. In the classroom you may want to think about using these with care.

- **If** implies choice, so avoid it - unless you want to allow choice (e.g. 'If you do that again' immediately implies the possibility of repeated bad behaviour).
- **But** negates what has been said - therefore, if you don't want your last thing to be forgotten or discounted use another word.
- **Try** implies the possibility of failure. If success is what you want, use another word.
- Another interesting command is **don't**.

Don't think about a blue elephant, right now!

Be aware that when you use 'not' you may be putting exactly what you don't want into people's minds (e.g. don't run, don't fail, etc.).

3. Connecting words or linkage language

You may also have begun to notice that another key element in influential language is the connecting of things that are agreed, or factual, to things that are being suggested. For example: *As you read this* (fact) *you could begin to think about all the ways in which this could be useful to you* (suggestion). Words like: *could, can, will, might, should,* etc. are all useful in this respect and are called model operators (these are discussed further below). Finally, notice the effect of the word *all* in the sentence above. This is a big generalisation and leaves the listener required to search inside for meaning – meaning which is also theirs. This makes their acceptance of the suggestion far more likely than if a specific detail was mentioned.

You can use linkage language to create more subtle embedded commands using words such as: *and, as, while, during,* and using the pattern *if x then y,* for example:

> *As you <u>sit down</u> and <u>open your books</u> you can begin to <u>quieten down now</u> and <u>if</u> you can do that now <u>then</u> we can finish early.*

Here what we want is a class to quieten down, so we preceded that instruction with how they get to the quieten down place, followed by an 'if then' instruction with a reward associated to it. Clever, *isn't it?*

Use soft language such as *maybe . . ., perhaps . . ., can . . ., I'm wondering . . ., I'm curious . . ., I'd like to invite you to . . ., you can . . .* to precede an instruction. This helps to reduce resistance and polarity responses (people doing the opposite to what you said – some people have a natural programme for doing this!). For example:

> *Perhaps you will <u>stand up</u>, <u>walk over</u> and <u>shut the door.</u>*

4. Reframing a negative and making use of these

'I can't' is often one of the biggest thought barriers to learning. When we say I can't do something we will have an internal representation (picture, sounds and feelings) about that activity. For instance, if a child says 'I can't swim' it's likely that the internal representation will be of them drowning, standing on the edge feeling frightened or in the water thrashing about. In order to respond to this in a positive way it is helpful to use our language to change the internal representation to something more positive. Saying 'yes you can' or 'there's no such thing as can't' does nothing to shift the picture, sounds and feelings in that person's mind. The first step is to agree by saying 'that's right' (or something similar) and then add the word 'yet' to whatever the activity is. For example, you might say: <u>*That's right*</u> *– you can't swim <u>yet</u>.* This statement helps to create in the mind of the receiver an internal representation of swimming in the future – a much more positive result.

We can become even more sophisticated with our language when dealing with 'I can't' by using a language pattern called 'chains of modal operators'. This sounds very fancy but is in essence is very simple. *Can't* is a 'modal operator of impossibility' – having loosened the internal representation by using the word *yet* we can further move the person's internal representations by connecting a number of operators together. Here are examples of modal operators:

- modal operator of impossibility – *can't*
- modal operator of possibility – *can, may, could, possibly*
- modal operator of probability – *might, probably*
- modal operator necessity – *must, will, have to, should.*

Here is a 'chain' using the swimming example from above:

> <u>*That's right*</u> *– you <u>can't</u> swim yet, and soon you'll find you <u>can</u> swim a few strokes and when you get used to that you'll <u>probably</u> be able to swim across the pool. Then very soon you <u>will</u> be able, just like the others, to swim a length or more.*

Learn more about this

John Grinder was an associate professor of linguistics at Santa Cruz University and in his modelling, with Richard Bandler, of the hypnotherapist Milton Erickson, he used ideas about the hidden meaning in sentences (presuppositions). These ideas were developed from ideas about the deep and surface structure of language and from the work of a leading figure called Lauri Karttunen. Karttunen had made in depth studies of presupposition in everyday language. Applying these to hypnosis revealed the structure of suggestion and influential language patterns – what Bandler and Grinder later called the Milton Model.

> **Read some more about hypnotic language**
>
> - Read Chapter 5, 'Don't think about chocolate cake', in *NLP for Teachers: How To Be a Highly Effective Teacher* (page 49)
> - If you want to know more about the structure of hypnosis from an NLP perspective read *Trance-formations: Neuro-Linguistic Programming and the Structure of Hypnosis* by John Grinder and Richard Bandler

When else can you use this?

There are many times when you need to think carefully about the language patterns that you are going to use (for example, when working with challenging parents). You can also use these tools in the following ways.

- Run a role play as part of an inset day and get some feedback on the language that you use.

- As a leader be clear about what you want and what the goal is. Make sure that the way you talk about this presupposes the outcome that you want. Notice your own internal dialogue and self-talk – does it presuppose success?

What are you going to do with this?
(Your ideas and thoughts)

Personal development and effectiveness			
Self-awareness	Self-management and resilience	Relationship awareness and influencing skills	Influencing and relationship management
* * *	* * *	* *	* *

46 If

How to develop your practice and effectiveness with positive presuppositions

The internal dialogue and ideas we have about life, particularly our beliefs, play a key role in determining our behaviour – particularly when we are stressed or just acting automatically. At such times, our unconscious 'mind' processes take over and we can find ourselves back on that old train track to where we always were before, even if we don't want it. Just noticing our beliefs and thinking about our thinking can free us from some of the automatic responses that serve us badly.

Here's how

In their studies of highly effective communicators and highly effective people, Richard Bandler and John Grinder identified a number of key beliefs that these sorts of people tend to have. Over the years through ongoing modelling by a number of NLP researchers, the list has become modified and adapted and is frequently referred to as 'the presuppositions of NLP'. In other words, they are beliefs that presuppose positive and effective behaviours and ways of thinking. Can you think about a belief that you once had as a child but don't have any more? What was it like to have that belief? When did it change? What are the benefits of your new belief? You see, beliefs are like items of clothing – they determine our identity. But as with clothes we have the power to change them – just by deciding to. Below you can find a presuppositions worksheet. This contains developments and adaptations of the classic NLP presuppositions that we have developed as a result of our work and research with teachers.

1. Read all the presuppositions through and then work through the questions.

2. As you read through the list for the first time you may like to reflect on the implications of each presupposition in relation to: the way in which you organise learning, how you deal with children and how you work with other teachers in the school.

3. Decide on your priority for development. Write your new belief on a card and carry it with you. Have a day when you keep it in mind, so that you consider it in each context you encounter. At the end of the day reflect on the benefits and imagine yourself in the future using it more often.

NLP presuppositions	What is my current belief?	What would be the benefits of adopting this NLP presupposition from now on?	What will be the implications for my current practice?	What will be my first and next step?
We are always communicating (the words we use, small changes in our facial expression, the way we stand, how we arrange our classroom, where we stand, etc.)				
The meaning of your communication is the response you get				
Resistance is the result of a lack of rapport				
The map that we create in our mind's eye is not reality				
The person who sets the frame controls the communication and the actions that happen				
Everyone has all the internal resources that they need				
Feedback is information – there is no such thing as failure				
The person with the most flexibility has the most influence				

Learn more about this

Reflecting on and developing your beliefs is not only a positive thing from a personal development point of view – it can also have a positive effect on the children that you teach. Evidence from education research suggests that negative beliefs can exist with or without teacher awareness,

Read some more about presuppositions

- Read Chapter 1, 'What's in a name?', in *NLP for Teachers: How To Be a Highly Effective Teacher* (page 1)

and can have an effect on learning. Learning to develop awareness of beliefs will give you much greater flexibility and in turn help you to develop more resilience when you find yourself in challenging situations.

When else can you use this?

Every time we interact with the world we do so through the filter of our beliefs – this is particularly true in teaching contexts. The presuppositions of NLP can be helpful in a wide range of situations.

- Use the presuppositions as discussion points when supporting groups of newly qualified teachers.

- Incorporate into teacher training activities.

- Use as a 360-feedback tool by getting others to fill in a worksheet about you. Compare what they say to what you say – so that you can get a feel for how well your beliefs play out in relation to your actual behaviours.

- Use with children to help develop social and emotional aspects of learning.

- Use as a basis for strategic discussions about school improvement.

What are you going to do with this?
(Your ideas and thoughts)

Personal development and effectiveness for teachers

Personal development and effectiveness			
Self-awareness	Self-management and resilience	Relationship awareness and influencing skills	Influencing and relationship management
*		* *	* * *

47 Let it go

How to free yourself from limiting past experiences

You know how sometimes things from the past just keep popping back into your mind in ways that affect you now? Teaching is a tough job and we have all had experiences with children, parents, classes or even other members of staff that we would rather park in our minds and move away from. Below, you can find a strategy for dealing with some of those everyday irritations that just won't go away so that you can begin to let go and focus on what is really important. This tool makes use of two NLP techniques: anchoring (the association of feelings to a stimulus) and submodality changes (visualisations that involve changing small details of your internal pictures, sounds and feelings).

Here's how

This tool involves some self-coaching and visualisation. So first of all find yourself somewhere comfortable where you can work through the process in your own mind without being disturbed. Alternatively, you could find a colleague or a friend to coach/facilitate you through the process. As we are dealing with things that may be slightly uncomfortable, start by setting yourself a positive anchor first.

Setting a positive anchor

1. Decide where in the room to moor your anchor. Walk over to the spot, but don't stand on it yet. Imagine a positive time when you felt resourceful just about to be in control and happy (or something similar) and turn the feelings up. When they are at their strongest stand on the space in the floor so that you associate that state of mind with standing there. Notice what you see, hear and feel.

2. Step out and notice what it is like to be back in the room again without those feelings and then step back in to test your anchor. Run this a few times if you need to so that you have it working before you start. Now if you feel like you need those resources at any time during the process below you can simply return to the space to feel comfortable again.

Now in your mind

3. Think of the thing that you have being holding on to for some time that keeps pulling you in an emotional or behavioural direction that you really don't want to go in any more – something that you would like to let go of. Imagine it in your hands like a rope pulling you. Ask yourself if you can let go of it? If you could, would you? What would you get by letting go? What would the benefits be?

4. Now in your own mind imagine yourself drawing a picture or taking a photograph of yourself letting go of something that you let go of once before in the past. Notice how pleased you were to be finally rid of this thing. Where in the room around you does that image belong? Take it and place it there. As you look over to the you in the picture, think about what resources you had then that enabled you to do this effectively. Think of a symbol or image that sums that up.

5. Now go and stand in that space in the room and imagine the thing that you no longer need to hold on to, the thing you know you want to let go of. Notice the rope in your hand pulling you towards those old feelings and behaviours and notice the feeling of the rope slipping away as you let go of the rope and see it drift into the past . . . further and further away until it disappears over the horizon. Finally, imagine yourself in the future dealing with a situation without that old baggage. What do you see, hear and feel? What will the benefits be?

Learn more about this

The inherent biases we carry round as teachers, which are often the result of past experiences and negative associations, can affect the way we are today. Education research shows that not only are these beliefs and biases influential but they can easily remain unconscious. Sometimes it's just a good idea to have a clear out in your own mind and let go of stuff that really is not helpful any more.

> **Read some more about submodalities**
>
> - Read Chapter 8, 'Memories are made of this', in *NLP for Teachers: How To Be a Highly Effective Teacher* (page 91), to find out more about strategies for dealing with negative past memories and experiences and how to use submodalities

When else can you use this?

- Run the process at the end of term so you start the holiday having let go of all the things you need to move away from.

- Use when starting a new job so you can really make a fresh start.

- Run the process after a hard lesson. Once you know how you can do this quickly in your mind, imagine letting go of any negative emotions and see them disappear into the distance.

What are you going to do with this?
(Your ideas and thoughts)

48 Mixing desk

How to develop flexibility and change your behaviours

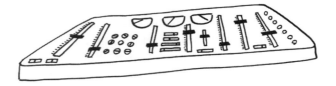

The meaning of your communication is the response you get. We cannot control others, only ourselves, and therefore if something you are doing is not working the way you want (and you are not getting the behaviours you want) you are just going to have to be more flexible! 'Mixing desk' is a self-coaching approach that can be applied to any context in which there are a number of variables that are influencing a situation, and our behaviours in that situation. In the example below we have integrated this NLP tool with some fundamental thinking from psychology about personal needs and wants.

Here's how

If you have never done any work with intrapersonal NLP tools before, or even if you have, you may want to just spend a few moments noticing your current internal state. Close your eyes and notice how happy you feel at the moment? Imagine a dial that you could turn up to increase that feeling of happiness, even if it is quite low at the moment. Now in your mind turn the dial up so that you begin to experience how you can choose to manage your own feelings. You may want to imagine a specific feeling of happiness in the past and turn up those feelings a little at a time. Now . . .

1. Think of a situation, an issue or someone that you currently have difficulty comprehending and which you would benefit from understanding more.

2. On a scale from 1 to 10 where are you at the moment with this?

3. Now reflect on what you will get from having a better understanding. What do you want instead? Imagine the details of this: What will you see, hear (externally, what others say; and internally, your own words to yourself) what will you feel (physically and emotionally)?

4. Now imagine a mixing desk in front of you. The sort they have in recording studios. Notice three big sliders on the desk labelled: inclusion, control and affection.

5. Adjust each of the sliders to their current level in relation to how you behave at the moment: How much do you include others at the moment? How much do you express control over the situation to others? How much affection do you express?

6. As you think about this remember that *the meaning of your communication is the response you get*. This also affects the 'loop of communication' that we have with others – because people often assume that we want back from them what we put out ourselves.

Personal development and effectiveness for teachers

7. Now take each slider in turn and think about what you actually want from each of these areas, compared to what you are expressing to others. Are you expressing as much inclusion to others as you currently want back from them, or are you receiving more inclusion than you currently want because others are responding to your behaviours, etc.?

8. Work through each of the sliders adjusting them to what you actually want from others. Now project yourself to a specific context in the future and imagine yourself with this new set of behaviours. What will you see, hear and feel? What will you get from this new flexibility?

Top tip

Some people learn to visualise really quickly, others take some time and others need to work at it. There's no right place to be but you may find it helpful to draw the mixing desk on a piece of paper and mark out the points on the slider. If you find yourself feeling uncomfortable at certain levels on one of your sliders just adjust it a little and then readjust the levels of the other areas of your life.

Learn more about this

Will Schutz, the famous American psychologist, did a lot of work in the 1960s exploring people's internal needs and wants. His research showed that what people want (and demonstrate to others in their behaviours) is not necessarily what they need back from others. Because people can only see and hear your behaviours and language they therefore respond to this, rather than to what you actually want in your own mind. Schutz's work was later used with nuclear submarine teams and resulted in the creation of a personality questionnaire and development tool called FIRO-B, which is great for team, leadership and personal development.

Read some more about working with internal representations

- Invest in a copy of *The Truth Option* by Will Schutz which is full of great tools for self-development
- Get deep into submodalities by reading the *Insider's Guide to Sub-Modalities* by Richard Bandler and Will MacDonald
- Find out about getting FIRO-B feedback yourself or from your team

When else can you use this?

There are many times when you need to be flexible in a school. This is true in the classroom and the staffroom as well as when working with groups of stakeholders, such as parents.

- Adapt the tool so that you have different areas of life represented by each slider. This works well with metaprograms (see the Index to find chapters which use these).

- Teach children to use the tool to think and work through relationship problems and issues such as bullying.

Personal development and effectiveness for teachers

- Use the slider idea in discussions about problems and solutions around school improvement when facilitating active sessions in team meetings. Each slider can be used to represent a different area of school improvement. Where are we now? Where do we want to be? How are we going to get there?

- Plan your career goals using a mixing desk of sliders with a slider for each of your goals. Check in regularly to visualise the extent to which what you are doing at the moment is contributing to a specific goal or what you want overall.

- Use when coaching a colleague to help them to explore work–life balance issues. Draw the mixing desk and ask them to label each slider with an aspect of their life (work, home, leisure – whatever they want). Again, where are they now and where do they want to be? What are they going to do about it?

What are you going to do with this?
(Your ideas and thoughts)

Personal development and effectiveness			
Self-awareness	Self-management and resilience	Relationship awareness and influencing skills	Influencing and relationship management
* * *	*	*	* * *

49 Pace, pace, lead

How to develop your influencing skills

Have you ever tried to influence someone else and not succeeded? Or perhaps you got instant push back about a really good idea that you were convinced the other person would want to take up? At the end of the day we are constantly seeking to influence others as part of our job as teachers: children, parents, colleagues, etc. People, however, have very different maps and the way in which we explain things to them can be critical to whether people go along with it or not. There are three key ways to pace and lead:

- Notice whether you are in rapport with the other person. If not match or mirror some body language or the types of words that the person likes to use (e.g. visual, auditory or kinaesthetic).

- Notice the person's metaprogram preferences (the way they see the world and the language they use that illustrates this) and explain the situation or idea from that perspective (e.g. if they are 'away from' motivated, explain the problems that will be avoided by doing it). See the Index for tools that include more about metaprograms.

- Use language that relates to the person's current experience and use this to link to the ideas that you are presenting or the ways of thinking that you want them to adopt. It is this area that we will look at in more detail in this tool.

Here's how

Bandler and Grinder spent much of their time modelling the work of leading therapists, in particular, Milton Erickson (the world famous and academically respected hypnotherapist). Out of this work emerged the Milton Model of communication. A key part of the processes that they observed was the initial phase, sometimes known as 'pacing a person's current experience'.

Pacing and leading with language

It works like this.

- Before you make a suggestion or propose an action you mention something that is currently true or part of the person's current experience.

- Having done this you connect the idea, suggestion or action that you want them to adopt to this thing.

For example:

> *As you read this sentence* (pacing current experience) *you could begin to think about the last time that you had to give an instruction in the classroom . . .* (leading)

There is something about pacing experience linguistically that creates an internal 'yes' (as it were) in the heads of the people who are listening. In hypnosis, hypnotists might say something like this:

> *As you sit there, listening to my voice, being aware of the sounds in the room* (pacing) *you could begin to feel more relaxed* (leading), *and as you feel more relaxed right now* (pacing), *you can start to notice all the things that . . .* (leading).

Notice in the example above how, once a suggestion has been accepted as fact (and therefore part of current experience), it can then in turn be paced.

In the classroom you might say:

> *As you look at the maps and resources that you have in front of you* (pacing), *you could begin to think about all the ways in which these sorts of resources are going to be useful to you* (leading). *Thinking about that* (pacing) *you can now make a list of these* (leading).

or

> *Now that you have got the first step right* (pacing) *you will begin to find the next part of the learning easy* (leading).

Connecting words

You have probably begun to notice some of the words that are helping this process along (e.g. we have used the word *as* at the start of the sentence examples above). There are lots of 'transition' words that can be really helpful in making these types of connections, for example, *and*, *as* and *while*.

Even stronger suggestions can be made by using words that have a time implication, for example, *before, during, since* and *when*.

The three steps to effective linguistic pacing and leading are:

1. Know what it is that you want to say.

2. Phrase it in the positive.

3. Notice something that is going on that is currently part of the experience of the person you want to influence.

4. Use a pattern which first paces current experience and then make the suggestion.

Top tip

When it comes to pacing and leading generally, particularly in a leadership context or with other adults, it is always good to seek to pace and lead in the proportions 2:1 or 3:1 (e.g. pace, pace, lead or pace, pace, pace, lead). This is not always easy to do linguistically, but remember there are lots of ways to pace and lead. Just by listening to the other person for longer and by asking open questions before making any suggestions you will have done more pacing, built more rapport and increased your effectiveness as an influencer. Questions are great (as long as they are not leading questions) because they allow someone else to talk about their current experience (a form of pacing in itself).

Learn more about this

Very occasionally, and increasingly rarely these days, we hear an objection to teaching influencing skills to teachers 'because it is manipulative'. As with all tools it is your intention that is important. We doubt that there are many teachers who joined teaching with the intention of harming children. We believe that the potential benefits of better language and influencing outweigh any negatives and offer teachers even more tools to help ensure that all children achieve their fullest possible potential.

Read some more about pacing

- Read Chapter 5, 'Don't think about chocolate cake', in *NLP for Teachers: How To Be a Highly Effective Teacher* (page 49) on hypnotic language
- If you want to read much more, get a copy of *Trance-formations: Neuro-Linguistic Programming and the Structure of Hypnosis* by John Grinder and Richard Bandler

When else can you use this?

We all go into teaching to make a difference and this frequently involves persuasion and effective influencing.

- Use to encourage positive attitudes in the classroom.

- Be more effective in giving behavioural instructions.

- Be more persuasive when you need to influence parents.

What are you going to do with this?
(Your ideas and thoughts)

Personal development and effectiveness for teachers

Personal development and effectiveness			
Self-awareness	Self-management and resilience	Relationship awareness and influencing skills	Influencing and relationship management
* * *	* * *	*	*

50 Present state, desired state planner

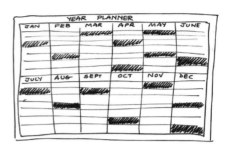

How to access the secret heart of personal development

Have you ever noticed your current emotions and feelings getting in the way of what you want the most? At the heart of NLP is the core notion of adding personal resources to achieve what we desire and set ourselves as a goal. Remarkably, this sort of process not only helps with motivation but when used effectively can also help you to understand and recognise what it is that you really need to do to be effective. The tool below works well as a self-coaching tool but you can also use it with other people or find someone to facilitate you through the process.

Here's how

1. Look at the planner on the next page. The planner is organised in three vertical columns: present state, resources and desired state. There are also horizontal 'levels' of thinking to explore for each of these areas:

   - The environment around you
   - Your behaviours
   - Your skills
   - Your beliefs (what you think is true in this situation)
   - Your values (what's important to you)
   - Your identity (who you are)
   - Your purpose.

2. Begin by exploring Step 1 and think about the current problem or issue and what is happening at each of the levels of thinking.

3. Now ask yourself the question in Step 2 at the right hand side of the planner. Record what it is like in the future at each level of thinking.

4. Now (Step 3) continue to imagine yourself in the future, having achieved your desired outcome, and explore how you did it and what resources you added in order to get there at each of the levels of thinking.

Top tip

When you have completed the planner run a visualisation of yourself in the future achieving the goal that you want and a second visualisation of you taking the first step on the journey (adding those first essential resources). As with many journeys in life, the first step is often the hardest.

Present state, desired state planner

	Present state	Resources	Desired state
Adding resources / Levels of thinking	**Step 1** Ask yourself, what is the current situation or problem? Think about it from each of the following perspectives and write down your thoughts.	**Step 3** Continue to imagine yourself in the future having achieved your desired state. What resources helped you to get there?	**Step 2** If you woke up tomorrow and everything was solved, what would it be like? What do you see? What do you hear? What do you feel?
What is this like at each of the levels below?			
The environment around you			
Your behaviours			
Your skills			
Your beliefs (what you think is true in this situation)			
Your values (what is important to you)			
Your identity (who you are)			
Your purpose			

Learn more about this

Our consciousness and working memory is quite restricted and may only be limited to seven plus or minus two pieces of information at any one time. Therefore we can sometimes find ourselves so focused on the problem that we are unable to see the solutions and answers that, in many cases, are simply staring us in the face. Visualising what you really want as an outcome can often release you from the tyranny of 'problem-focused' thinking and help us to identify what we really want, how we can get there and what resources (internal and external) we will need in order to get there.

Read some more about values and NLP

- Read Chapter 15, 'Instant training day' in *NLP for Teachers: How To Be a Highly Effective Teacher* (page 177) to learn how to include a present state, desired state activity in a staff training day

When else can you use this?

The tool is brilliant for use in any situation where there are problems and thinking needs to be moved on.

- Use with a colleague to support in peer coaching.
- Use as a manager when line managing colleagues and doing performance reviews.
- Use for coaching children, particularly in relation to career development and examination preparation.

What are you going to do with this?
(Your ideas and thoughts)

Personal development and effectiveness			
Self-awareness	Self-management and resilience	Relationship awareness and influencing skills	Influencing and relationship management
* * *	* * *	*	*

51 That's not what I meant at all

How to explore what you do, why you do it and how you can change

Is there something that you do that you don't like or don't want to do any more? Something that doesn't serve you well, yet you still do it? In the classroom, staffroom, as a leader or in your personal life? In NLP we say that all behaviour has a purpose. Our minds, brains and behaviour are all moving towards something, some goal or object, but we may not be consciously aware of what that is. Stop for a moment and think about the last time you saw something that you did not like (either in your own behaviour or that of others). Now ask yourself, what was the intention behind that behaviour?

Here's how

Asking about and thinking about intention can be wonderfully liberating and can help you to be more aligned with your own needs and sense of purpose in life. It can also be the door to changing some of those previously hard to shift behaviours. Learn to honour the positive intention, not the behaviour.

1. Look at the activity sheet on the next page. You will notice a series of questions and spaces to write your answers.

2. The activity sheet is organised from the bottom up – to reflect the idea that we are going to be 'chunking up' to find the real intention behind the behaviour.

3. In order to really change effectively and for our unconscious mind and automatic part of our behaviours to accept any new behaviour, we are going to need to ensure that (a) we replace the old behaviour with something new and (b) whatever that new behaviour is, it fulfils the core intention that the old behaviour was fulfilling.

4. When you have completed the activity sheet, close your eyes and visualise yourself doing the activity as if you were an observer. Tell yourself what the benefits will be when you are doing this. Now see it through your own eyes in rich detail as you will be doing it in the future (What do you see? What are you hearing? What do you feel?).

Intentions and behaviour change activity sheet

(Start at the bottom and work up)

Continue until you have identified your core intention. Write it here. **My core intention is:**	Identify an alternative behaviour that you will do instead that also fulfils this intention.	**Write your new behaviour here.**
Write your **answers** to the C questions here and then ask the D questions about what you have written.	**D. Questions** What is important about doing . . .? What does this do for you? What do you get out of it?	↑
Write your **answers** to the B questions here and then ask the C questions about what you have written.	**C. Questions** What is important about doing . . .? What does this do for you? What do you get out of it?	↑
Write your **answers** to the A questions here and then ask the B questions about what you have written.	**B. Questions** What is important about doing . . .? What does this do for you? What do you get out of it?	↑
	A. Questions What is your positive intention in doing what you do? What does this do for you? What do you get out of it?	**Write the behaviour you want to change here.**

Top tip

Some behaviours shift the first time, some take a couple of goes and some may need to be worked on. It is well recognised in studies about addiction, for example, that the journey towards freedom from an old behaviour is sometimes one in which we will slip back briefly to the old behaviour before moving on to a further step in the progression. If you find yourself slipping back, simply see it as a stage on the journey and revisit your intentions (which may themselves have changed slightly and require further explanation).

Learn more about this

Creating awareness of our behaviours is a key way of changing and modifying them. Without such awareness we can find ourselves back on autopilot – which is fine for the behaviours we want but not so good for the ones we don't.

Read some more about achieving outcomes with NLP

- Read Chapter 2, 'Blockbuster movies', in *NLP for Teachers: How To Be a Highly Effective Teacher* (page 9)

When else can you use this?

How many times have you heard someone talk about the idea of moving from unconscious incompetence to conscious competence without telling you how to make a start? This tool is a great way of starting the process with yourself and others.

- Apply the same ideas to help you to analyse and reflect on the intentions and behaviours of the children you teach.

- Use the activity sheet in a one-to-one context when mentoring a child with behavioural difficulties.

- Use in a coaching context when supporting a colleague or apply it as a group process for school improvement planning to challenge why the school does things the way it does.

What are you going to do with this?
(Your ideas and thoughts)

Personal development and effectiveness for teachers

Personal development and effectiveness			
Self-awareness	Self-management and resilience	Relationship awareness and influencing skills	Influencing and relationship management
* * *	* * *	* *	* *

52 The chuffed-o-meter

How to have some self-coaching fun with a serious point

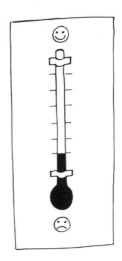

How often in life do we take time to check in on our emotions and feelings about something? Or just ask ourselves the question 'How do I feel about this?' The chuffed-o-meter is a fun way to give yourself some time for self-reflection and to check in on your life from the perspective of different levels of experience. It is also a great tool to use when coaching others or working with children one-to-one in a counselling-type context.

Here's how

NLP draws on what is called the TEA model that suggests that all of our subjective experience can be viewed through three basic positions: thoughts, emotions and actions. Change one and you affect the others; however, we can often find ourselves neglecting one of these areas and particularly how we feel.

The chuffed-o-meter on the next page combines noticing your internal emotional feelings with Robert Dilts's levels of thinking tool. This suggests that our subjective experience can be defined by a series of levels of thinking, some of which are more deeply influential than others (e.g. purpose and identity). Dilts proposed that when things are going less well for us, or when we are feeling uncomfortable about a situation, we are likely to find that one of these levels is out of alignment with the others – because we have not paid enough attention to it or are addressing it in a way that is not ecological from the perspective of the whole system of levels.

1. Read through the levels on the left hand side of the chuffed-o-meter so you get the big picture first.

2. Now associate yourself into the specific context that you want to reflect on. Imagine yourself in that situation doing what you always do. What do you see? What do you hear (the sounds around you and your self-talk)? What do you feel (physically and emotionally)?

3. Once you have a strong sense of being connected with this context, as if you are really there doing it, begin to mark on the chuffed-o-meter how chuffed you feel about each level. Complete the questions, reflections and action planning thoughts.

Level of thinking	How chuffed are you about this aspect of life in relation to the context you are thinking about?	What is missing for you at this level?	What do you need to do?
Environment (the physical context around me)	Not chuffed at all — Well chuffed		
Behaviours (my current behaviours as seen by others)	Not chuffed at all — Well chuffed		
Capabilities (the skills and knowledge I have that support my behaviours)	Not chuffed at all — Well chuffed		
Values and beliefs (what is important to me and what I think about the world)	Not chuffed at all — Well chuffed		
Identity (who I am at heart)	Not chuffed at all — Well chuffed		
Purpose (what my life purpose is)	Not chuffed at all — Well chuffed		
Spirituality (my sense of place in the universe)	Not chuffed at all — Well chuffed		

Personal development and effectiveness for teachers

175

Learn more about this

Where we used to think about logic and reasoning as separate from emotions and feeling, recent neuroscience has led to a different way of understanding the role of emotions. In particular, Antonio Damasio has pointed out that all consciousness involves feelings and it would be more accurate to say that human consciousness is the consciousness of feeling. Therefore, you cannot separate feelings, emotions and the body from the processes of thinking.

Read some more about self-reflection

- Read Chapter 11, 'The teacher within', in *NLP for Teachers: How To Be a Highly Effective Teacher* (page 131) to find out about other ways to use Dilts's levels of thinking
- Read *The Feeling of What Happens: Body, Emotion and the Making of Consciousness* by Antonio Damasio

When else can you use this?

Taking time to reflect on all levels of thinking in a school is a valuable way of beginning any change activity. You can also:

- Use with children to help them to explore their feeling in a particular context and to help them to develop emotional awareness.

- Use when you are reviewing areas of your work as well as your personal life and career planning.

- The Dilts levels are also useful for exploring areas of professional development to improve teacher effectiveness and some teachers have found it helpful when planning new lessons – as sometimes we tend to focus only on the levels of knowledge that we are transferring to children and less on the values and beliefs that we intend to put across, the capabilities that we want the children to develop, their identity as learners when they are doing it and the core purpose of the learning.

- Use it when you have just had a difficult lesson to help you reflect on what levels you need to pay more attention to, or may have been ignoring, in relation to your own self-management and what you did.

What are you going to do with this?
(Your ideas and thoughts)

Personal development and effectiveness			
Self-awareness	Self-management and resilience	Relationship awareness and influencing skills	Influencing and relationship management
* * *	*	* *	* * *

53 The own child test

How to speak to a parent about a child's behaviour with greater effectiveness

Have you ever been unsure about whether or not to phone a parent to talk about their child's behaviour? Or are just not sure what to say when you do? In NLP we talk about using perceptual positions to gain insights when working with others. This tool is a variation on this process and uses a 'second position' to help. We go into second position when we imagine the world from someone else's point of view.

Here's how

1. Read the Here's how section in Chapter 21 ('Ori-goal-me').

2. Take a few moments to ask yourself some key questions:

   - *If this was my child what would I want to know?*
   - *How would I expect to be involved?*
   - *What information would I expect to be given?*
   - *How would I want to be spoken to?*

3. Set up two chairs and imagine yourself speaking to the parent who is sitting in the other chair. Rehearse what you are going to say. Remember to be specific about what behaviours you don't want and specifically what you do want to see instead. If this was your child, what would you want and expect from the teacher?

4. Now sit in the other chair and imagine yourself as the parent you have just spoken to. Sit as they sit and imagine the world through their eyes.

5. Now give yourself some feedback about what you said and how you said it. What would you do to improve?

Top tip

If you have had to phone a parent to talk about poor behaviour, always phone back when the behaviour has improved to tell the parent that this has now happened. Doing this is a powerful way to reinforce the behaviours that you want to see. Be specific about what is now happening. It is good to let the parent know that you will be phoning back when you make the first call.

Learn more about this

Without preparation, phoning parents to talk about a child's behaviour can be stressful. It can be particularly worrying if you are new to teaching or if you have not had to do it before. Taking some time to rehearse what you are going to say and to reflect on how that will be received will enhance the outcome for you, the parent and the child.

Read some more about perceptual positions

- Read Chapter 7, 'Knowing me, knowing you . . . aha!', in *NLP for Teachers: How To Be a Highly Effective Teacher* (page 73)

When else can you use this?

You can do the own child test in any context where you need to understand different points of view.

- Use the two chair test whenever you have something to deal with and are unsure about how to handle it.

- Add in the third perceptual position in order to gain more information and feedback (see the situation as if you were a detached observer, and ask 'What would that person say?').

- Run the process as a role-play with a colleague or integrate into a training day for other members of staff.

What are you going to do with this?
(Your ideas and thoughts)

Personal development and effectiveness			
Self-awareness	Self-management and resilience	Relationship awareness and influencing skills	Influencing and relationship management
* * *	* * *	*	* * *

54 The self-think 360

How to align what you do with who you are and what is important to you

Have you ever felt that something is not quite right with your work as a teacher, but you can't quite put your finger on it? Or maybe you sometimes feel as if things could be improved but don't quite know where to begin your thinking to do this? It's easy to say that teachers need to be reflective practitioners – how to do it simply and easily is not such a straightforward matter. In the levels of thinking tool below you can explore areas of your classroom practice using a model developed by Robert Dilts.

Here's how

You can do this in your head, by drawing it on a piece of paper or do it by standing in your own classroom (in the centre of the room to begin with). In this example we are going to run the tool as if you were doing it in your classroom (this involves a bit of desk moving, however, many people find that this helps them to connect with their real-life situation and circumstances). Alternatively, you can simply photocopy the activity sheet and make notes on it as you ask yourself the questions on the sheet.

1. Make a space in the centre of your classroom or teaching space.

2. Look at the resource sheet below. Write each of the words on a piece of paper and arrange them on the floor going out from the centre. Imagine a set of concentric circles with the word *Purpose* at its core.

3. Stand on the piece of paper with the word *Purpose* on it and reflect on the purpose questions in the activity sheet.

4. Move through each of the different levels exploring each of the questions and reflecting on them.

5. Notice if there are any levels of thinking that feel out of alignment with your purpose. How does this feel? What do you need to change in order to feel more aligned and comfortable? What other resources do you need?

6. When you have worked through all the levels of alignment and ended up at the *Environment* level, step off the circle and sit in one of the seats that your learners sit in. Imagine a lesson you taught recently that you were unhappy with. Play it in the cinema of your mind from the learner's perspective. Ask yourself:

- *What would the children I teach say about the environment and the experience that they have?*

- *Would my learners recognise my purpose, identity and values from the environment I create, the behaviours I use and the skills and capabilities that I demonstrate?*

7. Finally, look back at the circle and decide if you need to return to any of the spaces in order to reflect further.

Learn more about this

Teaching is a busy and at times frantic occupation and we do not always spend enough time reflecting on our practice and why we do what we do. Sometimes we can get so caught up with the delivery of subject content and the processes and concepts (that we need to teach to our learners) that we forget to check in with ourselves to be sure that the way in which we are teaching and behaving is aligned with who we are and what we believe in. Feeling comfortable in your own skin as a teacher, and the ways in which you work, can help to develop resilience and help you to deal with the more difficult day-to-day challenges, because knowing why you do things can reinforce their importance and keep you on track.

Read some more about levels of thinking

- Spend some time reflecting on ideas such as your moral purpose (see *The Moral Imperative of School Leadership* by Michael Fullan)
- If you need some input on skills and capabilities, read more about teacher effectiveness in *Teacher Effectiveness* by Daniel Muijs and David Reynolds

Self-think 360 activity sheet

Questions to ask yourself:

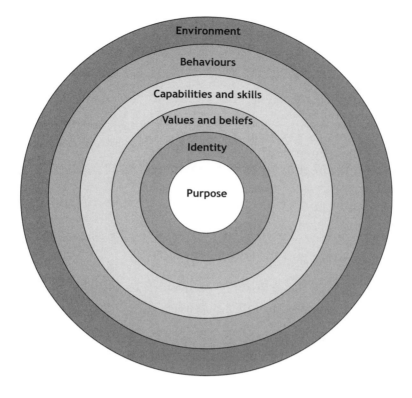

Purpose

What is your purpose? Why are you here? What is your life purpose?

Identity

Who are you? If you were to complete the statement: *I am* . . . in relation to yourself as a teacher, what would you say? If this were an invisible badge that you wear what would it say?

Values and beliefs

What is important to you about the way you teach? What are your values? What are your beliefs about teaching, learning and children?

Capabilities and skills

What capabilities and skills do you need to have/develop in order to achieve alignment with your purpose, identity and values and beliefs? Are there any development gaps you need to address?

Behaviours

Thinking about values and beliefs, identity and purpose, what behaviours should your learners see you doing consistently? Are there any behaviours that do not help you or which do not serve your purpose?

Environment

What do your learners experience when in your classroom? Looking at the classroom environment you create, does it reflect your purpose and is it aligned with this and other levels? What do you need to change in order to gain better alignment?

When else can you use this?

Taking time out to reflect on your practice is essential in any profession to improve performance and effectiveness. You can also:

- Share your values with the children that you teach so they are clearer about why you do what you do and what the reasons are.

- Use the activity sheet in a coaching context with newly qualified or trainee teachers to help them begin their teaching career as reflective practitioners.

- Use with children, as part of learning to learn activities, to help them reflect on themselves as learners.

- Get a colleague to coach you through the process.

- Use the tool to reflect on other areas of your work as a leader, manager or in relation to an area of school improvement that you lead.

- Use for whole school planning and development work to assess whether all the levels in your school are focused on the core purpose and whether this purpose relates to every child.

What are you going to do with this?
(Your ideas and thoughts)

Personal development and effectiveness			
Self-awareness	Self-management and resilience	Relationship awareness and influencing skills	Influencing and relationship management
*		* *	* * *

55 Yes you can

How to advance your emotional awareness and self-management

To use the tools in this section you first need to have learned about spatial anchoring and simple kinaesthetic anchoring. To get the information and basic skills you need to read Chapter 35 ('On the spot') and Chapter 58 ('Are you relaxed and focused?'). Make sure that you are happy with both these techniques before you apply them in the ways below. You may also want to read Chapter 9 ('Anchors away!') in *NLP for Teachers: How To Be a Highly Effective Teacher*, which will give you even more information and practice activities.

Here's how

Not only can we use anchoring to create single positive emotional states (or states with a combination of emotions) we can also use anchoring to help us move from one state to another by connecting emotional states. This can be a very powerful tool in coaching and personal development. We called this process 'chained anchoring'.

Chained anchors

We learned how to create simple anchors in earlier chapters of the book, and how to make use of these to change our state in situations of challenge or just to make us feel more motivated. There are times when our negative states are just too far away neurologically and emotionally from the desired state we want. In these situations using a chained anchor is a more efficient way of re-routing to a desired state. We can think of this as creating stepping stones from negative to positive states.

| Fear | Indifference | OK | Go for it! |

This can be done spatially using the spotlighting method in Chapter 35 ('On the spot'). Simply create a set of states in a series of spaces on the floor (using the technique in Chapter 35) that you associate with the emotional states in the chain. You will need to take some time first in designing the chain and thinking about the states you will need. Once you have created each state in a specific place and elicited these states in yourself (or the person you are working with), you can walk through the states leading from negative to positive, gradually moving yourself from the current state to the desired state – accessing fully each state as you move from one to another.

Examples of chained anchors

In the examples below, as above, you would create four anchored spaces on the floor and then, starting from the beginning, walk your issue, problem or situation through each of the stages until you are able to feel the positive state of mind you wanted associated with the area you were seeking to change.

Negative state	More neutral states		Positive state
Insecure	Comfortable	Secure	Confident
Hesitation	Checking	Stop	Go for it
Upset	Detached	Inspired	Excited
Confusion	Doubt	Revelation	Understanding

Chaining anchors kinaesthetically

Chained anchors can also be set using a simple kinaesthetic method. Again this tool won't make any sense unless you know how to do simple kinaesthetic anchoring so read and practise the skills in Chapter 58 ('Are you relaxed and focused?') before you use this tool. A good way to do this is to use the knuckles on one hand. We have illustrated this as if you were doing the technique for someone else. However, it works just as effectively when done on yourself. This is an advanced technique so practise and rehearse the process on yourself a few times before you support someone else. You may find the photos helpful, as well as the description.

1. Get in rapport.

2. Set the frame – *In a moment we are going to do anchoring, is it OK with you to do it?* Give an illustration by getting the person to access a positive past experience and choose a word for this. This may be helpful later as you can use this to help the person if they feel at all negative. When we do this we call this a 'bail out anchor'.

3. Identify the undesirable present state (or emotions) by asking questions.

4. Ask the person to decide on a positive desirable and resourceful end state that they would like to have.

5. Help the person to decide on what intermediate states could lead from the undesirable to the desirable state. The more these come from them the more likely this is to be successful.

6. Design the chain or set of stepping stones.

Present state	Intermediate	Intermediate	End state
State #1	State #2	State #3	State #4

7. Elicit and anchor each state separately, beginning with the present state through to the end state (using the simple kinaesthetic anchoring technique in Chapter 58) with one state on each consecutive knuckle. Make sure that the person you are working with is out of the previous state prior to anchoring the next one.

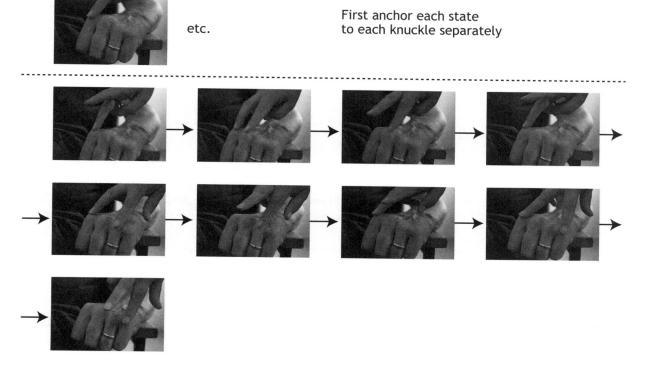

etc.

First anchor each state
to each knuckle separately

8. Fire the present state anchor #1 and when at its peak, release and fire the intermediate anchor #2. Test fire anchor #1 again and check that this is now the same as #2. Fire present state anchor #1, watch subject go into present state and check intermediate state #2. At peak, immediately add state #3. Test fire #1, check #2, check #3.

9. Add each intermediate anchor in the same way:

Fire #1, check #2, check #3, add #4.
Fire #1, check #2, check #3, check #4, add #5.

10. Fire present state, and the subject should go through all the states and end up at the desired state.

11. Break state by getting the person to think of something completely unrelated.

12. Test the final anchor and get the person to imagine a time in the future when they would be able to use it.

Top tip

If you find this tool interesting and exciting you may well be ready explore the therapeutic or more advanced personal development side of NLP and do an NLP practitioner and master practitioner qualification.

Learn more about this

How often have you been told, in recent years, about emotional intelligence but rarely had anyone explain to you how to do it? One of the fascinating things about NLP is that it seems to offer ways not only to understand what emotional literacy is, but also ways to develop and enhance it.

Read some more about anchors

- See Chapter 9, 'Anchors away!', in *NLP for Teachers: How To Be a Highly Effective Teacher* (page 105)

In this respect anchoring is probably one of the most useful tools to learn. The tools above are particularly helpful where really strong emotions are involved which cannot be resolved without some intermediate steps.

When else can you use this?

People really enjoy learning this stuff, so have a go at structuring a change workshop with a team using the approach. You could use the four corners of a room for the different states. Have a discussion first to agree the present state and desired state and then the intermediate steps. Get the whole team to stand in the spaces and discuss them one at a time. You can also:

- Use with children as part of one-to-one behaviour management strategies.

- Use on yourself – by writing the names of the states you need to access in turn on pieces of paper which you then place in a line on the floor.

What are you going to do with this?
(Your ideas and thoughts)

PENS

Personal development and effectiveness for teachers

Part 5

Leading with NLP

56 Aha! Developing a 'high reliability mindset'

How to explore your mindset and behaviours

One of the key moral imperatives, if not the most important one, for the public sector in the 21st century is the question of high reliability. How much we can learn from other organisations that have a mindset of high reliability is perhaps as much open to debate as is how we could do it – but we probably can't avoid the question.

Here's how

NLP is all about modelling (looking for examples of excellence and taking on those characteristics). In this tool we explore two interesting examples from therapy and school research. If you were retraining in some of the other helping professions (e.g. psychotherapy) you might well find yourself required to reflect on your developing practice in concepts like the Treatment Triangle.

1. Take a look at the diagram overleaf and reflect on the four dimensions: diagnosis (using evidence to assess what is the issue and what is needed), contract (making an agreement with the person who is to be helped), treatment plan (committing to what you will do) and safety (making sure that you leave things in a better state than when you started).

2. Now imagine yourself in the classroom actually teaching an individual child. Where are the parallels? What are the challenges of thinking this way about your current practice? Which areas of the triangle do you emphasise more or less than others (e.g. you might think about contracting in terms of personalisation, and safety both in terms of emotional climate and attainment/achievement)?

3. Use the question grid to help you record your thoughts and also to reflect on the implications for your organisation in relation to concepts of high reliability.

4. Now ask yourself: what is the one thing that I could do now that would make the biggest difference? Imagine yourself in the future doing that. See it through your own eyes (What do you see, hear and feel?). Step out of yourself and be an observer for a moment – What internal resources do you need to add (beliefs, values, identity, sense of purpose)? What external resources do you need (skills, behaviours, changes to the environment)?

5. Re-imagine yourself achieving these goals through your own eyes and take a look back. What did you do that got you to where you are now?

High reliability thinking tool

The Treatment Triangle

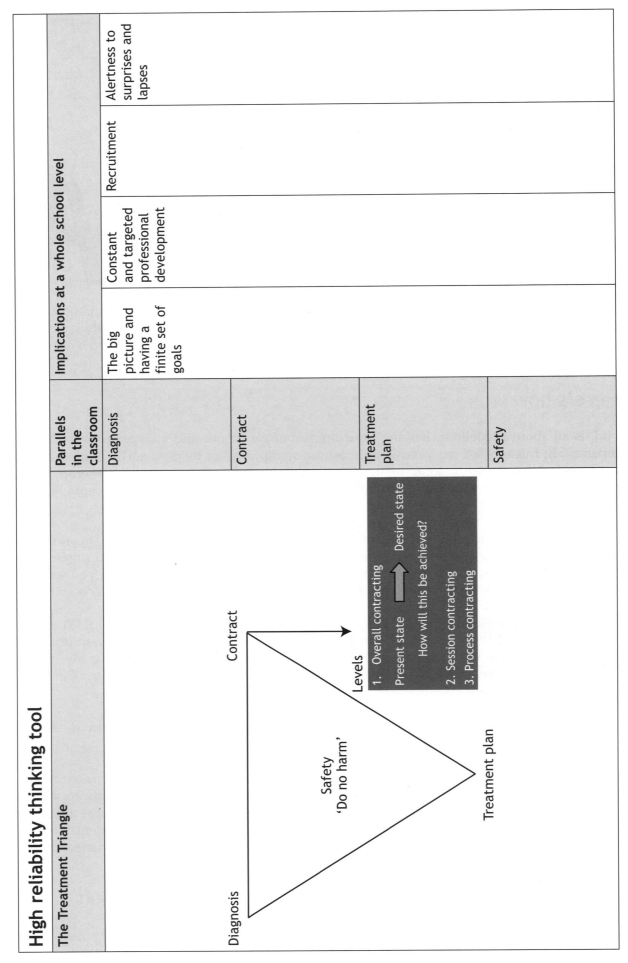

Parallels in the classroom	Implications at a whole school level			
	The big picture and having a finite set of goals	Constant and targeted professional development	Recruitment	Alertness to surprises and lapses
Diagnosis				
Contract				
Treatment plan				
Safety				

(Diagram: The Treatment Triangle with vertices labelled Contract, Diagnosis, Safety 'Do no harm', and Treatment plan. Dark box: Present state → Desired state; How will this be achieved? Levels: 1. Overall contracting; 2. Session contracting; 3. Process contracting.)

If you went through the whole process above you will have begun to experience a number of the core processes and elements of NLP:

- Modelling – identifying the 'difference that makes a difference' in relation to highly effective people or approaches.
- Identifying your present state and visualisation of your outcome or goal.
- The identification of resources (internal and external) and the development of motivations to become flexible to take on the characteristics of effectiveness and to put them in place.
- Finally, taking action – doing something about it in the real world, not just in your mind!

Learn more about this

Traditionally the notion of high reliability has been applied to organisations where safety is paramount (e.g. airlines). Applying ideas about high reliability to schools in Wales has been shown to increase attainment. Although the research did not apply a specifically clinical approach, nonetheless the mindsets of high reliability and the role of the professional were similar and based on similar premises. Specifically, research into high reliability and schools showed that high reliability was associated with: a heightened awareness of the big picture, a clear and finite set of goals, constant and targeted professional development, aggressive recruiting of new staff and alertness to surprises or lapses.

Read some more about high reliability mindsets

- Read about research into teacher effectiveness more often (e.g. *Effective Teaching: Evidence and Practice* by Daniel Muijs and David Reynolds)
- Read Chapter 15, 'Instant training day', in *NLP for Teachers: How To Be a Highly Effective Teacher* (page 177) to learn about applying the concept of present state to desired state in a training day
- Read the 2008 CfBT Education Trust research paper, 'Improving Secondary Students' Academic Achievement Through a Focus On Reform Reliability: Four- and Nine-Year Findings from the High Reliability Schools Project' by Sam Stringfield, David Reynolds and Eugene Schaffer

When else can you use this?

- Use as the basis for training day discussions and activities.

- Apply as a starting point for school improvement discussions and planning.

- Use to support your thinking in other areas of school life.

What are you going to do with this?
(Your ideas and thoughts)

Leading with NLP

Leading with NLP			
Self-awareness	Resilience	Relationship awareness and influencing skills	School improvement
* * *	*	* *	

57 Another point of view

How to be more effective in team meetings as a leader

Have you ever said something in a meeting and got immediate push back from the group or from one person and then thought 'Gosh, I knew that – if only I'd taken a moment to think'? Perceptual positions can be a very simple way of quickly working through the potential responses of others in your own mind in order to decide on what you are going to do or say.

Here's how

1. Take moment to learn and reflect on the different windows through which we can view the world in our minds. These are called perceptual positions. There are three basic ones:

   First position (self)

   Seeing the world from your own point of view, through your own eyes associated into your own thoughts, sense of self, values, feelings and with all the past experiences that have made you who you are. From this perspective you are most likely to react as an individual without thought for others but just in terms of meeting your own needs.

   Second position (other)

   Seeing the world from the point of view of somebody else, entering their map of the world, stepping into their shoes and seeing the world through their eyes. What does it look like from their point of view? What would they say? How would they receive a particular piece of communication?

   Third position (observer)

   The detached 'fly on the wall' perspective. Imagining yourself as a detached observer, someone who is new to the situation or not involved in it other than by virtue of watching the events transpire. What would that person say or think? What would they advise you to do or to say? What does the situation look like from out there observing?

2. To help get into **second position (other)** imagine that you are sat in the same seat as the person you are talking to. Adopt a similar body language and then imagine that you are a television camera placed where they are.

3. **Third position (observer)** is, as we noted earlier, sometimes referred to as the 'fly on the wall' perspective. Say to yourself, 'If I was that fly, what would I see from up there?'

4. Take a moment to note what perceptual position you are operating from before you start the meeting.

5. Remember to adopt all perceptual positions in turn so that you collect as much information as possible and as many possible points of view.

6. Seeing the world from somebody else's point of view doesn't necessarily mean agreeing with them. By adopting someone else's 'world view' you can often influence someone to agree with your ideas, simply by explaining things through their map of the world. It is often the way things are said or expressed which creates push back rather than the content of the ideas or suggestions themselves. The greatest leaders in the world have often influenced others to adopt actions or ideas by first showing empathy and rapport with the group that they were seeking to lead.

Top tip

Adapt your language to change the perceptual position of others

When you notice that someone else in the meeting is stuck or only operating from a single perceptual position, you can change their inner mindset by adapting your language. For example, if you have someone only operating from the 'self' or 'observer' perspective. You might say:

> *If we were to look at this through the eyes of [name of person] what would it look like from there?*

Or when a meeting lacks objectivity:

> *If we were an external person looking in, or listening to this conversation, what would they say?*

Learn more about this

In NLP we say 'the person with the most flexibility controls the system (or situation)'. Although what we are talking about here is our behaviour, as seen by others, having flexibility of behaviour all starts in your mind. Our map of the world and the way that we see things are unique to us; it takes effort and a different perception to be able to imagine the world from the point of view of someone else. However, the benefits can be enormous. We tend to have a preference for one or two perceptual positions. Learning to step out of your preference can be immensely rewarding and give valuable insights when seeking to influence or persuade someone else.

Read some more about perceptual positions

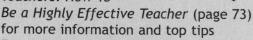

- Read Chapter 7, 'Knowing me, knowing you . . . aha!', in *NLP for Teachers: How To Be a Highly Effective Teacher* (page 73) for more information and top tips
- For an early NLP discussion on perceptual positions, see *Frogs into Princes* by Richard Bandler and John Grinder

When else can you use this?

You can use this tool any time that you find yourself coaching people that you manage. Get people to stand on spaces on the floor or just use the tool conversationally (e.g. *If you were an observer, what would you say to that?*). You may also like to have a go at the ideas below.

Leading with NLP

- Before you lead a meeting take a few minutes to imagine how the agenda will be perceived by all of the attendees in turn and then adopt the third position (observer) and give yourself some good advice.

- In a strategy-type meeting where you are discussing action plans which may affect others in the school (parents, children, teachers and other stakeholders) run your thinkstorming by having flipcharted discussions about the impact of any strategy or action from the self-perspective of the team deciding, the others who will be affected and from the perception of an external objective, critical friend.

- You could even have sections of a meeting agenda orientated to the three different positions. Some schools have found this helpful in preparing for Ofsted (or other forms of school inspection) and in developing their school self-evaluation process.

What are you going to do with this?
(Your ideas and thoughts)

58 Are you relaxed and focused?

How to be relaxed

Has there ever been a time when you have been stressed and wished you could find a way to quickly relax? Would it be useful to have a relaxed state on tap any time you needed it – to help you overcome stress and be more resourceful? The process of kinaesthetic anchoring is a very simple one and very effective for creating resourceful emotional states in oneself and others. The process puts you in control of your emotional state so that you can be more effective when you need to be. Anchoring harnesses the natural stimulus response mechanism that lies within all human beings. By applying a step-by-step process, and providing you follow the instructions, the result should be that you're able to generate a resourceful state with a simple touch. This is one of the most powerful techniques in NLP and is well worth learning. By using it regularly we can begin to condition our mind and body to support us in our day-to-day navigation of the world.

Here's how to create a kinaesthetic anchor

Having relaxed states on tap can assist us in many aspects of our working and home life. By reducing stress and initiating relaxed states we can be more flexible in our behaviours. The bonus is that the more we do this, the more our unconscious mind will automate the process so that in time those places that we used to find stressful will become places where we will be relaxed. Start by identifying a situation in which you would like to be relaxed.

1. Choose a unique place to anchor the emotional resource you are going to create – a touch on a specific part of the body that is repeatable (knuckles or thumb and an opposing finger are usually best).

   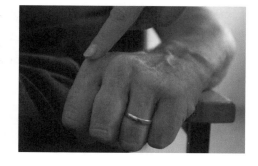

2. Recall an experience in which you were very relaxed – the greater the intensity the better. Then 'step back in time' into that experience. Go back to that scene and replay it – as if you were there again. As you mentally replay it make sure that you are associated (imagining the event as if it were real, seeing it through your own eyes, hearing what you heard and feeling what you felt). Notice the colours and make them brighter, listen to the sounds and make them louder or softer. Make your picture bigger. Does it have a frame or border to it? If it does, make it panoramic. And while you play with these aspects of your event, notice what happens to the way you feel – some of the changes will make the feelings stronger. When you have found out which changes give the best feeling run the event through (with the changes) and as the feelings start to grow . . . (move to Step 3).

3. Anchor the state by applying pressure to the place that you chose in Step 2. As you touch yourself think back to the experience again. Apply pressure for about 5–15 seconds until the state comes in and approaches its peak, and remove it just before the intensity reaches its peak. 'Break state' by thinking or doing something as a distraction, something that has nothing to do with the process (e.g. by thinking of breakfast or the colour of your front door).

4. Test the anchor by firing it – applying pressure to the precise spot. This should lead to a return of the resource state. If the anchor needs to be stronger, repeat the process with a more intense memory or add more memories – one on top of another. Imagine the situation that you identified as the one you want to be relaxed in. Fire the anchor and notice how the experience can be different in future. Wait a moment – relaxed states tend to emerge slowly. Just wait and enjoy.

Learn more about this

Creating an effective emotional climate is not only essential for learning in a school, it is also essential for school leadership – as leaders our emotional state affects others and in turn affects learning. Managing yourself is the key. In this context the benefits of anchoring are almost too many to list.

Read some more about anchoring

- Read Chapter 9, 'Anchors away!', in *NLP for Teachers: How To Be a Highly Effective Teacher* (page 105)

This technique is simple yet effective and gives us control over the chemicals that moment-by-moment flow through our body and our brain. Instead of being at the mercy of our moods and states we can begin to make conscious choices around just how we want to be and be at our best in any given situation.

When else can you use this?

- Choose different positive emotions and have a series of anchors that you use (e.g. confident, calm, focused, successful).

- Relax when you get home so that you are refreshed and get some 'me time'.

- Relax during a stressful day or before you have to deal with something difficult.

What are you going to do with this?
(Your ideas and thoughts)

PENS

Leading with NLP			
Self-awareness	Resilience	Relationship awareness and influencing skills	School improvement
* * *	*	* * *	*

59 Comfort zone

How to develop others through an awareness of individual programming

People are different, right? But have you ever stopped to think about the ways in which people are different from each other? Understanding some of the key ways in which people's preferences differ from each other and how these affect behaviours can be a powerful way of supporting your own personal development and a useful tool when developing others in a line management or coaching context. With practice you will also be able to notice the metaprograms of people who are really good at something and therefore begin to recognise where you need to flex yourself in order to be successful in that context too – a process known in NLP as 'modelling'.

Here's how

Metaprograms are like the software routines we run in response to a particular context or stimulus. Recognising these in ourselves and in others can give us greater flexibility in our behaviours and in the way that we react to and influence others so that we can step out of our comfort zone and really develop.

1. Carefully read the activity sheet below. Identify the specific context that you would like to develop in yourself. Now imagine yourself in that context. Close your eyes and imagine what you see, hear and feel through your own eyes.

2. In the central column circle the place on the continuum that best expresses your natural preferences. Preferences are our first inclinations. (To experience this – sign your name. Now try to sign your name with your other hand. What does that feel like? We all have preferences.) As you read the questions you will begin to notice similar feelings of comfort and discomfort when you read the questions. Now imagine yourself looking at someone else doing the activity that you were thinking about. This person is someone who is really excellent at the task or activity. What are the perfect metaprograms for this activity? What does this person see, hear and feel? Imagine it through their own eyes. Now complete the final column.

3. Compare your metaprogram answers with those of the other person or imagined person. Where do you differ? In which areas do you think that you need to be more flexible? What will you do about this?

Learn more about this

In Bandler and Grinder's early modelling work, they noticed that there were some very common patterns of attention and thinking which frequently occurred and which were common to everyone. These they called metaprograms. Over 40 metaprograms are now described in NLP literature and 11 of these have been validated through research and accreditation by the British Psychological Society as described in the CDAQ personality questionnaire. It is these 11 questions that appear in the activity sheet below. Interestingly, metaprograms (unlike traits and other forms of personality preference) appear to be more strongly contextual. In other word we may adopt different patterns when doing different things.

Read some more about metaprograms

- For a description of over 40 metaprograms, see *The User's Manual for the Brain*, volumes 1 and 2, by Michael Hall and Bob Bodenhamer

When else can you use this?

- Interview someone who you admire about a specific thing that they do that you see as outstanding. Get them to imagine themselves doing the activity and complete the worksheet. Look for those areas that differ to the way you work.

- Use the sheet when working with others in a coaching context. Get the person you are coaching to do the imagining. You can do this in relation to leadership development, classroom development, lesson observation or any other context in which interpersonal skills are critical.

- Notice the metaprograms of others when you are seeking to influence people and make your point from the perspective of their metaprograms. This is particularly effective when you are working with someone who is the opposite from you in relation to the 'towards' or 'away from' motivation metaprogram.

- Have a day when you work on flexing in relation to one metaprogram and notice the benefits. Or if you have been in conflict with someone take time to reflect on which metaprograms you have that are opposite to the person you find it difficult to work with. Often conflict is the result of our behavioural preferences rather than the content of the situation.

What are you going to do with this?
(Your ideas and thoughts)

Metaprograms – Self and others' development and modelling activity sheet

Metaprogram	Questions to ask yourself to identify metaprograms			How useful is this metaprogram in this context? Does it help or hinder? What would be the ideal metaprogram to have?
Internal-external	I know when I have achieved something because I feel it inside	1 2 3 4 5 6	I know when I have achieved something because others tell me	
People orientation-activity orientation	I notice the people things first	1 2 3 4 5 6	I notice task and activities first	
Possibility-reality	I tend to think of options and possibilities	1 2 3 4 5 6	I like to focus on grounded and existing things	
Towards-away from	I am motivated by future goals and solutions	1 2 3 4 5 6	I am motivated by avoiding mistakes and problems	
Options-procedures	I like choices	1 2 3 4 5 6	I like to follow agreed steps	
Same-difference	I notice the differences between things first	1 2 3 4 5 6	I notice similarities between things first	
Accept-evaluate	I tend to accept what others say	1 2 3 4 5 6	I pause and evaluate what people say before accepting it	
Active-reflective	I like to do first	1 2 3 4 5 6	I like to think first	
Global-detail	I think big picture	1 2 3 4 5 6	I think detail	
Perfecting-optimising	I like to get things right	1 2 3 4 5 6	As long as it works it's OK	
Closure-non-closure	I like things to have an end point	1 2 3 4 5 6	I can leave things open ended	

Leading with NLP

60 Feedback sandwich

How to give effective feedback easily in performance reviews and other contexts

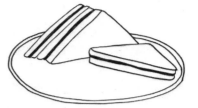

The subject of feedback can be very contentious and unless the feedback process is handled well it can cause many misunderstandings, upsets and become a de-motivator. On the positive side, feedback is often called the 'breakfast of champions' and, no matter where we look in the world, we see that high performance, whether in the field of sports, business or education, never happens without effective feedback. No one argues that to become a Lewis Hamilton or Paula Radcliffe, one of the most vital components is being able to receive and incorporate feedback. However, if you are responsible for performance reviews and for developing high performance in your team, then being skilled in the art of delivering feedback is a critical capability.

Here's how to give well-formed feedback

The RAF aerobatic team the Red Arrows have a very comprehensive and strictly adhered to process for delivering feedback. In order to execute the types of manoeuvres and aerial acrobatics that they perform, done at high speed and often flying only a few feet apart, being able to deliver and receive feedback is a life-saving activity. In their case, to depersonalise the feedback they do not use names but their flight position numbers in the squadron. They are all expected to provide feedback to other members of the team. The feedback is specific and designed to provide improvements – as their goal is to fly at all times in the perfect formation required for the manoeuvre. Using the sandwich formula well, with everyone understanding the purpose, can deliver huge shifts in performance.

1. The first part of the sandwich: the best feedback is based on accurate information and observations and the first task is to collect together all of the information that is to be used for the review. Go through this information and identify firstly all the areas where the person being appraised has performed well and therefore needs recognition.

   For each of these areas note down the specifics of what and how that person has achieved and the results. Make sure you have specific behavioural evidence, clear language and an appropriate attitude – with results-based observations that provide clear advice and which are founded on unambiguous evidence. This ensures that the person knows and will be able to repeat the high-performing behaviours.

2. In the second part of the sandwich, look for instances where the person being appraised could make performance improvements. For each area choose one thing only for improvement. Be specific about what and how that improved performance can be

achieved (just saying 'you could do better here' is not sufficient or useful feedback). Where behavioural, linguistic or a skills improvement is needed be prepared to demonstrate how they can go about changing what they are doing or saying, and if necessary how to acquire the skill.

3. The third part of the sandwich is to give an overall positive assessment of the trends and progression in a particular area, and the overall change or movement in this area – you would expect to see when the improvement is incorporated. Use the Quick start sheet at the end of the tool to guide your feedback process.

Top tips

- Have a direct and straightforward manner.
- Avoid the use of 'need to' as you will send a message that things didn't go well – this is neither clear nor sufficiently specific.
- Give the feedback with care and respect.
- Avoid 'yes buts' language.
- Give your feedback in person.
- Always state observations and not interpretations.

Learn more about this

The benefits of feedback when delivered in the right manner will bring performance improvement to individuals and teams. Adopting the right attitude and approach when delivering feedback can make the difference between someone being able to take on the feedback and improve their performance or feeling hurt, squashed and de-motivated.

Read some more about feedback

Effective relationships in management and leadership often depend on good body language, so read:
- Chapter 3 ('We like like' - page 23) and Chapter 6 ('Streetwise body language' - page 68), in *NLP for Teachers: How To Be a Highly Effective Teacher*

When else can you use this?

- Use with children when doing one-to-one reviews. Or use a short version to give feedback on homework (one specific positive, one improvement, overall praise).

- Useful at parents' evenings to deliver information about a child and maintain rapport.

- Use for reporting back on projects at team meetings.

Quick start – The feedback sandwich

Area:

Part 1: What the person did that demonstrated performance

What specifically showed high performance? (Behaviours, Language, Attitude, Skill)	
Where did it take place?	
When was it?	
What was the result?	

Part 2: One thing that could improve performance

What specifically could be improved?	
How can the performance improvement be gained? (Behaviours, Language, Attitude, Skill)	
Where specifically is this to be implemented?	
What demonstration is needed?	
How is the skill to be acquired?	

Part 3: Overall positive assessment of the trends and progression

Overall progression and trends	
What you would see, hear and feel when the improvement is incorporated?	

Final positive statement:

What are you going to do with this?
(Your ideas and thoughts)

Leading with NLP			
Self-awareness	Resilience	Relationship awareness and influencing skills	School improvement
* * *	* * *	* * *	*

61 In quick fix coaching mode

How to help a stressed out colleague get back on track

We all get stressed out at times. Finding solutions to problems when we are in a stressed state or making decisions is not easy. This resource is based on the NLP 'present state to desired state' model. Although deceptively simple, when used with rapport and care it can dramatically help to turn around a stressful situation.

By helping a person in stress to move out of that state we can bring about clearer thinking, generate a more positive state and create the ability to focus and find solutions that will bring about the change that is desired. In this model we are more concerned with the desired state than going over the problem. By moving our focus to what the person wants we can engage the brain's ability to solve problems – something that is always best accomplished from the standpoint of knowing where we want to go (even if we're not sure how to get there).

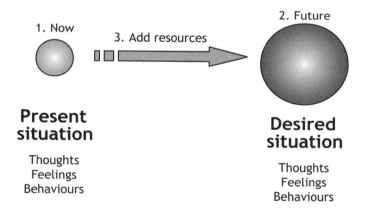

Here's how

This quick fix method takes ten minutes and is designed to rapidly move somebody out of a stressed state into a more resourceful place – where solutions can be found.

The best way to work with this model, when using it as a quick fix coaching method, is to stay strictly to the timings.

1. Find a quiet place where you can sit and talk for around ten to fifteen minutes.

2. Explain to your colleague how this is going to work and that the timings are important.

3. Ask your colleague to take just two minutes to describe the present situation. Ask questions about what is happening now, rather than allow your colleague to talk about the past and the events that led up to the present situation.

4. Once the two minutes are up, stop your colleague and move on to the desired state. In order to facilitate this you can ask the miracle question:

    Imagine you woke tomorrow and the situation is fixed in the best way possible:

    - How is it now that it is sorted?
    - What are you seeing, hearing, feeling?
    - What are you enjoying most?
    - What is important about this change?
    - What else becomes possible?

5. Spend eight minutes or so facilitating your colleague to answer these questions. Help them stay focused on the desired state and discourage any slipping back to the present state or searching for how to solve the problem. Do all this with open questions.

6. When you have observed a change in your colleague, and a shift to a positive state (with a reduction in stress), this is a good time to stop. Then arrange a longer coaching session where you can coach your colleague in more depth.

Learn more about this

This surprisingly simple tool can be highly effective in getting our brains out of habitual patterns of thinking – where we tend to run round and round the same problem without coming up with any answers. Having a clear idea of where we're going will often facilitate an approach and an attitude that gets us halfway there. The 'present state to desired state' is a core NLP model. Knowing what you want, not only in the big things but also in the small things, makes a big difference. So many of us, when we have a problem, can spend a lot of time talking about what we don't want to happen. A few minutes spent examining what we do want can bring a dramatic shift in state and also can create the conditions in which our mind delivers the solutions we want.

> **Learn more about outcomes**
>
> - Read Chapter 2, 'Blockbuster movies', in *NLP for Teachers: How To Be a Highly Effective Teacher* (page 9)
> - Or read how to use this during a training day in Chapter 15, 'Instant training day', in *NLP for Teachers: How To Be a Highly Effective Teacher* (page 177)

When else can you use this?

People get stuck all the time and so do children. This is a brilliant tool for use anytime that you need to release someone from their 'thinking traps' and delete their problem thinking.

- Quick planning of activities where your thinking feels a bit stuck.

- Sorting out what to say at parents' evenings.

- Run a meeting with this format to help people move away from current thinking.

- Plan an activity in the classroom by imagining what you want at the end.

What are you going to do with this?
(Your ideas and thoughts)

---

62 It's a syn!

How to overcome barriers in your own mind

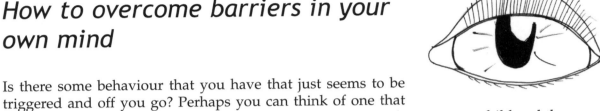

Is there some behaviour that you have that just seems to be triggered and off you go? Perhaps you can think of one that you would like to get rid of? It might be just seeing a particular parent or child and there you go getting those feelings again or perhaps behaving in the same way. Eye movements seem to be associated with feeling although no one is quite sure why. The tool below makes use of this phenomenon to reprogramme our mind in the same way that you can create a restore point on a computer. By wiping ourselves clean of old emotions in a situation we can prime ourselves to have more useful and resourceful behaviours.

Here's how

In NLP we often talk about how associated memories can bring back negative or positive feelings. Often these can be triggered by a single memory or image. This association of visual image (or auditory stimulus) with feelings is known in NLP as a synaesthesia. This is a slightly different use of the term than you will find in other fields of study but is derived from the same concepts and ideas about how we process sensory information. Like many NLP techniques you can do this for yourself or it can be applied when working one-to-one with someone else. Choose something that always triggers a reaction (e.g. if they always feel a little apprehensive if they see a particular child).

1. Ask the person you are working with to think of something that triggers a negative experience in them (this is best used for simple problems – phobias and more embedded negative experience requires more advanced approaches, such as the fast phobia cure (which is taught as part of NLP practitioner training).

2. Elicit the visual image that the person has associated with this experience. Collect lots of information so that they really have a clear image in mind.

3. Hold the palm of your hand out in front of their face and ask them to imagine that image in the centre of your palm. Tell them to follow your hand movement keeping the image in the centre of your hand.

4. Move your hand smoothly up to your right diagonally so that their eyes track as far as they can up to their top left. Hold this position for a few seconds and track back to the centre position.

5. Repeat this for side right, diagonal right down, diagonal left down, side left, diagonal left up, returning to the centre after each track. Hold rapport with the person as you are doing this.

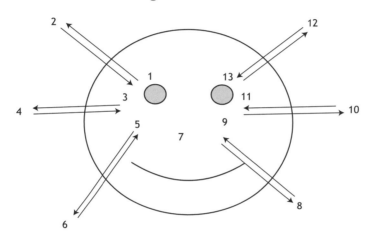

6. Once you have come back to the centre for the last time repeat the cycle again but this time return backwards, as in the diagram below.

7. Break state (for example, ask the person you are working with an unusual question) so that their mind is no longer occupied with the activity.

8. Check with them what differences they notice and how they feel about that old experience (use time-related language).

9. With practice you can also 'unwire' auditory associations. This is particularly useful where people have repeat negative self-talk that they keep revising. Just get them to imagine the sound in the palm of your hand (buzzing like the feeling of touching a piano when it is being played).

Top tip

This is a great tool to use with a colleague. Take it in turns to learn the strategy and run it with someone who you often work with or share practice with.

Learn more about this

Although controversial, eye movements are increasingly being incorporated into therapy, the most well known version of which is eye movement desensitisation and reprocessing (EMDR) which was developed by Francine Shapiro. Although some use EMDR for various problems, its research support is primarily in relation to disorders that stem from distressing life experiences. A number of NLP tools and techniques also make use of similar phenomena.

Read some more about internal representations

- Read Chapter 13, 'It's in your eyes . . . among other things', in *NLP for Teachers: How To Be a Highly Effective Teacher* (page 153)

When else can you use this?

This is a fast and effective tool to use before an important meeting or activity that you are going to run. It is particularly useful in situations where you do not currently feel comfortable. You can also:

- Run the pattern with children as part of a behaviour management programme for those children that are hard to reach. It is fun as well as being highly effective.

- Use the pattern as a starting point for noticing those hidden triggers and biases that you may have to certain contexts or people, and make some critical changes.

What are you going to do with this?
(Your ideas and thoughts)

Leading with NLP			
Self-awareness	Resilience	Relationship awareness and influencing skills	School improvement
*	* *	* * *	* *

63 Negotiating with NLP

How to work with others to create win-win agreements

It takes all sorts to make a world and we are all made up of different experiences, values and beliefs. It is not surprising therefore that sometimes we disagree. Understanding how to negotiate with others in order to agree a joint solution is a critical leadership skill and one that is easily acquired with some basic knowledge and a little practice.

Here's how

Planning to negotiate is a little like writing a play or a good story. There should be a beginning, a middle and an end. Not only should you plan in advance for the process but you should also ensure that you follow up and have a closure process.

Before you begin the meeting (planning ahead)

1. Decide what is it is that you actually want. Think about what is important to you. You would be amazed by the number of people who begin a negotiation process without a clear outcome in mind. If you don't know where you want to go, how will you possibly get there? Decide on what your ideal result would be and what your minimum 'bottom line' is.

2. Think about what will be your next step if you cannot get agreement – it's not always possible.

3. Decide what emotional state you will need to be in to negotiate effectively. Imagine what it will be like to have those feelings. Set this with an anchor (a particular way you will hold your hands or a word that you will say to yourself etc.). Do this before you start so that you can put yourself into that resourceful place again when you need to and right from the start.

4. Think about the details of what you will see, hear and feel when you have achieved the outcome that you want.

5. What body language will you need to use to be really effective?

6. What frame of thinking will you need to set with the person you are talking to?

During the meeting

7. Build rapport with the other person. Spend time listening to them. Notice the visual, auditory and kinaesthetic words they use so that you can explain your position using similar types of language. Notice their physiology and details of their voice tone. If you are practised in strategies for matching and mirroring use these. Alternatively, imagining a bridge of light connecting you with the other person until you feel a sense of warmth and trust develop and then think about where they are coming from.

8. Use perceptual positions during the course of the discussion. See the conversation through the other person's eyes, as well as your own, and when you need even more information imagine yourself as an observer watching the conversation. What advice would that person give you?

9. 'Chunk up' out of the details to find something that you both agree upon (e.g. the purpose of what you are both attempting to do or the bigger picture).

10. Once you have a common agreement on something general you can then 'chunk down' to agree more specific things.

At the end of the meeting

11. Make sure that you summarise and clarify what was agreed. Include in that process some discussion about what both of you will see, hear and feel in the future when these actions are in place and working.

12. Take some time afterwards to visualise the outcome in your own mind. Send a clarifying e-mail later that day and invite comments to check for agreement.

Learn more about this

In NLP studies of effective people their common characteristics emerged. In particular, excellent communicators and effective people apply a similar sort of strategy – what you might call an 'excellence formula'. It works like this:

> **Read some more about outcomes, rapport and framesetting**
>
> To find out more see the following chapters in *NLP for Teachers: How To Be a Highly Effective Teacher*:
>
> - Rapport – Chapter 3 (page 23)
> - Outcomes – Chapter 2 (page 9)
> - Framesetting – Chapter 5 (page 49)

- Excellent communicators know what it is that they want – they identify clear and achievable outcomes in their own minds. They know what the purpose and direction of their communication and action is and will be. They have clear internal pictures, sounds and feelings which come together to create an internal representation of the future action.

- Effective people know and look to see if they are getting what they want – they sharpen their senses so that they notice the responses of others in order to provide sensory feedback on how they are doing. Small things are important to notice as well as the big things.

- They have the flexibility to change and are flexible in their behaviour, language and internal feelings. They continually adapt in order to influence and involve others in their outcome.

- Excellent communicators take action – there is a real world out there. What goes on in your own mind, and in the cinema that plays in front of your mind, is just a map. You have to do something to make things happen – just thinking is not enough.

When else can you use this?

You can use the same underlying processes when leading teams and influencing in meetings and group discussions. You may also want to have a go at the following ideas:

- Apply the excellence formula to other areas of life: when you start a new job or role, in a job interview, when you have to begin leading a new team.

- Adapt the processes to support in preparing for Ofsted to help staff to think through what is really important in relation to last minute preparation.

- Use the mental preparation processes and in meeting processes when you know that you are going to have to negotiate with a difficult parent to agree a behaviour contract for a child.

- Apply the process in one-to-one counselling and behaviour management contexts with difficult children.

What are you going to do with this?
(Your ideas and thoughts)

PENS

---

64 Put it another way

How to change mindsets

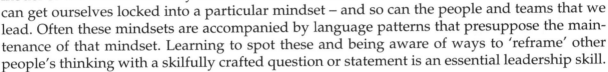

Language is one of the key ways in which we build a mental model of the world. The only trouble is that sometimes we can get ourselves locked into a particular mindset – and so can the people and teams that we lead. Often these mindsets are accompanied by language patterns that presuppose the maintenance of that mindset. Learning to spot these and being aware of ways to 'reframe' other people's thinking with a skilfully crafted question or statement is an essential leadership skill.

Here's how

Robert Dilts, one of the early developers of NLP modelling, conducted a study on how language can be used to impact on people's lives and emotions. Specifically, Dilts's research showed that influential leaders in business and from the past made use of a number of language patterns that act as 'verbal reframes' and so shift and reframe the beliefs and mental maps that people are operating from – Dilts called these 'sleight of mouth' patterns.

Current mindset

Ideas, thoughts, concepts etc. that are inside the current frame

All the other possible ways of thinking that are outside of the current frame

We are constantly talking from, or thinking within, frames and our conscious mind and working memory are quite limited in terms of what we are actually aware of processing at any one time. Therefore, there are always many things that are outside of the frame that we are operating from. The trick is to notice the frame that someone else is in (in their mind) and take them somewhere more productive in their thinking.

1. Notice the limiting belief that someone is currently operating from (the frame that they have set around their thinking and their mindset).

2. Ask yourself what type of mindset this is. There are two basic types:

    i. Cause and effect (where cause is assumed)

        e.g. The children's attainment is the result of their background.

ii. Complex equivalence (where meaning is inferred)

> *e.g. These children's background means a lack of attainment.*

3. Think about the type of mindset you would rather see in place and select a frame from which to make a statement or adopt a questioning approach from a particular frame.

4. There are 14 basic patterns. Look at the list below and read about the different approaches and examples.

5. Select an example of a limiting belief that you have heard recently and have a go at reframing it.

Quick start – The 14 sleight of mouth patterns

Intention reframe – Direct the person's attention to the purpose or intention behind their mindset.

> *What's your intention in believing that and how does it help you?*

Redefine reframe – Swap a word in the sentence that they have used that means something similar to what they have said but for which the mindset implications are different.

> *Learning is part of a child's background isn't it, so surely their attainment is also the result of their learning?*

Consequence reframe – Direct the person's attention to the effects and consequences of holding that belief.

> *If that is the case then what is the point of school?*

Chunk down – Direct the person's attention to the details that are assumed in a way that challenges the idea.

> *Thinking about children who have succeeded from less advantaged backgrounds, how did they do it?*

Chunk up – Generalise part of the mindset expressed so that they get the bigger picture.

> *Teachers and all those involved in education have background too – what are we going to do about that?*

Analogy reframe – Make an analogy to move thinking forward.

> *I guess ensuring attainment is a bit like a glass of water – you probably only get out what you put in?*

Change frame size – Alter the size of the frame that the person is operating from.

> *If everyone believed that, what would that be like?*

Another outcome reframe – Switch to a different goal.

> *Is attainment all that there is?*

Model of the world reframe – Re-evaluate the statement from a different view of the world.

> *What does that belief look like from the point of view of the children?*

Reality reframe – Point out that people's perceptions of the world are really what they operate from.

> *What is it from your perspective that makes this look so? By the time they have finished in this school at 19 won't their experience here also be part of their background?*

Counter example reframe – Give an example from a different frame of thinking.

Do you remember John Smith who passed all his exams, wasn't he from the Downs Estate? There seem to be many examples of this, aren't there?

Hierarchy of criteria reframe – Use a criteria that is more important than the current one used in the mindset.

So what's the purpose of education if everything is so set?

Apply to self reframe – Illustrate to the person their frame and perspective so that they recognise that there are other frames out there.

Yes, there are some people who believe that children's attainment is the result of their background.

Meta frame – Establish a belief about the belief.

What other ways are there of seeing this? If you were to think about it differently how would you do that?

Learn more about this

Often as leaders we can get bogged down in thinking about the tasks that we and others have to do, and how to go about them, without paying much attention to the mindsets of the people that we are leading. The reality is that you have to change people's mindsets as well as the tasks that they do. Sleight of mouth aims to identify the positive intention behind the limiting beliefs and values that drive this and find more appropriate ways of thinking that can also fulfil these needs. As a leader you have to spend time debating, discussing and even arguing your case to ensure that beliefs are changed as well as other more environmental aspects of the organisation.

Read some more about reframing

- Read Chapter 10, 'Verbal ju-jitsu', in *NLP for Teachers: How To Be a Highly Effective Teacher* (page 117) for more information about skilful language
- Buy a copy of *Sleight of Mouth: The Magic of Conversational Belief Change* by Robert Dilts

When else can you use this?

Noticing the frame that people are operating from, and thinking about where you need them to be, is a really effective way of beginning the influencing process. Of course, once you have reframed in the first instance you may need to do more reframing and further influencing. You can also use this technique to:

- Notice limiting beliefs and mindsets in the classroom and practice reframing with your learners as well.

- Be aware of the mindset that you are setting with others through the language you use.

- Notice your own internal limiting beliefs in the internal dialogue you use with yourself and the things that you say about your own capabilities and do some personal reframing.

What are you going to do with this?
(Your ideas and thoughts)

65 Rescue me

How to coach more effectively

Have you ever said something, or told someone to do something, and then realised later that if you'd had a little more information things would have gone better? Or maybe you have noticed that a good question can be a far better way of getting people to do something? Questioning is more challenging than telling because when you ask a good question people have to think. When people are thinking there is the potential for behaviour change.

Here's how

Coaching skills are now widely recognised as not only important for leaders in a line management and one-to-one context but also as an essential tool for leadership in general. Good questioning is at the heart of coaching and leadership; however, sometimes when we are coaching or leading we can find ourselves stuck for a good question to ask. At these times 'rescue questions' can be a great way of ensuring that you continue to stay in a coaching model without having to come up with that 'killer question' every time. Rescue questions are also great in the classroom to promote more thinking and to get children to talk more about the things they are learning.

1. Take time when coaching, leading or working with others to shift your communication style from a telling one to a coaching and questioning one.

2. When you find yourself itching to jump in and offer a solution, just take a moment to pause and instead ask another question.

3. Recognise that sometimes when people ask for advice what they are really doing is exploring your reactions. Find out more by asking a validation question.

   For example, if someone were to ask you:

   Do you think that we should . . .?

   Instead of jumping in with a solution of your own ask them what they think, for example:

   What's your view on this?

4. Take a moment to look at the rescue questions below and look for opportunities to ask them.

Great coaching questions

- Tell me more about that . . .
- What's that like?
- Specifically, what do you mean by that?
- What do you want out of this?
- What else?
- What do you want instead?
- How should it be?
- If you were to wake up tomorrow and everything was how you want, what would that be like?
- If you pretended you could, what would you do?
- What stops you?

Learn more about this

Most of people's behaviour happens quite automatically and in response to contexts and situations. Think about the last time you drove somewhere – are there any bits missing from your memory? When we think and notice what we are doing or saying there is much more potential for us to change our behaviour. Also people are much more motivated if they feel that they have had an input into the solution or process that they are being asked to contribute to. Good questions asked at the right time do both of these.

Read some more about questioning skills

- Read Chapter 10, 'Verbal ju-jitsu', in *NLP for Teachers: How To Be a Highly Effective* Teacher (page 117)
- Read some books on coaching: *Coaching with NLP: How To Be a Master Coach* by Joseph O'Connor and Andrea Lages is a great place to start

Top tip

You know when you have asked a really good question because you get silence from the person you have asked – during which time they have had to go inside to think hard about the answer to the question you have asked. You will know when this happens by paying careful attention to small facial movements and in many cases you will start to notice interesting eye movements. Just wait and give the person time to think.

When else can you use this?

Developing your questioning skills is a key way to improve your effectiveness. This is as true with children as it is with colleagues and parents. You can also use these skills in following ways.

- In meetings be the person who clarifies the way forward by asking good questions – you will soon get a reputation for being a consensus creator as a leader.

- Use rescue questions with yourself, particularly when you are unsure of what to do – *What do you really want?* is a great question to start with.

Leading with NLP

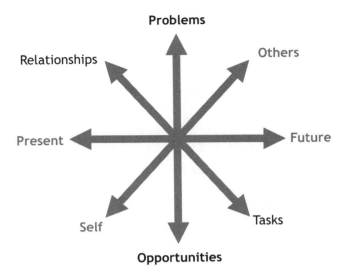

Problems

Others

Relationships

Present ⟷ Future

Self

Tasks

Opportunities

If your coachee can't see beyond a particular barrier,
or way of thinking, take them somewhere
else in their thinking. Ask a question that targets
the opposite of what they are talking about.

- When you notice that someone's thinking is stuck in a particular frame of mind ask them a question related to an opposite concept. For example, if they are stuck and only talk about the task ask them a question about relationships. If they are stuck and only talking about themselves ask them about others. You may find the coaching compass (above) helpful as a way of conceptualising this type of questioning. This process is often known as reframing.

What are you going to do with this?
(Your ideas and thoughts)

PENS

66 Showing appreciation

How to think more effectively in line management, performance review and school improvement contexts

Have you ever been responsible for developing others and yet found yourself struggling to find a framework that challenges conventional thinking really effectively? Or maybe you just need a structure to work with when helping others? NLP often works well when synthesised with other approaches. The tool below contains elements of NLP and appreciative inquiry (AI). David Cooperrider proposed a theory for living and working with change that he called appreciative inquiry. This involves taking people through four stages of thinking that he called the 4D cycle (discover – dream – design – deliver). Combining this model with NLP questioning and coaching techniques works really well and can promote deeper thinking about learning and development. It can also be a good framework for school improvement, development planning and for facilitated team meetings and discussions.

Here's how

1. **Get the person** you are meeting with to identify an area that they want to develop.

2. **Starting strengths** – ask them to take a moment to remember something that they have done which sums up positively all of their skills and attributes which may be useful to them in this developmental context.

3. **Ask them** to estimate their level of self-confidence on a scale from 1 to 10, with 10 defined as totally confident and resilient.

4. **Ask them** what they feel and where in their body this belief and their current sense of confidence is located. Ask them to describe the feelings they are experiencing.

5. **Affirming existing skills** – ask them to talk about what they already do well and what is important to them about that. How do these skills illustrate the person that they are deep down?

6. **Discovering** – ask them to think about the area they want to develop and reflect on what is currently working well. How does this relate to their starting strengths? Can they think of examples in the past where they have been able to apply their strengths to the area they want to develop?

The diagram below may help you to conceptualise the whole process.

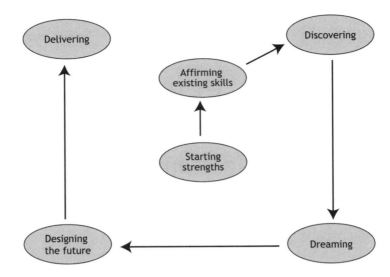

7. **Dreaming** – ask them to reflect on the aspect of their work that is going well. What would they get by developing this area further? Picture the results and consider what might be. How could they apply these skills elsewhere?

8. **Designing the future** – get them to reflect on the ideal future. What would that be like? Ask them to imagine themselves there. What do they see, hear (external sound and their own internal dialogue) and feel (physically and emotionally)? Elicit lots of details from them. Now ask them to look back from the future and talk about how they got there. What steps did they take? Get them to imagine watching a film of themselves doing it and the journey they travelled. Ask them to describe what they see.

9. Ask them to check inside again to look at their skills and capabilities. On a scale of 1 to 10 how much more confident do they now feel? Where in their body is this feeling? What other resources do they need to improve this further?

10. **Delivering** – now ask them to return to the present keeping all those skills and images with them and talk about what they will do next. What resources will they need and how will they go about it?

Learn more about this

Sometimes when we realise that we have to embrace change we can end up forgetting about our existing strengths and skills. However, every team, individual or organisation has something that already works well and can be built on or extended. What we focus on becomes our reality – so focusing on strengths makes change and devel-

Read some more about appreciative inquiry

- Find out more about AI by reading *Appreciative Inquiry: A Positive Revolution in Change* by David Cooperrider and Diana Whitney

opment not only easier but also more likely to be effective. People are more likely to change and develop when they take with them what has been of value or use in the past.

When else can you use this?

This tool is a great way to develop your NLP skills further – for example, by coaching someone using this tool as a 'spatial sort'. To do this simply write the name of each of the questioning zones on different pieces of paper (see the diagram above) and then get the person you are working with to stand on the different spaces when you are coaching them.

- Use this structure when 'think-storming' ideas about school improvement. Have a different flipchart for each of the questioning zones and use the structure as the basis for your team or group facilitation.

- Use with children in the classroom as a structure to support problem-solving activities or to plan design projects or extended independent learning projects.

- Use when working one-to-one with students in a career planning and development context.

- Facilitate the 'spatial sort' described above with a whole team or group. Use corners and spaces in the room to hold discussions.

What are you going to do with this?
(Your ideas and thoughts)

---

67 The iceberg for school improvement

How to analyse your school using a levels of thinking tool

Just like an iceberg, a major part of a school's philosophy, beliefs and values lie below the waterline and out of sight during the working week. It is only when we come to make changes, in an effort to bring about improvements, that the issues that are below the waterline can (like an iceberg) sink our improvement ship. Robert Dilts, one of the developers of NLP, developed a useful model that he called neurological levels of change (i.e. these are the levels of thinking that affect our language and our mind when we start the change process). You can use this model to map out the sort of improvement and changes that would work best. During the process you can find any sticking points that lie below the waterline and decide how to address them.

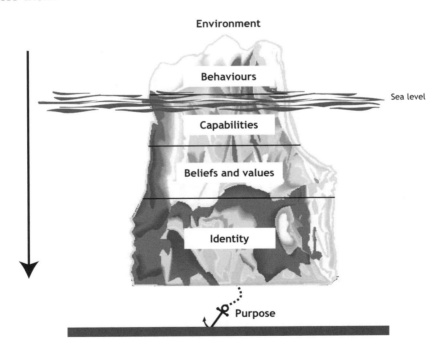

The iceberg has six levels – three of which are visible above the waterline and three lie below.

These three are observable and are often paid more attention:

- Environment
- Behaviours
- Capabilities (or skills) – only visible when they emerge as behaviours. This level includes the untapped talent in your school.

The next three, which are often invisible, are part of the unspoken traditions that all institutions tend to generate over time. By paying attention to these categories we can begin to create school improvement plans that will fit our needs and aspirations:

- Beliefs and values
- Identity
- Purpose.

Here's how

Study the Quick start sheet below and familiarise yourself with the categories and the types of questions that are helpful to ask. Begin your analysis with the environment category and work towards the purpose level, identifying the gaps and answering the questions. The questions below are a guide and you may want to add your own questions in each category, taking care not to mix the categories together. This will very much depend on the context in which you are using the tool.

Quick start – School improvement planning with thinking levels

Levels		Key questions to ask
Purpose	Vision	What is our overarching purpose for existing? What is our purpose in particular areas? What is our intention?
Identity	Role and mission	Who are we in our context? What is our role? What is our mission? What specifically do we want to achieve?
Values **Beliefs**	Motivation – what is seen as important How thinking about the situation is expressed at the moment	In the context of this review: Why are we doing it this way? What are our values? What are our states of mind? What are our limiting beliefs? What are our empowering beliefs?
Capabilities	Perceptions Direction	What are our capabilities? What capabilities do we lack? What are the strategies currently being applied? What do we need to change?
Behaviours	Actions Reactions	What behaviours support the current situation? What behaviours do not support the current situation?
Environment	Constraints and opportunities	What is our context? School infrastructure Cultural connections Social and societal connections Financial constraints Human resources What are the opportunities?

Once you have completed your survey you can begin to map the essential parts of your improvement plan.

1. This time start with the vision – make it short, clear and succinct to bring clarity (see present state to desired state resources (on page 168) for ideas about how you might do this – particularly if your thinking is still stuck in problem mode). Define your mission. Make a comparison between the current values and beliefs that you uncovered in your review and any new values and beliefs that will be needed in order to complete the mission. Are there any new capabilities that will be required in order to fulfil the vision and mission and actualise the beliefs and values needed? What behaviours are useful in building the capabilities?

2. Finally, what changes are needed in the environment in order to support the vision, mission, values and beliefs, capabilities and behaviours? Your aim is to create alignment of categories so a supportive framework is built and improvement can be a success. Create some detailed plans and an execution strategy. Aim to take the level of thinking in the iceberg that is currently most out of alignment with the overall purpose and mission.

Learn more about this

The importance of values and moral purpose for effective school improvement is recognised by a number of writers, particularly Michael Fullan. Fullan suggests that it is important for leaders in schools to practise and develop the behaviours that go with the values associated with moral purpose and that real breakthroughs in

> **Read some more about levels and values and how you can use them**
>
> • Read Chapter 11, 'The teacher within', in *NLP for Teachers: How To Be a Highly Effective Teacher* (page 131)

development come not just from doing but also from 'thinking about the doing'. Other writers, like John West-Burnham, also stress the importance of the moral dimension in school leadership as well as the spiritual. The levels tool, particularly when used in a group context, prompts us to think at a purpose, values and identity level by challenging our thinking to go much deeper than just thinking about those things that appear in the environment around us.

When else can you use this?

• Use it to help develop your own thinking about your purpose as a leader and whether your behaviours and values are aligned with this. Run a team session in which you explore all the levels on flipcharts

• Use it as a coaching tool. Write each level on a piece of paper and walk your coachee through the process – what in NLP we call a 'spatial sort'.

• In the classroom use as a framework for teaching creative writing to help with character creation in stories or to help understand a famous historical figure in a historical context.

What are you going to do with this?
(Your ideas and thoughts)

---

68 Time bomb

How to use the language of time

Whether you notice it or not we are constantly placing ideas and concepts on a chronological timeline – past, present, future. That we make use of tenses is not only an interesting linguistic curiosity; placing things in time creates powerful presuppositions about future behaviours. Knowing this will give you the ability to influence more effectively.

Here's how

Take a look at the opening paragraph and notice the time-based language elements that we used. Notice the effect of placing your attention in the present for the first part of the paragraph and then the presuppositions of the potential of these skills for you in the future.

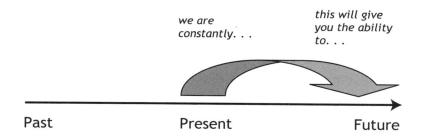

Now think about how different the effect would have been if we had said something like: *At some point in the past you may have noticed time language. You may even be able to think of a time in the past when you used such patterns well.* Although this sentence brings to mind thoughts about these skills it does not presuppose the potential of them for you in the future.

As leaders and teachers we are constantly required to influence others, whether they are other teachers or children. How we use time-based language can make a real difference to how effective we are; this is because the language we use affects the minds of others and the frames of thinking that they adopt when they receive language.

Ways to use this

1. When talking about 'problems' be careful about which time-based presuppositions you use. Placing the problem in the past creates the presupposition that there is another possibility now and in the future. For example:

   School attendance has been a problem.

Notice the difference between this and:

School attendance is a problem.

or

School attendance will be a problem.

The third example is what is sometimes called a 'limiting presupposition' or 'limiting suggestion' because if you accept the suggestion implied in the sentence then you also accept that you may not be able to solve the problem in the future. Therefore you become limited to the current or past situation.

2. As well as verbs, adverbs and phrases also presuppose time frames and even the order in which events are to/might have or are happening.

Think about the different effects of

- Before
- During
- After
- While
- Yet
- At the same time
- Once you have
- Until
- Previously
- Never!

Imagine where your mind would be sent on a timeline as a result of each of these words and phrases.

Now notice the difference between:

- *Before we do an action plan we should talk to staff.*
- *After we do an action plan we should talk to staff.*
- *While we do an action plan we should talk to staff.*

Imagine what each of those sentences would look like on a timeline.

Top tip

Again, as with all NLP, decide on the outcome that you want before speaking. What do you want others to agree to, or what frame of mind do you want them to be in to accept this? Once you have an outcome in mind, think carefully about what time-based language you will need to use in order to help you to achieve this.

Learn more about this

Evidence from areas of research such as cognitive linguistics suggests that the language that we use is not incidental but is rather the result of fundamental cognitive processes and reflects these. In this way we may be sorting and organising events, memories, behaviours and actions in a sort of 360 degree internal space within our heads. Think about it for a moment and imagine a happy memory from your childhood – where in the 360 degree space around you would that be if you were to point to it? Now think of an important future event and point to that. When you shift time-based language you may actually be moving and affecting the internal spatial processes of other people.

> **Read some more about time and NLP**
>
> * Read Chapter 12, 'You can do it . . . and it's about time', in *NLP for Teachers: How To Be a Highly Effective Teacher* (page 143)
> * Read some NLP books on timeline therapy such as *Time Lines* by Bob Bodenhamer and Michael Hall

When else can you use this?

Use effective time-based presuppositions in the classroom to more effectively explain learning. You can also:

* Presuppose future behaviours in ways that replace thought about past actions when dealing with behaviour issues.

* Change some of your own internal dialogue so that it reflects better what you want in the future.

What are you going to do with this?
(Your ideas and thoughts)

Leading with NLP			
Self-awareness	Resilience	Relationship awareness and influencing skills	School improvement
* * *	*	* * *	* * *

69 Walt Disney wouldn't do it that way!

How to get creative in meetings

Creativity is not as easy as it seems, especially when teams of people are involved. Have you ever had to manage a creative meeting and found that no one had any ideas – or worse still, there were plenty of ideas but no one had any idea how to put them into practice? Or maybe when the ideas came out they were quickly criticised and so evaporated? These situations are common in meetings in a range of work contexts. This tool will help you run creative meetings in a way that not only allows the ideas to be generated but will also focus time and energy on both developing realistic plans and constructively criticising those plans, in order to come out with projects that are really workable.

Here's how

Perhaps you have a new initiative or school project that needs creative thinking? This strategy was 'modelled' by Robert Dilts (one of the pioneers of NLP as a research tool) in his study of Walt Disney. Dilts found that Disney had three distinct personas that appeared at different times during the creative process. Dilts named these the *dreamer*, the *realist* and the *critic*. Dilts found that by encouraging people to move between these personas, during the creative process, ideas and plans could be developed quickly and effectively. We all have these personas inside ourselves and they often get mixed up. Sometimes the critic comes in too soon and our dreams die before they've even had a chance to breathe. Sometimes we can have great dreams but do not know quite how to put them into action and so they stay dreams. Through a structured approach (like the one modelled from Walt Disney) this strategy allows the creative process to deliver a fully formed and tested idea.

1. Create an agenda for your meeting. Divide your meeting up into four time segments. Study the Quick start table below.

2. The first segment of the meeting should be devoted to the dreamer. In this part of the meeting any ideas are allowed with no absolute criticism accepted.

3. The second segment is for the realist. Here's where you take the ideas and work out how you can put them into practice.

4. The third segment is devoted to the critic, providing constructive criticism. This segment is designed to take the plans from the realist and find any pitfalls or obstacles that would prevent it working.

5. The fourth segment is used to tidy up any loose ends, and a short dreamer or realist phase may be needed to generate extra ideas and plans to overcome obstacles found in the critic phase.

6. This is an iterative process so a number of cycles may be needed to bring an idea fully into being. The main point to remember is that the critic always needs to be separated from the dreamer otherwise the flow of ideas may dry up.

Quick start – Disney strategy

Stage	What you would see if you were an observer
The dreamer Have lots of fun, creative items to hand (A3 paper, coloured pens, sticky notes and a flipchart). Ensure a relaxed fun atmosphere.	• The generation of ideas, no matter how crazy or strange. • No criticism – encouragement only. • Dreams and ideas are allowed to unfold and grow. • Exploring of ideas freely. • A belief that for every one good idea you may need to generate many others.
The realist Have available tools and resources that help with planning (calendars, paper with grids on, paper for making lists, useful directories). Create a more serious working atmosphere – a place to get the job done.	• The turning of ideas into reality and the development of working models. • No new ideas are needed except those related to making the dreams become reality. • Planning. • Preparing. • Identifying and gathering resources.
The critic In this phase your plans, resource lists and timing need to be clearly laid out so that the critic can be constructive and ensure that your plan will be successful.	• Looking at the plans, resource lists and working models. • Applying positive critical skills to iron out the wrinkles and make a plan workable. • The criticisms are then turned into questions for the realist, which helps the development of new ideas to be cycled through the process. • When a final plan has passed the critic's scrutiny it is ready to be put into action.

Learn more about this

There are many ways in which creative processes can be stimulated. Here are just a few from the past: Balzac wore a monk's cowl and ate enormous amounts of fresh fruit; Kipling needed very heavy black ink to express himself; Descartes wrapped his head in towels and buried himself in bed to do his best work; Proust also did the same and sealed off his room from any wandering air currents; Kant worked in bed with a curious arrangement of blankets and used a tower as a focus while working on *Critique of Pure Reason;* and Milton composed with his head leaning over his easy chair.

Read some more about the Disney strategy

Read:
• *Tools for Dreamers: Strategies for Creativity and the Structure of Innovation* by Robert B. Dilts, Todd Epstein and Robert W. Dilts
• Chapter 15, 'Instant training day', in *NLP for Teachers: How To Be a Highly Effective Teacher* (training exercise 6)

This leaves the question that there must be a simpler way to get creative! The Disney strategy model of creativity provides an easy way to stimulate creativity in almost everybody. The process is now widely used in many contexts from individuals working out their own futures and dreams to multinational companies using the process to design new business models and products. The concept of being able to separate out these different functions is simple and elegant to use in many contexts.

When else can you use this?

- Create spaces in your classroom where your students can adopt the different creativity archetypes when studying a topic.

- Use the process to help in teaching the writing of essays, articles and reports.

- Plan an inset day using the strategy.

- Of course, the strategy also works brilliantly for art students to help them plan and implement projects as has been shown by Sharon Beeden's research (see page 255).

What are you going to do with this?
(Your ideas and thoughts)

70 Well well

How to create an effective school development vision

Being able to create a well-formed outcome in your mind and in the minds of others is not only a key skill in NLP – it is also an essential capability for leadership. Any initiative that is not well formed, thought through and planned may fail for reasons other than the quality of your enthusiasm and potential beliefs in its efficacy.

Here's how

To give yourself the best chance of succeeding and bringing your vision into reality, create a well-formed outcome to give a solid start to your enterprise. The well-formed outcomes structure was modelled from studies of successful people and provides a set of questions that identify and clarify: intentions, actions and thoughts and how these contribute to a particular outcome. Start by writing down your outcome. There are many formulas which help you do this – one favourite that you already may know is called SMART. We have made a couple of modifications to this formula that we have found helpful in leadership and other contexts – which we call PURE. Once you have a SMART and PURE outcome in mind, use the Quick start at the end of the tool to add depth to your outcome and develop your motivations further.

1. Start by writing your vision according to the SMART criteria:

    S – Specific. Be specific about what your vision encompasses and add details of what it will be like.

    M – Milestones. Work out when your vision should come into being, then work back in three-month increments (or other units of time relevant to the project length). At each increment specify what will have been accomplished by this time – again give details.

    A – As now. Write your vision in the present tense (e.g. start with something like 'It is now November 2020 and . . .' (those of you reading the book after then will need to make the appropriate adjustments!)).

    R – Realistic. Talk to someone else about your vision – have them do a 'sanity check'. Is your outcome realistic? Do you stand a good chance of achieving it?

    T – Timing. When will you start moving towards your outcome?

My SMART outcome is:

2. Now check what you have written down and modify it to make sure it is PURE.

   P – Positively phrased. Leadership goals are always best expressed in the positive and as a 'towards' motivation.

   U – Under your control. Is this something that you are able to influence? If not then you may need to rethink the goal or identify another goal (or outcome) which is under your control and which might be the first step.

   R – Right sized. Is this goal or outcome the right size for your organisation and for you?

   E – Ecological. Are there any unintended consequences of having this outcome – things that would make it un-ecological if you were to take a really big picture view of it?

3. Now you should have a goal that you can express clearly and easily both to yourself and to others.

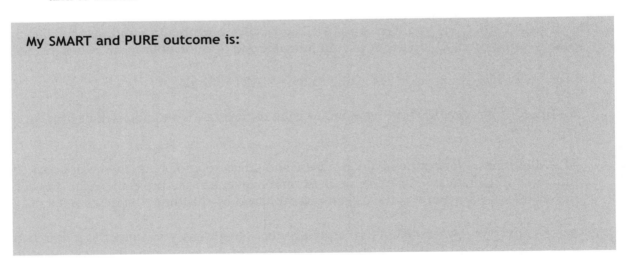

My SMART and PURE outcome is:

4. Once you have your outcome answer the questions in the Quick start table (which you can find at the end of this tool). These questions will help you to explore your outcome further and connect the goal to your personal motivations. This makes a great coaching exercise so you may like to have a colleague ask you the questions (with them writing the answers) so that you can concentrate on your thinking.

Learn more about this

There has been much research regarding outcomes, vision and effective leadership – particularly in relation to effective school improvement. It has also been found that just the process of writing down an outcome can make you more likely to achieve it. Even today, when we are surrounded by electronic technology, there is something about writing that just seems to make things seem more important. Of course, it's entirely possible that when you have completed this process, or even got halfway

Read some more about well-formed outcomes

• Read Chapter 2, 'Blockbuster movies', in *NLP for Teachers, How To Be a Highly Effective Teacher* (page 9)

Or explore another school improvement tool in this book like:
• Chapter 67, 'The iceberg for school improvement'

through, you may find that the vision you started with needs changing or even discarding. However, it is much better to spend a few hours on a paper exercise than days or weeks actualising your vision only to find it won't work! You might also like to have a go at drawing a rich picture metaphor that sums up this vision for you and what it means to you. Pictures, metaphors and stories can be hugely influential. Ask yourself: if my leadership vision were a garden, what would it be like?

When else can you use this?

This is a process tool that is really useful whenever you have something important to do that needs thinking through.

- Use this in combination with the tools in Chapter 67 ('Iceberg for school improvement'). Use as part of performance review processes to support the people you line manage.

- Run the process as part of a team meeting or school improvement planning meeting.

- Apply the process when you are starting departmental projects or when starting to implement government or district initiatives.

- Use yourself as a career planning tool to help you to think through applying for that next step or new job.

What are you going to do with this?
(Your ideas and thoughts)

Quick start – Having a well-formed outcome for your leadership vision

1	What do you want? State in positive terms your SMART and PURE outcome/objective/goal.	
2	How will you know when you've got it? Stated in sensory specific terms. Create a strong internal mental representation. • What will it be like when you achieve your outcome? • Create a detailed sensory internal representation. What will you see, hear (your self-talk, what others say and the sounds around you) and feel (physically and emotionally)? • Ensure that this is juicy and appealing. Does it draw you towards it? • Describe it to a friend or colleague – imagine yourself doing this.	
3	What resources do you need to get it? Identify all the resources you will need (from equipment and materials to help from colleagues – you may need extra pages for this bit).	
4	How will achieving your vision benefit you? State at least three benefits.	1 2 3

234

5	Do you want this outcome in any other situations? If so, where, when and with whom do you want it? Where, when and with whom do you NOT want it?					
6	How will succeeding in implementing your vision affect other aspects of your work and life?					
	These next four questions are designed to make you think differently. Ask them and then notice how they change the way you perceive your outcome.					
7	What would happen if you did succeed?					
	What would happen if you didn't succeed?					
	What wouldn't happen if you did succeed?					
	What wouldn't happen if you didn't succeed?					

Leading with NLP

Leading with NLP			
Self-awareness	Resilience	Relationship awareness and influencing skills	School improvement
*	* * *	* * *	* * *

71 You've been framed

How to get what you want when leading meetings

Some meetings are very effective, some take a while to get going and others seem to wander off track. Perhaps you have been to a meeting where you thought you were turning up for one thing and never got to discuss it. If you are involved in meetings that tend to run off at tangents or where discussions seem not to be relevant, then the concept of setting frames (sometimes called ground rules) can be a powerful way to give a meeting direction and make them more effective. As with many tools in NLP, we start with the basic idea that before we can go anywhere we need to know the purpose and the outcome. The same is also true with meetings.

Here's how

Let's take purpose first of all. Meetings are called for many reasons and it is vital that those who come to meetings understand the purpose of the meeting. See below for some of the reasons that we hold meetings.

Once we have clarity in our mind, as a leader, about the purpose of a meeting then setting frames at the start of the meeting becomes easy and group agreement tends to follow on. Framesetting is a key skill and in NLP we often say:

The person who sets the frame controls the communication.

236

This is particularly true in leadership and especially in team or group contexts.

1. Decide on the purpose for the meeting. Put this at the top of the agenda or if the agenda is going to be sectioned make sure the purpose is clearly stated before each section.

2. Send out any paperwork and the agenda well before the meeting so everyone knows the purpose. Once you have a team used to seeing the benefits of this you can even mark items with a code so that everyone knows what the aim of the meeting is:

   - PS – Problem solving (state the problem that needs to be solved)
   - IG – Information giving
   - IS – Information seeking (state the topic that the information is required about)
   - DM – Decision making

3. Well before the meeting ensure that members of the meeting have the agenda with the purpose and paperwork required.

4. Study the Quick start table below so that you can plan your frames before the meeting.

5. At the meeting, either on a flipchart or whiteboard in full view, write on it the meeting purpose. Set agreed outcomes for the meeting and add these in priority order. Agree milestones to measure the progress of the meeting. Set any other frames either overtly or conversationally that you need to. Simply stating the purpose and the frame at the start is a very powerful way of ensuring focus throughout the meeting.

Using the Quick start below

Take a few minutes to reflect on a meeting that you are going to be leading in the future with a team that you have responsibilities for. What is the purpose of that meeting? What do you want to have achieved by the end of the meeting? What will you see, hear and feel if this has been successfully achieved? Now take a few moments to read the Quick start below and decide which frame or frames you are going to need to set the start of the meeting in order for the outcome to be achieved. If your meeting looks like it is going to cover too many of these then the scope of the meeting may be too wide and you may need to think about holding a series of meetings with a logical order between them.

Quick start – Framesetting for meetings	
Frame type	
Outcome	Set agreed outcomes not only for the content of the meeting but also for how the meeting is going to be conducted. This is especially important for meetings that may be contentious. Agree an outcome for what you will all have accomplished by the time you walk out of the door.
Evidence frame	This frame is related to the outcome frame and is useful to consider on its own. The key question is: *How will you know when you have reached your outcome - what will you see, hear, feel, know or experience?* This frame can be used to assess how well you are progressing towards your outcome, if corrective action should be taken or if a new or modified outcome needs to be set.
Milestones	Agree how far you should have got with the agenda items at one quarter, half and three quarters of the way through the meeting.

Relevancy	Once you have set the two parameters above then it is possible at points where the meeting is going off track for you to gently and with curiosity ask the following question: *[Name] I wonder if you could clarify how your current point is relevant to . . . [state the agreed outcome]?* Usually only one or two relevancy challenges need to be made during a meeting to keep things on track. Without an outcome and milestones relevancy challenges are impossible and so meetings can get off track.
Backtrack	Agree with everyone in the meeting that if they wish to go back to a previous item, or wish to comment on a previous item, they need to ask permission to do this – so that everyone can agree to this change in direction and follow the progress of the meeting. If the backtrack is not relevant then time may be wasted going over old topics. If people have to ask then you are in a stronger position to manage their response (e.g. you can then get agreement to 'park' the point until later).
Silence is acceptance	In meetings where consensus is required this frame can be very useful. It simply says that if you don't speak up around the topic or decision then you are accepting the decisions made.
As if	The 'as if' frame is useful when meetings get stuck and solutions cannot be found within current constraints – for a period of time participants generate ideas and suggestions with no boundaries. This will often free up creativity and allow new ideas to come forward that can be modified or adapted to create a solution. For an outcome, act as if you have already achieved your outcome. Below are some examples: • If an essential person is not present, you may say, 'Let's act as if [name] is here. What would he think, feel or suggest?' • For planning projects act as if the project has been successfully completed and then ask what steps were necessary to reach this outcome.
Open	The open frame should be used with care as once we open the meeting to questions without qualification the meeting can then go in any direction. The biggest open frame that most organisations have on their agendas is 'any other business'. If your agenda is organised then there is no need for any other business; in fact, many meetings are derailed when any other business takes over leaving people feeling de-motivated or worse that the meeting was just an excuse for someone to put their point of view. Use language to avoid open framing. 'Are there any questions on [the item] before we move on.' This restricts questions to the matter in hand.
Study of consequences	In a decision-making meeting this is an important frame to set. Before beginning the discussion ask: *What are the consequences of taking this decision?* This frame helps to ensure that actions are related to the real world and can support motivations to carry out actions following a meeting.
Contrast	This is another useful way to un-stick a topic. Shift the conversation to the extremes of what you are talking about to help people see the middle ground.

Learn more about this

Setting frames allows us to set the context and provide focus, direction and guidance for thoughts and actions. Frames assist us in being clear about what is included and what is excluded from the particular context we are discussing. By using frames we can increase our ability to be congruent around decisions that are taken during meetings. We don't have to be in charge of the meeting to set frames – sometimes it is possible to suggest these things at the beginning of the meeting which will go a long way towards keeping things moving in the right direction.

Read some more about frames

- *Precision: New Approach to Communication* by Michael McMaster and John Grinder
- *The Hidden Art of Interviewing* by Roger Terry and Neil McPhee

When else can you use this?

Any situation in which a particular outcome is desired may need you to set strong frames to guide the people that you are working with.

- Reflect on your own internal frames before you deal with a difficult situation as a leader.

- Set frames in letters to parents or staff.

- Set frames when coaching students or colleagues in one-to-one meetings.

- Use frames in tutor groups and when dealing with behaviour issues.

- Take time to notice the frames that are being set by other people.

What are you going to do with this?
(Your ideas and thoughts)

PENS

Glossary of commonly used NLP terms

Accessing cues A term used when talking about the observation of body language and facial expressions. Accessing cues are subtle behaviours or micro signals. These help to indicate how a person is thinking and feeling. Typical types of accessing cues include eye movements, voice tone, tempo, body posture, gestures and breathing patterns. Matching this sort of information is a key way to develop rapport.

Ambiguity Ambiguity is the use of language which is vague or ambiguous. Ambiguous language is used in therapy as a form of waking hypnosis and can be used to create deeper trance. Using ambiguous language is one way of leading people through an influencing process.

Analogue Having shades of meaning (i.e. on a continuum), as opposed to digital, which has a discrete (on/off) meaning. For example, in relation to submodalities (the subtle details of memory representations), something is either black and white or colour; however, brightness is a continuum from very light to completely dark.

Anchoring The process by which an internal response is associated with an external trigger (similar to classical conditioning), so that the response may be quickly and sometimes covertly re-accessed. Anchoring can be visual (as with specific hand gestures), auditory (by using specific words and voice tone) or kinaesthetic (as when touching an arm or laying a hand on someone's shoulder).

Associated In memory, when you appear to be looking through your own eyes, hearing what you heard and experiencing the feelings as if you were actually there. This is sometimes called an associated state.

Auditory Relating to hearing or the sense of hearing.

Away from Away from is a type of metaprogram. It is when a person's preference is to move in the opposite direction from what they don't want, as opposed to moving towards what they do want (e.g. *I don't want a nine to five job* as opposed to *I want flexibility of hours*).

Beliefs The generalisations we make about ourselves, others and the world. Beliefs act as self-fulfilling prophecies that influence all our behaviours. Beliefs are locked in place by the language we use to describe them – changing this language is an effective way to change limiting beliefs.

Break state When someone 'breaks state' they are suddenly interrupting their current emotional state and are moved into a different one. Typically, a break state is used to pull someone out of an unresourceful state into a neutral one, so that they are more easily able to do what is required to achieve their outcome. When using NLP therapeutic or personal development tools, a break state is often used deliberately in order to ensure that the states being worked with are clearly separated from each other and therefore are 'clean'.

Calibration The process of learning to read and interpret another person's unconscious, non-verbal responses and micro signals.

Chunking Organising or breaking down an experience into bigger or smaller pieces. Chunking up involves moving to a larger, more abstract level of information. Chunking down involves moving to a more specific and concrete level of information. Chunking laterally involves finding other examples at the same level of information. The term chunking is also applied to Milton and meta model language.

Congruence When all of a person's internal beliefs, strategies and behaviours are fully in agreement and oriented towards securing a desired outcome they are said to have congruence.

Cross matching Matching a person's body language with a different type of movement (e.g. tapping your foot in time to their speech rhythm).

Deep structure The sensory maps (both conscious and unconscious) that people use to organise and guide their behaviour. In terms of language the deep structure is the meaning that is inherent in what has been said but which has not been stated.

Deletion Within language deletion this is the process by which portions of the deep structure are removed and, therefore, do not appear in the surface structure representation (e.g. if someone were asked how they got to work and their reply was simply, *I caught the bus*, clearly a lot more happened; however, this information has been deleted). When this process occurs in relation to beliefs or outcomes, this can result in people omitting key information that they need in order to be more in touch with reality.

Digital The opposite of analogue; see above.

Dissociated In a memory when one appears to be looking at oneself, as if in a picture doing whatever you were doing, as opposed to seeing the event through your own eyes.

Distortion In language where someone 'distorts' what has happened or what is happening.

Downtime When a person's attention is inward or when they are paying attention to their internal world and representations. Daydreaming is a form of downtime.

Ecology Ecology is the study of the consequences and effects of individual actions on the larger system. In NLP this same concept is applied to an individual. In other words, when carrying out changes or deciding on outcomes it is important to consider the whole life picture, including value, beliefs, etc.

Elicitation The art of uncovering internal processes through questioning.

Eye accessing cues Movements of the eyes in certain directions that may, through calibration, give clues to people's inner thoughts, processing and feelings.

First position *See* perceptual position.

Framing To set a context or way of perceiving something upfront and, as a result of this, influence the outcome.

Future pacing The process of mentally rehearsing and anchoring changes in yourself to a future imagined situation. This helps to ensure that the desired behaviour will occur naturally and automatically.

Generalisation In language, generalisation is the process by which a specific experience comes to represent an entire category of experience. For example, *X always happens.*

Gustatory   Relating to the sense of taste.

Identity   Our sense of who we are. It is our sense of identity that drives our beliefs, capabilities and behaviours.

Installation   The process of facilitating the acquisition of a new strategy or behaviour.

Internal representation   Patterns of information we create and store in our minds in combinations of images, sounds, feelings, smells and tastes. Internal representations are the way we store and encode our memories in representational systems and their submodalities.

Kinaesthetic   Relating to body sensations. In NLP the term kinaesthetic is applied to all kinds of feelings including tactile, visceral and psychomotor.

Leading   Changing your own behaviours with enough rapport for the other person to follow. Effective leading is always preceded by pacing.

Matching   Adopting parts of another person's behaviour for the purpose of enhancing rapport.

Meta model   The model developed by John Grinder and Richard Bandler that identifies categories of language pattern. Meta model language chunks down into details to restore the generalisation, deletions and distortions in people's language and beliefs.

Metamessage   A message about a message. Your non-verbal behaviour is constantly giving people metamessages about you and the information you are providing. Sometimes these can contradict what you want to communicate.

Metaprogram   A level of mental programming that determines how we sort, orient to and chunk our experiences. These correlate to traits, preferences and schemata in applied psychology and cognitive neuroscience. We tend to behave according to our metaprograms and therefore we can be influenced by the matching of them.

Milton model   Hypnotic language – specifically the language patterns of Milton Erickson. These work as the opposite of the meta model by chunking up out of detail into generalisations, distortions and deletions.

Mind reading   In NLP terms, this does not refer to the idea of telepathy, but rather to the assumptions that one sometimes makes about other people's thoughts or opinions.

Mirroring   Matching portions of another person's behaviour as if in a mirror.

Mis-matching   Adopting different patterns of behaviour to another person, breaking rapport for the purpose of redirecting, interrupting or terminating a meeting or conversation.

Modelling   The process of observing and mapping the successful behaviours of other people in order to apply them to self and others.

Neurological levels of change   A practical model proposed by Robert Dilts for organising the elements of human experience. There are a number of tools that take people through these levels to help them to solve problems and feel more aligned in their life.

Olfactory   Relating to smell or the sense of smell.

Pacing   A method used to quickly establish rapport with people by matching certain aspects of their behaviour and/or experience. Pacing with language is a key part of the hypnotic process. Typically to influence, the pattern *pace, pace, lead* is required as a minimum.

Pacing current experience   This is the linguistic process of deliberately alluding to the present experience of another in order to pace and influence (e.g. *As you read these words . . .*).

Perceptual filters   Our unique combinations of values, beliefs, metaprograms, senses and language that shape our model of the world.

Perceptual position   A particular perspective or point of view. In NLP there are three basic positions one can take in perceiving a particular experience. First position involves experiencing something through our own eyes, associated in a first person point of view. Second position involves experiencing something as if we were in another person's shoes (in doing so the world would appear through the other person's eyes). Third position involves standing back and perceiving the relationship between ourselves and others from a dissociated perspective.

Presupposition   An underlying meaning hidden in a sentence, as opposed to what it appears to say.

Rapport   The process of being liked and trusted by another person. In NLP there are specific techniques for doing this. *See also* cross matching, matching, mirroring, pacing.

Reframing   A linguistic process by which a person's current thinking is shifted.

Representational systems   In NLP the term representational system applies to all things related to the five senses: seeing, hearing, touching (feeling), smelling and tasting.

Resources   Central to NLP is the notion that people have all the internal resources that they need. The word resource is therefore applied to anything that can support the achievement of an outcome: positive memories, internal emotional states, physiology, language patterns, etc.

Resourceful state   When a person feels emotionally resourceful and congruent.

Second position   *See* perceptual position.

Sensory acuity   The process of learning to make finer and more useful distinctions about the sense information we get from the world. One of the benefits that comes from studying NLP is the realisation that so much more is going on than we are normally aware of. Specifically, the term is often applied to the development of the awareness of facial and physiological micro signals.

Spatial anchoring   This is a term referring to the method of using physical location as an anchor.

Spotlighting   Using spatial anchoring in the classroom to influence group behaviour.

State   A person's state of mind and emotions at any moment in time.

Strategy   A set of explicit mental and behavioural steps used to achieve a specific outcome. The modelling of strategies is at the heart of NLP's study of excellence.

Submodalities The subtle distinctions in memories, either visual, auditory or kinaesthetic. In a visual memory these might include whether the memory is colour or black and white, light or dark, etc.

Surface structure The opposite of deep structure; see above.

Swish pattern A process by which visual internal representations are switched to facilitate changes in behaviour or to give more options.

Third position *See* perceptual position.

Timeline The internal representation of memories on a chronological line.

Trance When our conscious experience appears to be an altered state of consciousness, e.g. daydreaming. Trance can be induced by a range of processes including hypnotic language or just open questioning.

Transderivational search for meaning (TDS) The process of locating meaning by going into a trance.

Uptime This is the opposite of downtime, and means when the individual is paying attention to what is going on externally to them in their environment and not to their internal processes.

Values In NLP the term values is applied to those things that are important to you – not objects or people, but rather experiences or feelings such as learning, health, wisdom, respect. They are the non-physical qualities that we seek to have more of in our life.

Visual Relating to sight or the sense of sight.

Well-formed outcome A well-formed outcome is an outcome that is positively stated, under the person's control, right-sized and ecological to their values, beliefs and life conditions.

Alphabetical list of chapter titles

A chronological bibliography of key texts in the development of NLP

Bandler, R. and Grinder, J. (1975a). *The Structure of Magic: A Book about Language and Therapy*, vol. i, Palo Alto, CA: Science and Behaviour Books.

Deep and surface language structure
Deletion
Distortion
Generalisation
Eye movement model
Meta model language
Predicates
Presuppositions

Bandler, R. and Grinder, J. (1975b). *Patterns of the Hypnotic Techniques of Milton Erickson, M.D.*, vol. i, Cupertino, CA: Meta Publications.

Milton Model
Modelling
Primary experience and secondary experience

Bandler, R. and Grinder, J. (1975c). *Patterns of the Hypnotic Techniques of Milton Erickson, M.D.*, vol. ii, Cupertino, CA: Meta Publications.

Congruence
Lead system
Transderivational search

Bandler, R. and Grinder J. (1976). *The Structure of Magic II: A Book about Communication and Change*, Palo Alto, CA: Science and Behaviour Books.

Addition of digital representation system
Congruence
Incongruence
Input channels
Meta model
Representational system
Russell's Theory of Logical Type (application of)
Satir Categories of communication

Bandler, R., Grinder, J. and Satir, V. (1976). *Changing with Families: A Book about Further Education for Being Human*, Palo Alto, CA: Science and Behaviour Books.

Meta model
Representational systems
Satir Categories

Bandler, R. and Grinder, J. (1979). *Frogs into Princes*, Moab, UT: Real People Press.

> **Accessing cues**
> **'All communication is hypnosis'**
> **Anchoring**
> **Change personal history**
> **Dissociation patterns**
> **Ecology**
> **Eye movement model and relationship to representational system**
> **Flexibility of behaviour**
> **Future pacing**
> **Mirroring**
> **Pacing and leading**
> **Perceptual positions**
> **Phobia cure**
> **Polarity response**
> **Rapport**
> **Reframing**
> **Strategy**
> **Transderivational search**

Bandler, R. and Grinder, J. (1979). *Reframing*, Moab, UT: Real People Press.

> **Reframing**

Dilts, R., Grinder, J., Bandler, R., Bandler, L. C. and Delozier, J. (1980). *Neuro-Linguistic Programming: The Study of the Structure of Subjective Experience*, Cupertino, CA: Meta Publications.

> **Definition of NLP as the study of the structure of subjective experience**

Grinder, J. and Bandler, R. (1981). *Trance-Formations: Neuro-Linguistic Programming and the Structure of Hypnosis*, Moab, UT: Real People Press.

> **NLP training approaches to hypnosis and waking state hypnosis**

Bandler, R. and Andreas, C. (1985). *Using Your Brain for a Change*, Moab, UT: Real People Press.

> **Submodalities**

Bandler, R. and MacDonald, W. (1988). *An Insider's Guide to Sub-Modalities*, Cupertino, CA: Meta Publications.

> **Submodalities**

Selected articles and publications
by Roger Terry and Richard Churches that include NLP and may be of interest to teachers and school leaders

Austin, N. and Churches, R. (2009). 'Coaching with Impact', *School Leadership Today* 1: 3: 46–49.

Carey, J., Churches, R., Hutchinson, G., Jones, J. and Tosey, P. (2009). *Neuro-linguistic programming and learning: teacher case studies on the impact of NLP in education*, Reading: CfBT Education Trust.

Churches, R. (2008). 'Improving Teacher Effectiveness with NLP', *Learning and Teaching Update*,12: 4–6.

Churches, R. (2009). 'Look Into My 'i's: A Conversation about Leadership as Hypnosis', Society for Organisational Learning in the UK seminar, University of Surrey School of Management, 19 March 2009 (available from www.sol-uk.org).

Churches, R. and Terry, R. (2008). 'Connect More Than Four in Your First Year: A TES Essential Guide for New Teachers', *Times Education Supplement*, 12 September, 4–6.

Churches, R. and Terry, R. (2006). 'Don't Think About Chocolate Cake: An Introduction to Influential Language Patterns', *Teaching Expertise*, 11: 15–16.

Churches, R. and Terry, R. (2006). 'Feng Shui in the Classroom', *Teaching Expertise*, 12: 22–24.

Churches, R. and Terry, R. (2008). 'Hypnotise Your Class', *Times Educational Supplement*, 11 January, 26–29.

Churches, R. and Terry, R. (2007). *NLP for Teachers: How To Be a Highly Effective Teacher*, Carmarthen: Crown House Publishing.

Churches, R. and Terry, R. (2005). 'NLP for Teachers: Starting with the End in Mind', *Teaching Expertise*, 9: 50–51.

Churches, R. and Terry, R. (2008). 'Ready to Watch and Learn', *Times Educational Supplement*, 4 January, 26–29.

Churches, R. and Terry, R. (2005). 'Streetwise Body Language', *Teaching Expertise*, 10: 50–51.

Churches, R. and Terry, R. (2008). 'The View from Elsewhere', *Times Educational Supplement*, 28 January, 26–29.

Churches, R and Terry, R. (2006). 'You Can Do It and It's About Time', *Teaching Expertise*, 13: 25–27.

Churches, R., Terry, R. and Partridge, E. (2008). 'Windows on the World', *Primary Choice*, July: 28–29.

Churches, R., Terry, R. and Tosey, P. (2008). 'Re-thinking Teacher Effectiveness', *Teaching Thinking and Creativity, 9*(2): 60–63.

Churches, R. and West-Burnham, J. (2008). *Leading Learning through Relationships: The Implications of Neuro-Linguistic Programming for Personalisation and the UK Government Children's Agenda*, Reading: CfBT Education Trust.

Churches, R. and West-Burnham, J. (2009). 'Leading Learning through Relationships: The Implications of Neuro-Linguistic Programming for Personalisation and the UK Government Children's Agenda', International NLP Research Conference, Surrey University, 5 July 2008.

Hutchinson, G., Churches, R. and Vitae, D. (2006). *The Consultant Leader Programme in London's PRUs and EBD Schools, Impact Report 3: Towards System Leadership*, Reading: CfBT Education Trust for the London Leadership Strategy.

Hutchinson, G., Churches, R. and Vitae, D. (2007). *NCSL London Leadership Strategy, Consultant Leaders to Support Leadership Capacity in London's PRUs and EBD Schools, Impact Report: February 2007*, Reading: CfBT Education Trust and the National College for School Leadership.

Hutchinson, G., Churches, R. and Vitae, D. (2007). *NCSL London Leadership Strategy, Consultant Leaders to Support Leadership Capacity in London's PRUs and EBD Schools, Impact Report: July 2007*, Reading: CfBT Education Trust and the National College for School Leadership.

Hutchinson, G., Churches, R. and Vitae, D. (2008). *Together We Have Made a Difference, Consultant Leaders to Support Leadership Capacity in London's PRUs and EBD Schools, Final Programme Report: July 2008*, Reading: CfBT Education Trust and the National College for School Leadership.

Terry, R. and McPhee, N. (2007). *The Hidden Art of Interviewing People: How To Get Them To Tell You the Truth*, London: Wiley.

Bibliography of education perspectives and research

Papers and research that are supportive of the use of NLP in education

Contrary to popular opinion, and some academic writing which has not been based on a substantial literature review, there have been a number of academic and semi-academic publications on NLP which are supportive of its use in schools and education in general. In contrast, there have been few critical publications (only five of which are research evidenced). Fifty of the publications below, as well as containing positive perspectives, also contain positive research evidence (both qualitative and qualitative). For an extensive commentary on the literature see Carey et al. (2009).

There is a general tendency for NLP research papers to be self-referential and not to reference earlier studies – perhaps because of the assumption that there is little other research. If you are carrying out research into NLP yourself, perhaps as part of a Masters in Education or Masters in Teaching degree, you can use the bibliography below as a toolkit to build your literature review at the start of your research. Most of the papers or their abstracts are available on-line.

Creativity and self-expression

Beeden, S. (2009). 'Applying Dilts' "Disney creativity strategy" within the Higher Education arts, design and media environment', in P. Tosey (ed.), *Current research in NLP; Volume 1, proceedings of the first international NLP research conference, University of Surrey, 5 July 2008*, South Mimms, Hertfordshire, UK: ANLP International CIC.

Ronne, M. (1998). *A theoretical approach to creative expression for school counselling*, PhD Thesis, The Union Institute.

Winch, S. (2005). 'From frustration to satisfaction: using NLP to improve self-expression', in *Proceedings of the 18th EA Educational Conference 2005*, Surry Hills, NSW.

e-learning

Ghaoui, C. and Janvier, W. A. (2009). 'Interactive e-learning', *International Journal of Distance Education Technologies*, 2: 3: 2: 26–35.

Sheridan, R. D. (2008). *Teaching the elderly effective learning strategies in relation to internet use*, PhD Thesis, University of Brighton.

Zhang, N. and Ward, A. E. (2004). 'On the adaption of e-learning content to learner NLP input sensory preference', International Conference on Innovation, Good Practice and Research in Engineering Education, 131–137, Wolverhampton, 3–4 June.

Emotional, social, behavioural and learning difficulties

Beaver, R. (1989). 'Neuro-Linguistic programme as practised by an educational psychologist' *Association of Educational Psychologists Journal*, 5: 2: 87–90.

Bull, L. (2007). 'Sunflower therapy for children with specific learning difficulties (dyslexia): a randomised, controlled trial', *Complementary therapies in clinical practice*, 13: 1: 15–24.

Childers, J. H. (1989). 'Looking at yourself through loving eyes', *Elementary School Guidance and Counseling*, 23: 3: 204–209.

Esterbrook, R. L. (2006). *Introducing Russian Neuro-Linguistic Programming behavior modification techniques to enhance learning and coping skills for high-risk students in community colleges: an initial investigation*, Doctoral Dissertation, George Mason University, Fairfax, VA.

Fruchter, H. J. (1983). 'Sensory reinforcement in the service of aggression maintenance in children: a treatment study', *Dissertation Abstracts International* 45(3) 1013-B, Syracuse University.

Renwich, F. (2005). 'The "A Quiet Place" programme: Short-term support for pupils with social, emotional and behavioural difficulties in mainstream schools', *Educational and Child Psychology*, The British Psychological Society, 22: 3: 78–88.

Squirrel, L. (2009). 'Can Neuro-Linguistic Programming work with young children who display varying Social, Emotional and Behavioural Difficulties?', in P. Tosey (ed.), *Current research in NLP; vol 1: proceedings of the first international NLP research conference, University of Surrey, 5 July 2008*, South Mimms, Hertfordshire: ANLP International CIC.

English as a foreign language

Harris, T. (2001). 'NLP if it works use it. . .', *CAUCE, Revista de Filología y su Didáctica*, 24: 29–38.

Knowles, J. (1983). *The old brain, the new mirror: matching teaching and learning styles in foreign language class (based on Neuro-Linguistic Programming)*, paper presented at the Northeast Conference on the Teaching of Foreign Languages, Baltimore, MD, 28 April–1 May.

Further and higher education

Johnson, S. (2004). *'Strategies for success': integrating Neuro Linguistic Programming into the undergraduate curriculum*, paper presented at The 12th Improving Student Learning Symposium, Oxford Centre for Staff and Learning Development, Oxford Brookes University, Birmingham, 6–8 September.

Murray, P. and Murray, S. (2007). 'Promoting sustainability values within career-oriented degree programmes: a case study analysis', *International Journal of Sustainability in Higher Education*, 8: 16–300.

Skinner, H. and Croft, R. (2009). 'Neuro-Linguistic Programming techniques to improve the self-efficacy of undergraduate dissertation students', *Journal of Applied Research in Higher Education*, 1:1: 9–38.

Language and learning

Eckstein, D. (2004). 'Reframing as an innovative educational technique: turning a perceived inability into an asset', *Korean Journal of Thinking and Problem Solving*, 14: 1: 37–47.

Marcello, M. (2003). *Language and identity: learning and the learner*, paper presented at the Tenth International Literacy and Education Research Network Conference on Learning. Institute of Education, University of London 15–18 July.

Mathison, J. (2004). *The inner life of words: an investigation into language in learning and teaching*, PhD thesis, University of Surrey.

Mathison, J. and Tosey, P. (2008c). 'Riding into Transformative Learning', *Journal of Consciousness Studies*, 15: 2: 67–88.

McCabe, D. (1985). 'Meeting language needs of all types of learners', *Academic Therapy*, 20: 5: 563–567.

Millrood, R. (2004). 'The role of NLP in teachers' classroom discourse', *ELT Journal*, 58: 10–37.

Leadership and management in education and in general

Dowlen, A. (1996). 'NLP – help or hype? Investigating the uses of neuro-Linguistic Programming in management learning', *Career Development International*, 1: 27–34.

Helm, D. J. (1994). 'Neuro-Linguistic Programming: establishing rapport between school administrators and the students, staff and community', *Education*, 114: 4: 625–627.

Hutchinson, G., Churches, R. and Vitae, D. (2006). *The consultant leader programme in London's PRUs and EBD schools; impact report 3: towards system leadership*, Reading: CfBT Education Trust and the National College for School Leadership.

Hutchinson, G., Churches, R. and Vitae, D. (2007). *NCSL London Leadership Strategy, consultant leaders to support leadership capacity in London's PRUs and EBD Schools: impact report: roll-out, July 2007*, Reading: CfBT Education Trust and the National College for School Leadership.

Hutchinson, G., Churches, R. and Vitae, D. (2008). *Together we have made a difference: consultant leaders to support leadership capacity in London's PRUs and EBD schools, final programme report*, Reading: CfBT Education Trust and the National College for School Leadership; San Diego, California: Jensen Learning.

Jones, J. and Attfield, R. (2007). *Flying high: some leadership lessons from the Fast Track teaching programme*, Reading: CfBT Education Trust. Unpublished.

Young, J. A. (1995). 'Developing leadership from within: a descriptive study of the use of Neurolinguistic Programming practices in a course on leadership', Dissertation, Ohio State University, *Abstracts International*, Section A: Humanities and Social Sciences, Vol 56 (1-A).

Metaprogrammes in the classroom

Brown, N. (2003). 'A comparison of the dominant meta programme patterns in accounting undergraduate students and accounting lecturers at a UK business school', *Accounting Education*, 12: 159–175.

Brown, N. (2002). 'Meta programme patterns in accounting educators at a UK business school', *Accounting Education*, 11: 79–91.

Brown, N. (2004). 'What makes a good educator? The relevance of meta programmes', *Assessment and Evaluation in Higher Education*, 29: 5: 515–533.

Brown, N. and Graff, M. (2004). 'Student performance in business and accounting subjects as measured by assessment results: an exploration of the relevance of personality traits, identified using meta programmes', *International Journal of Management Education*, 4: 3–18.

Modelling

Day, T. (2005). *NLP modelling in the classroom: students modelling the good practice of other students*, paper presented at the British Educational Research Association New Researchers/Student Conference, University of Glamorgan, 14 September.

Day, T. (2008a). *A study of a small-scale classroom intervention that uses an adapted Neuro-Linguistic Programming modelling approach*, PhD Thesis, University of Bath. Parents

Munaker, S. (1997). 'The great aha! a path to transformation', PhD Dissertation, *Abstracts International*, Section A: Humanities and Social Sciences, Vol 57(11-A), May 1997.

Outdoor education

Lee, A. (1993). 'Outdoor education and Neuro-Linguistic Programming', *Journal of Adventure Education and Outdoor Leadership*, 10: 16–17.

Parents

Brandis, A. D. (1987). 'A neurolinguistic treatment for reducing parental anger responses and creating more resourceful behavioral options, California School of Professional Psychology', Los Angeles, Dissertation abstract, *Dissertation Abstracts International*, Vol 47(11-B), 4642, May.

De Mirandi, C. T., de Paula, C. S., Palma, D., da Silva, E. M., Martin, D. and de Nobriga, F. J. (1999). 'Impact of the application of neurolinguistic programming to mothers of children enrolled in a day care center of a shantytown', *Sao Paulo Medical Journal*, 4: 117(2): 63–71.

Hall, E., Wall, K., Higgins, S., Stephen, L., Pooley, I. and Welham, J. (2005). 'Learning to learn with parents: lessons from two research projects', *Improving Schools*, 8: 179–191.

Peer counseling

Dailey, A. L. (1989). 'Neuro Linguistic Programming in peer counselor education', *Journal of College Student Development*, 30: 2: 173–175.

Research methodology and NLP

Mathison, J. and Tosey, P. (2008a). 'Innovations in constructivist research: NLP, psycho-phenomenology and the exploration of inner landscapes', *The Psychotherapist*, 37: 5–8.

Mathison, J. and Tosey, P. (2008b). 'Exploring inner landscapes: NLP and psycho-phenomenology as innovations in researching first-person experience', *Qualitative Research in Management and Organization Conference*, New Mexico, 11–13 March.

Steinfield, T. R. and Ben-Avie, M. (2006). *A Brief Discussion of the Usefulness of NLP in Action-Based Education Research*, paper presented at the *NLP and research: a symposium*, Surrey University School of Management, University of Surrey, 16 June.

Spelling strategy

Loiselle F. (1985). *The effect of eye placement on orthographic memorization*, Ph.D. Thesis, Faculté des Sciences Sociales, Université de Moncton, New Brunswick, Canada.

Malloy, T. E. (1995). 'Empirical evaluation of the effectiveness of a visual spelling strategy', in K. H. Schick (ed.), *Rechtschreibterapie*, Paderborn: Junfermann Verlag.

Malloy, T. E. (1989). *Principles for teaching cognitive strategies*, University of Utah. (Available at www.kattmodel.se.)

Malloy, T. E. (1987). *Teaching integrated thought. Techniques and data*, paper presented at Annual Meeting of the Conference on College Composition and Communication 12–19 March. (Available at ERIC.)

Teacher perspectives and development

Carey, J., Churches, R., Hutchinson, G., Jones, J. and Tosey, P. (2009). *Neuro-Linguistic Programming and learning: teacher case studies on the impact of NLP in education*, Reading: CfBT Education Trust.

Churches, R. and West-Burnham, J. (2008). *Leading learning through relationships: the implications of Neuro-Linguistic Programming for personalisation and the Children's Agenda in England*, Reading: CfBT Education Trust.

Churches, R. and West-Bumham, J. (2009). Leading learning through relationships: the implications of Neuro-Linguistic Programming for personalisation and the Children's Agenda in England, in Tosey, P. (ed.), *Current research in NLP, vol 1: proceedings of the first international NLP research conference, University of Surrey, 5 July 2008*, South Mimms, Hertfordshire: ANLP International CIC, pp. 126–136.

Dragovic, T. (2007). *Teachers' professional identity and the role of CPD in its creation – a report on a study into how NLP and non-NLP trained teachers in Slovenia talk about their professional identity and their work*, International Society for Teacher Education, 27th Annual International Seminar at University of Stirling, Scotland, 24–30 June.

Teaching and learning in general

Childers, J. H. (1985). 'Neuro-Linguistic Programming: enhancing teacher-student communications', *Journal of Humanistic Counseling, Education and Development*, 24: 1: 32–39.

Dolnick, K. (2006). *Neuro-Linguistic applications to classroom management: reach them to teach them*, PhD Thesis, Capella University.

Girija Navaneedhan, C. and Saraladevi Devi, K. (2009). 'Influence of learning techniques on information processing', *US-China Education Review*, 6: 1 (Serial No. 50): 1–32.

Helm, D. J. (1989). 'Education: the wagon train to the stars/it's time to "jump start" learning through NLP', *Education*, 110: 2: 54–256.

Helm, D. J. (2000). 'Neuro-Linguistic Programming: enhancing learning for the visually impaired', *Education*, 120: 5: 790–794.

Helm, D. J. (1990). 'Neurolinguistic Programming: equality as to distribution of learning modalities', *Journal of Instructional Psychology*, 17: 3: 159–160.

Helm, D. J. (1991). 'Neurolinguistic Programming: gender and the learning modalities create inequalities in learning: a proposal to reestablish equality and promote new levels of achievement in education', *Journal of Instructional Psychology*, 18: 3: 167–169.

Hillin, H. H. (1982). 'Effects of a rapport method and chemical dependency workshop for adults employed in Kansas service agencies', *Dissertation Abstracts International*, 44(12), 3574-A, Kansas State University.

Kennedy, C. and And, O. (1994). *Study strategies: a formula for exceptional outcomes in the mainstream*, paper presented at the Annual Convention of the Council for Exceptional Children, 72nd, Denver, CO, 6–10 April.

Parr, G. and And, O. (1986). 'The effectiveness of Neurolinguisitc Programming in a small-group setting', *Journal of College Student Personnel*, 27; 358–361.

Ragan, J. and Ragan, T. (1982). *Working effectively with people: contributions of neurolinguistic Programming (NLP) to visual literacy*, paper presented at the Annual Meeting of the International Visual Literacy Association (13th, Lexington, KY, 31 October–3 November), in *Journal of Visual Verbal Languaging*, 2: 2: 67–79.

Raja, R. and Tien, N. (2009). *Exploring multi-modality tools of Neuro-Linguistic Programming (NLP) to facilitate better learning among primary school students* National Institute of Education, Singapore, Redesigning Pedagogy, International Conference 1–3 June.

Sandhu, D. S. (1994). 'Suggestopedia and Neurolinguistic Programming: introduction to whole brain teaching and psychotherapy', *Journal of Accelerative Learning and Teaching*, 19: 3: 229–240.

Schaefer, J. and Schajor, S. (1999). 'Learning with all one's senses: Neurolinguistic Programming in the teaching of pediatric nursing', *Kinderkrankenschwester*, 18: 7: 289–291.

Stanton, H. E. (1998). 'Reducing test anxiety by a combination of hypnosis and NLP', *Journal of Accelerated Learning and Teaching*, 23: 59–65.

Stanton, H. E. (1989). 'Using Neuro-Linguistic Programming in the schools', *Journal of the Society for Accelerative Learning and Teaching*, 14: 4: 311–326.

Tosey, P. and Mathison, J. (2003a). *Neuro-Linguistic Programming: its potential for teaching and learning in higher education*, paper presented at the European Educational Research Association conference, University of Hamburg, 17–20 September.

Tosey, P. and Mathison, J. (2003b). 'Neuro-Linguistic Programming and learning theory: a response', *Curriculum Journal*, 14: 3: 371–388.

Tosey, P., Mathison, J. and Michelli, D. (2005). 'Mapping transformative learning: the potential of Neuro-Linguistic Programming', *Journal of Transformative Education*, 3: 2: 140–167.

Thalgott, M. R. (1986). 'Anchoring: a "cure" for Epy', *Academic Therapy*, 21: 3: 347–352.

Woerner, J. and Stonehouse, H. (1988). 'The use of Neuro-Linguistic Programming model for learning success', *School Science and Mathematics*, 88: 516–524.

Zechmeister, E. (2003). *The impact of NLP on the performance and motivation of primary school children*, PhD Thesis, Leopold-Franzens-Universitat, Innsbruck.

Vocal training

Pruett, J. A. S. (2002). *The application of the Neuro-Linguistic Programming model to vocal performance training*, DMA Thesis, University of Texas, Austin.

Papers and research that question the use of NLP in education

Only papers from the 1980s contain formal research evidence that is critical. Furthermore, the methodologies used in these have been criticised – in most cases because of inaccurate application/interpretation of NLP techniques (See Carey et al., 2009). So far, no critical papers (since the 1980s) contain research evidence-based criticism that is the result of actual NLP research studies.

Research

Bradley, G. M. (1986). *The effectiveness of a Neurolinguistic Programming treatment for students test anxiety*, Melbourne: La Trobe University.

Cassiere, M. F. and And, O. (1987). *Gender differences in the primary representational system according to Neurolinguistic Programming*, paper presented at the Annual Convention of the Southwestern Psychological Association, 33rd, New Orleans, LA, 16–18 April.

Fremder, L. A. (1986). 'Generalization of visual dot pattern strategies to number pattern strategies by learning disabled students', *Dissertation Abstracts International*, 47(11), 4055-A Columbia University Teachers College.

Schleh, M. N. (1987). 'An examination of the Neurolinguistic Programming hypothesis on eye movements in children', *Dissertation Abstracts International*, 48(2), 584-B Biola University, Rosemead School of Psychology.

Semtner, E. A. (1986). 'An investigation into the relevance of using Neurolinguistic Programming (NLP) as an aid in individualizing college reading programs', *Dissertation Abstracts International*, 47(4).

Perspectives

Burton, D. (2007). 'Psycho-pedagogy and personalised learning', *Journal of Education for Teaching International Research and Pedagogy*, 33: 13–17.

Craft, A. (2001). 'Neuro-Linguistic Programming and learning theory', *Curriculum Journal*, 12: 125–136.

Lisle, A. (2005). *The double loop: reflections on personal development planning and reflective skills of undergraduates*, paper presented at the British Educational Research Association Annual Conference, University of Glamorgan, 14–17 September.

Marcus, J. and Choi, T. (1994). 'Neurolinguistic Programming: magic or myth?', *Journal of Accelerative Learning and Teaching*, 19: 3–4: 309–342.

Index

About the authors

Roger Terry

Roger Terry is an International NLP Master Trainer and public speaker. As an expert on neuro-linguistic programming and human value systems Roger leads seminars and consults with organisations in the UK, US, Europe and Middle East. He is the author of *The Hidden Art of Interviewing* and NLP and qualitative research. His published articles include regular contributions to *Teaching Expertise*, the *TES and Teach Primary* magazine with Richard Churches. Roger has, with Henrie Lidiard, trained over 1,000 Fast Track teachers in NLP. Eleven years ago he founded Evolution Training with his wife and business partner Emily. Previously his career was within the utility sector where he was responsible for new business creation and innovative organisational development. He now works with organisations and individuals, guiding them to evolve to their full potential.

Roger can be contacted at roger.terry@evolutiontraining.co.uk

Richard Churches

Richard Churches is Principal Consultant for National Programmes at CfBT Education Trust, the world's leading education consultancy. In recent years he has worked on a number of major UK government initiatives for the Department for Children Schools and Families and the National College for School Leadership. This has included being the national lead consultant for Fast Track Teaching, Managing Editor for the NPQH materials and consultant for the London Leadership Strategy. He is currently National Programme Manager for the support materials for the new secondary curriculum. Richard was an Advanced Skills Teacher in Greenwich and before that held senior management posts in two inner London schools. He has taught in primary and secondary phases and in a special school. He is a doctoral researcher in the School of Management at Surrey University and is a Fellow of the RSA.

Richard can be contacted at r.churches@surrey.ac.uk

Also available: *NLP for Teachers: How To Be a Highly Effective Teacher*
ISBN: 978-1845900632

The perfect companion to *NLP for Teachers: How To Be a Highly Effective Teacher*